M. K. Kellogg's Texas Journal, 1872

Miner K. Kellogg. Self-portrait. Cincinnati Art Museum, gift of Paul G. Pennoyer, New York.

M. K. Kellogg's TEXAS JOURNAL 1872

Edited with an Introduction by
LLERENA FRIEND

UNIVERSITY OF TEXAS PRESS
AUSTIN

Copyright © 1967 by Llerena B. Friend
First paperback printing 2014

All rights reserved

Requests for permission to reproduce material from this work should be sent to:
  Permissions
  University of Texas Press
  P.O. Box 7819
  Austin, TX 78713-7819
  http://utpress.utexas.edu/index.php/rp-form

Library of Congress Catalog Number 67-20417

ISBN 978-0-292-76869-7, paperback
ISBN 978-0-292-76870-3, library e-book
ISBN 978-0-292-76871-0, individual e-book

For Daisy and Curtis

PREFACE

Three little pencilled notebooks (averaging about 4 x 6.5 inches each) constitute the journal of Miner K. Kellogg's trip to Texas. The notebooks, entitled by Kellogg "M. K. Kellogg's Mems: Exploring Expedition to Texas, 1872," were left in library custody at The University of Texas when a history professor who was considering editing them moved to other campus scenes. Eventually the librarian got around to a cursory reading, a perusal which became exciting when Kellogg's account related the progress of a mineral expedition across a part of North Texas familiar to her. The account seemed to be an objective description of the Texas of 1872 by a non-Texan without preconceived notions, who, while he grumbled at discomforts and was discouraged by the company's failure to find the minerals it sought, did depict the local scenes in words refreshingly different.

Considerably later, when some information became available, Kellogg—world traveller, author, artist—was revealed as a journal keeper "from way back," who had begun recording his impressions with notes and sketches during travels as a teen-ager. His writing in the Texas notebooks was uniform and legible. Scarcity of paper plus the necessity for making his notes while being jerked in an ambulance over rough trails or by dim light in an army tent account for a general disregard of punctuation save for the extensive use of dashes. Often he jotted down phrase sequences separated only by spaces, noted herein by three hyphens. Seldom, however, did he fail to observe the convention of beginning a new sentence with a capital letter; for the reader's ease I have provided the initial capital for what Kellogg, by ending the preceding sentence with a period, obviously intended as a new sentence. But, otherwise, to retain in Kellogg's own written form a sense of the unfavorable conditions under which the artist wrote, I did not standardize his style according to modern conventions: the erroneous use of apostrophes, the inconsistencies of abbreviations, the misspellings, the run-on and fragmentary sentences are left as he wrote them.

On occasion Kellogg left blank spaces, obviously intending to fill them in later. The information lost in these blanks is negligible compared to the blank left by the loss of his sketches, the pictorial record of the trip and the reason for his employment on the Texas Land and

Copper Association Expedition. At least we know, from an entry in the first notebook, that his sketch-book block was 14.25 x 10.25 inches. Would that some farmhouse in Grayson County could produce a sketch from that block!

For the Kellogg diary to be meaningful two introductory sections seemed essential. Explanation of the Texas Land and Copper Association was needed, although what has been found concerning the genesis of the company and its seeming disappearance is disappointing and far from complete. It is to be hoped that the resultant brief presentation may stimulate research on this and similar companies created to exploit the "reconstructed" South. Particularly, I would like to know more of what lay in the future for those prime promoters A. R. Roessler and W. C. McCarty.

Biographical background on Kellogg the diarist was likewise necessary. An honest preface, detailing all of the editor's search for the author, would reveal a chasing after false clues, memory lapses, and a knack for discovering the location of material just after she had departed from the spot where it had been hidden. The ensuing sketch may explain Kellogg's background sufficiently to account in part for his feeling of frustration with the management and activities of the expedition. A study of Kellogg notebooks and other papers which I have not seen and an evaluation of the writer as an artist-explorer may eventually persuade an art critic to prepare a detailed biography.

A number of Kellogg's companions on his Texas tour remain unidentified, but not for lack of pursuit. Even the Missouri Historical Society could not identify the questionable "Missouri Bill"; and Constable Edwards is still a fugitive.

To those who contributed aid in so many of my quests I am greatly obligated. I am grateful to the Historical Society of Pennsylvania at Philadelphia, to the Archives of American Art at Detroit, and to the Indiana Historical Society Library at Indianapolis for permission to quote from their holdings.

First thanks go to The University of Texas for acquiring the Kellogg journal and for securing photocopies of several Kellogg pamphlets and some of his manuscript notes. My thanks also to Dr. Otis Singletary, who left the journal in my care and encouraged me to undertake the editing.

PREFACE ix

Interest, encouragement, information on the family, and copies of prints of various Kellogg pictures have been graciously supplied by Mrs. John Whitney Blemer, of Diablo, California, and by Mr. and Mrs. Paul Pennoyer, of Locust Valley, Long Island. Mrs. Blemer and Mr. Pennoyer are descendants of Kellogg's brother, Sheldon Ingalls Kellogg. Interest has been expressed by Mrs. Martha F. Butler, of Washington, D.C., who owns some of the early Kellogg journals and has collected Kellogg material for over a quarter century.

Librarians and curators have supplied information and leads to other information. At The University of Texas I am particularly indebted to Miss Kathleen Blow and Mr. Charles L. Dwyer, of the Library Reference Department, and to Dr. F. J. Hunter, curator of the Theater Arts Library. Mrs. Henry W. Howell, Jr., of the Frick Art Reference Library of New York City, guided me to Mrs. Blemer, who in turn led me to the Pennoyers. Miss Caroline Dunn, of the William Henry Smith Memorial Library of the Indiana Historical Society, was enthusiastically cooperative in selecting material for photoduplication. Mr. James J. Heslin, of the New-York Historical Society, and his organization supplied numerous identifications. Help came from Mr. E. P. Richardson, director of the Winterthur Museum; Mrs. Andrew N. Jergens, Jr., librarian of the Cincinnati Historical Society; Mrs. Irene McCreery, of the Toledo Public Library; Mr. Milton C. Russell, of the Virginia State Library at Richmond; Mr. Jack Livingston, of the Archives and History Division of the Department of Education, State of New Jersey; Mr. Richard A. Davis, Fine Arts Department of the Cleveland Public Library; Mrs. Manon B. Atkins, of the Oklahoma Historical Society; Mrs. Mabel R. Schell, of the Public Library of Cincinnati and Hamilton County, Ohio; Miss Adelaide A. Cahill, of the Metropolitan Museum of Art; and Miss Carolyn R. Shine and Mr. Richard J. Boyle, of the Cincinnati Art Museum.

Chief contributors in the way of eyesight, footwork, and patience are the members of the staff of Barker Texas History Library, The University of Texas. Their continued enthusiasm recalled me from the byways and urged me back to the tour.

CONTENTS

Preface vii
Introduction 1
   1. The Texas Land and Copper Association 3
   2. The Artist-Diarist 20
The Journal 57
   Notebook 1. M. K. Kellogg's Mems: Exploring
                 Expedition to Texas, 1872 59
   Notebook 2. Expedition to Texas—1872 cont. . . . 93
   Notebook 3. Texas Land and Copper Company,
                 Texas Expedition 126
Bibliography 165
Index 175

ILLUSTRATIONS

Self-portrait of Miner K. Kellogg, *frontispiece*

(Following p. 34)

M. K. Kellogg in Oriental Dress
Alvina Kilbourne Harris Kellogg
Charles Fraser Kellogg
Sheldon Ingalls Kellogg
Catherine Raynor Edmonds Kellogg
Kellogg's Caravan outside Jerusalem
Bust of Kellogg
Landscape Overlooking Arno Valley, Italy

(Following p. 98)

Sketch of Expedition's Encampment
Sketch of Dried Sunflower
Sketch of Mesquite Trees
Account of Indian Massacre in Kellogg Notebook
Last Page of Kellogg Notebook
Double Mountains from the Salt Fork

MAPS

(In half-tone section following p. 98)

Map of Texas by A. R. Roessler, 1872
Section of North Texas from Roessler's 1872 Map

(Following p.113)

Section Map of Texas Tracing Route of Expedition

INTRODUCTION

The Texas Land and Copper Association

Coronado and a multitude of his children have searched for wealth in Texas. The black gold which has given the state first rank in mineral production in the nation for a great part of the twentieth century is far different in texture from the metallic treasure pursued so eagerly and so long. For at least two decades in the latter part of the nineteenth century it was not the gleam of gold or silver but the duskier glow of copper that lured immigrants and prospectors, that incited creation of exploring companies, and that resulted in considerable wasted expenditure. From the vantage point of hindsight, since actual copper production has proved almost negligible even if always potential, we can almost be amused at the futility of the avid search for copper between 1866 and 1886 when companies were chartered and wagon trains were dispatched to the Texas frontier, the newcomers filled with great expectations based on glowing newspaper reports and geologists' predictions of vast mineral possibilities. Wartime profits accumulated in the East meant "risk" capital ready to finance projects to revitalize the frontier. Texas was more than eager to welcome newcomers and their capital. The Texas Bureau of Immigration, established by the Radical Republican administration of the Reconstruction period, advertised Texas as "The Home for the Emigrant from Everywhere" and offered treasure to lure those emigrants, for, as their brochure ran, "copper in almost inexhaustible quantities, is found in several counties, and promises to become a fountain of wealth for coming generations."[1] So said the Bureau of Immigration in 1873. In 1873, also, Edward King, a journalist known as a shrewd observer, journeyed up and down Texas to prepare for *Scribner's Monthly Magazine* illustrated articles which would depict the resources and condition of the people in the "States formerly subjected to the dominion of Slavery." King was especially eloquent about the immense copper deposit in the "wild Wichita regions," where the mines of Archer County had already proved profitable and where coal for smelting and requisites for building furnaces were available. He described the mountains as bold and romantic, the valleys as mysterious and picturesque, and the plains as covered with flowers and Indians, and then queried, "But who will let the ignoble savage stand in the way of mineral development?"[2]

Apparently it was not the savage natives but the niggardliness of mother nature in creating the poor quality, with low mining potential, of the copper that really stood in the way, and high hopes were pretty well exhausted by the turn of the century. On June 12, 1899, Frederic W. Simonds presented to the Texas Academy of Science a paper entitled "A Record of the Geology of Texas for the Decade Ending December 31, 1896." Concerning copper he said:

> The existence of copper ore in the Permian measures of Texas has long been known, and these ores have been, from time to time, the object of geological researches and mining developments. The most important of these efforts was made about ten years ago by the Grand Belt Copper Company of Texas, but it ended, after several years of fruitless labor, with an entire failure.[3]

---

[1]Texas Bureau of Immigration, *Texas: The Home for the Immigrant from Everywhere*, 8.

[2]Edward King, *The Southern States of North America: A Record of Journeys in Louisiana, Texas, the Indian Territory, Missouri, Arkansas, Mississippi, Alabama, Georgia, Florida, South Carolina, North Carolina, Kentucky, Tennessee, Virginia, West Virginia and Maryland*, I, 124.

[3]Frederic W. Simonds, "A Record of the Geology of Texas for the Decade Ending December 31, 1896," *Transactions of the Texas Academy of Science*, III (1900), 204. The president of the Grand Belt Copper Company was George B. McClellan, assistant and future son-in-law of Randolph B. Marcy, with whom he made the exploration of the Red River in 1852. In 1883 General McClellan sent a report to the trustees of the Consolidated Copper Syndicate of New York which was printed

Reviews of the state's geology made by University of Texas geologists in 1916 and again in 1944 mention various mining attempts in the red beds and trial shipments of copper ore from Baylor, Clay, Foard, Hardeman, King, Knox, and Stonewall Counties which resulted in financial fiasco despite the large deposits said to exist within the region.[4]

A day-by-day account of the experiences in one of these Wichita-area attempts, "the most completely and comfortably fitted out expedition which ever went to Texas," is the record kept by Miner K. Kellogg— "M. K. Kellogg's Mems: Exploring Expedition to Texas, 1872"—of his experiences with the Texas Land and Copper Association.

The briefest and most casual account of this exploring expedition to Texas in 1872 by the "company of Eastern Capitalists" seems to be that of H. H. McConnell in his *Five Years a Cavalryman*, printed in 1889, seventeen years after his employment by the Land and Copper Association. Because McConnell sets the stage, introduces the most interesting of the dramatis personae as "characters," and gives a capsule summary of the trip, his account is worth giving *in toto*.

Previous to the war some attention had been given to the deposits of copper supposed to exist along the tributaries of the Brazos and the Wichita, but the last prospecting party had been driven back by Indians, and for several years no effort had been made to look them up. In the early summer of 1872, a party, made up principally in Washington and Baltimore, and known as the "Washington and Texas Land and Copper Company," made their appearance at Fort Richardson, where they camped for some weeks previous to starting for their destination, which was at or near Kiowa Peak in Haskell county. This party had four or five good wagons and teams, several ambulances and hacks, and, including the mounted men, many of whom were hired at Jacksboro, made a total of perhaps sixty in all. My services were secured to accompany them, and had it not been that my sketch-book was stolen by some of the crowd, on our return to Jacksboro,

---

in The Grand Belt Copper Company, *Facts Relating to the Property of the Grand Belt Copper Company*. . . . (New York, J. K. Hetch, 1885). The story of the General's unsuccessful pursuit of a fortune in copper in the cedar brakes of West Texas is described in Floyd E. Ewing, Jr., "Copper Mining in West Texas: Early Interest and Development," *West Texas Historical Association Year Book*, XXX (1954), 17–29.

[4]J. A. Udden, C. L. Baker, and Emil Böse, *Review of the Geology of Texas* (*Bulletin* of The University of Texas, 1916, No. 4), 130; E. H. Sellards and Glen L. Haynes, "An Index to Texas' Mineral Resources: Descriptive List of Texas Minerals," *Texas Looks Ahead*, 98.

I am sure my account of the adventures of that famous party would have made some excellent reading.

The *personnel* of some of the *bosses* of the party were its distinguishing features, and never have I seen in one small crowd so many *characters*. The real head of the party was one Mr. Chandler, from Norfolk, Virginia, and a member of Congress in *ante bellum* days from that city; one Kellogg, an Oriental traveler, and author of several works on Egypt and the Holy Land; he was an artist as well, and made excellent water-color sketches of the beautiful scenery through which we passed; Professor Roessler, sometime State Geologist of Texas, and the most thorough and ideal crank of any age; one Troutman, a professional photographer, who accompanied the party in the capacity of its "official" artist; W. M. Beard was commissary, a fine young fellow, and since then Speaker of the New Jersey Legislature, and who has achieved eminence as a physician; and Dr. Loew, chemist to the expedition, a droll looking little fellow, about four feet and a half in height, and his pony yclept Bismarck, the latter animal requiring the whole command to catch it each morning. Besides these, there were several "disbanded" army officers who had been "surplussed" out of the army a year or two previously, notably Sam Robbins, one Plummer, and one Winklepaugh, all oddities in their way, except Robbins, who was a fine fellow, both officer and gentleman, and in regard to whom I could never understand his being mustered out. Last, but not least, was the *executive* boss of the crowd, one "Colonel" McCarty, whose home, I think, was Galveston, but who had been picked up by Mr. Chandler in Washington upon his (McCarty's) recommendation of himself as being familiar with the region, which proved to be humbug, as he soon convinced us that he had never been here in his life. His claim to the title of Colonel was based on his having been a Sergeant in a Confed. regiment, and he was the heroic and altogether unapproachable liar of my recollection. He told me confidentially once he was a nephew of "Barbara Fritchie" and had witnessed the incident on which Whittier has based his poem. He was a handsome fellow, wore his hair in true brigand style, a red silk sash around his waist, a splendid black horse, and silver-mounted Winchester completed his "outfit," and a bigger fraud never was seen. Early in June we rolled out across the West Fork, proceeded to "meander" around the forks of the Wichitas, turned south into Belknap (here I did a little of the "pioneer act" myself, having been here five years before), and then to Fort Griffin, where we left the howitzer gun we had with us, and also the supply of trinkets they had brought out to trade to the Indians! We proceeded to Kiowa Peak, located ten or twelve sections of land, returned to Fort Griffin and got rid of our Tonkawa guides, and reached Jacksboro early in September, where the party was disbanded and paid off. An account of this trip, such as I could have produced had my notes and sketches not been stolen, would have been a funny experience, such as seldom falls to the lot of any one to describe.[5]

At least three of McConnell's "characters" left written accounts of the Texas Land and Copper Association's Expedition; what tall tales the oral versions of other participants must have been one can only conjecture. Professor Roessler, "the thorough and ideal crank," submitted his views of the value of the lands located with the company's certificates in the form of a *Geological Report of the Property of the Texas Land and Copper Association,* dated in New York on December 18, 1872. In thirteen pages he summarized the most valuable mineral deposits to be found on the land and expressed his hope for the privilege of presenting a complete report with further observations on the subject. Roessler also collaborated with McConnell's "droll looking little Dr. Loew" in preparing a more detailed description of the Expedition. Edited by Albert S. Gatschet, their fifteen-page account entitled "Erforschung des Nordwesttheiles von Texas im Jahre 1872" appeared in *Petermanns mitteilungen* in 1873.[6] While factual and scientific, the report is also interesting in its inclusion of comments on the personnel of the company, an analysis of the nature and potential of the area explored, an account of the progress of the trip, and some description of communities, vegetation, and wild life encountered.

The impact that the experiences of the Expedition and that the area

---

[5]H. H. McConnell, *Five Years a Cavalryman; or, Sketches of Regular Army Life on the Texas Frontier Twenty Odd Years Ago,* 294–296. Over thirty years later, in his book called *On the Border with Mackenzie,* R. G. Carter, without benefit of any citation, used McConnell's exact words to tell his story of the "Washington Land and Copper Mining Company" and then added interesting vignettes of Loew, von Crenneville, and particularly of McCarty, whom he characterized as the "Bogus Colonel and Guide." Carter did have personal knowledge of the mining company personnel and he experienced encounters with McCarty in September, 1872, after the breakup of the expedition (R. G. Carter, *On the Border with MacKenzie,* 332–336, 350–352). Accounts of McCarty's later promotional schemes appear in the Dallas *Herald* for November 30, 1872, and May 1, 1875.

[6]Oskar Loew and A. R. Roessler, "Erforschung des Nordwesttheiles von Texas im Jahre 1872," *Petermanns mitteilungen aus Justus Perthes' geographischer anstalt,* XIX (1873), 453–457.

traversed made upon one individual is revealed in the journals kept by McConnell's "Oriental traveler," who, being actually the "official artist" of the party, made the water-color sketches of the country. His journal tells of the unfortunate abandoning of those water colors. Nor have any of the photographs taken by A. C. Troutman, the official photographer, been located; so the tour seems to be a lost expedition from the standpoint of illustration save for Kellogg's word pictures and the pencil sketches in his little notebooks. The word pictures grew fewer and less colorful as the summer grew hotter and the trip more arduous and as hopes of profitable accomplishment receded. Kellogg's despondency over the trip's apparent futility and his disgust and even suspicion because of its inept management or lackadaisical mismanagement demand an explanation of the Expedition.

According to Loew and Roessler, for fifty years rumors had circulated of the existence of an abundance of copper ore on the Staked Plains of North Texas. The first factual information resulted from Randolph B. Marcy's exploration of Red River in 1852. As his party traversed a ridge which divided Red River from its tributary Cache Creek (in present Oklahoma) they met "with numerous detached pieces of copper ore, mixed with volcanic scoria." A few miles south of their route they found specimens of a rich ore, later analyzed as a new species and named *Marcylite* by Dr. Charles U. Shepard of Amherst College after the leader of the expedition. The ore was coated with a thin layer of Atacamite or muriate of copper.[7] In his autobiography Marcy repeated the story of the 1852 findings and revealed that the party discovered traces of copper ore in other localities on Red River and also upon the Big Wichita in 1854, "but it generally occurred in small detached fragments, from the size of a pea to that of a hen's egg" and they saw no veins of ore. According to Marcy, Dr. Edward Hitchcock was of the opinion that it would not be strange if the Wichita Mountain vicinity should prove to be a prolific producer of copper. Marcy reported that specimens of surface copper ore near Fort Arbuckle were collected and sent via Fort Smith and New Orleans to

---

[7]Grant Foreman (ed.), *Adventure on Red River: Report on the Exploration of the Headwaters of the Red River by Captain Randolph B. Marcy and Captain G. B. McClellan*, 14–15, 17.

Liverpool, where they were smelted with enough proceeds resulting to pay the costs of transportation.[8]

The technical part of Marcy's report was made by Dr. George Getz Shumard of Fort Smith, Arkansas, geologist of the expedition. In 1858 Benjamin Franklin Shumard became state geologist of Texas. His first progress report of the Texas Geological Survey stated that small rounded masses of the oxide and carbonate of copper were distributed abundantly over the surface of the country toward the source of the Big Wichita, Brazos, and Red Rivers and that it was not improbable that productive veins of copper would be found in the region.[9]

Among B. F. Shumard's assistants on the Texas Survey were his brother George Getz Shumard and a draftsman named Anton R. Roessler. Roessler was born at Raab in Hungary and was educated in Vienna.[10] Just when he came to Texas is not clear, but his article on "Texas Minerals," printed in the Dallas *Herald* on June 8, 1872, mentioned that he had been making personal observations on the mineral resources of northwestern Texas for the last fifteen years. He lived in Austin, and seemingly moved in the best circles. Mrs. E. M. Pease wrote to her husband on October 7, 1860: "Miss Octavia was married last Tuesday night. They sent us cards and cake, and we called to see the bride and groom who are boarding at Mr. Smyths. Mr. Roesler is as black as an Indian and I found it difficult to understand his Hungarian English. He is to leave next week with Dr. Shumard." To her sister, Juliet Niles, Mrs. Pease wrote a month later: "Octavia Baker was married a short time since to Mr. Roessler a Hungarian."[11]

The year after his marriage, 1861, the Civil War came, and during the War years Roessler was chief draftsman at the arsenal established in 1862 in Austin for the casting of cannon. In February of 1865, in the dying days of the Confederacy, information from Roessler was the basis for a Union summary of ordnance potential in Texas. He said

---

[8]Randolph B. Marcy, *Thirty Years of Army Life on the Border*, 100–103.

[9]Texas Geological and Agricultural Survey, *First Report of Progress of the Geological and Agricultural Survey of Texas*, By B. F. Shumard, 14.

[10]Samuel Wood Geiser, "Men of Science in Texas, 1820–1880," *Field & Laboratory*, XXVII (1959), 187–188.

[11]Lucadia Pease to E. M. Pease, October 7, 1860; Lucadia Pease to Juliet Niles, November 9, 1860, Pease Papers, Austin-Travis County Collection, Austin Public Library.

that the foundry in Austin cast two guns per month from Mexican metal and that the local percussion-cap factory turned out 1,000,000 caps of inferior grade a month.[12] Those percussion caps used copper secured from Archer County. S. B. Buckley, assistant geologist and naturalist for the Texas Geological Survey, had made a trip into the Young, Archer, and Clay County copper regions in 1861.[13] It was probably on the basis of his reports that the Texas government, desperate for metals, in 1864 ordered the Texas State Troops at Fort Belknap, with Tonkawa Indian guides, into Archer County to secure copper ore to be transported to Austin. State Chemist William DeRyee said that the ore assayed about 70.68 per cent copper when he superintended its use for making the percussion caps.[14]

The need for metals and the arrival of the North Texas copper in Austin led to the creation of the Texas Copper Mining and Manufacturing Company, whose incorporation was approved in an act of May 28, 1864.[15] That company was fully organized by October, 1864, and its act of incorporation was amended in October, 1866, to provide that it could build and operate a manufactory for copper, iron, sulphur, and saltpeter at some site in the area of Clay, Wichita, Archer, Wilbarger, or Baylor Counties. In November, 1866, a second amendment extended the charter for a period of sixty years.[16] Original directors of this Texas company were M. D. K. Taylor, William R. Shannon, H. C. Lyon, William DeRyee, and E. Pendleton. Taylor and Shannon were both members of the Tenth Texas Legislature, which granted the 1864 charter. That same year J. W. Throckmorton and D. B. Culberson were in the Texas House of Representatives. Throckmorton was governor of Texas in 1866, when the charter was extended. In 1872 he was president of the mining company, and Culberson was one of the directors.

[12]Quoted in S. M. Eaton to Colonel C. T. Christensen, February 20, 1865, in *The War of the Rebellion: A Compilation of the Official Records of the Union and Confederate Armies* . . . , Series I, Vol. 48, Pt. I, p. 918.

[13]Texas Geological and Agricultural Survey, *First Annual Report of the Geological and Agricultural Survey of Texas*, By S. B. Buckley, 39.

[14]Texas Copper Mining and Manufacturing Company, *Charter and By-Laws of the Texas Copper Mining and Manufacturing Company . . . Prof. Wm. DeRyee's Geological Report*, 2.

[15]H. P. N. Gammel, *The Laws of Texas, 1822–1897*, V, 1623.

[16]Texas Copper Mining, *Charter and By-Laws of the Texas Copper Mining and Manufacturing Company*, 4–5; Dallas *Herald*, March 2, 1872.

The War events and disasters of 1864 and 1865 plus Indian devastation on the frontier precluded Texas geological activities or activities of the mining company until the end of the conflict. When the War ended, A. R. Roessler left Texas, his departure from the state seeming to coincide with the return of S. B. Buckley, who took over the revived Geological Survey. In 1866 Buckley's *Preliminary Report* to Governor Throckmorton stated that copper was said to be located on the headwaters of the Little Wichita in the buffalo country to which settlements had not extended. That same report complained of confusion in Austin because when the rooms once occupied by the Geological Survey had been used in the manufacture of percussion caps during the War the Survey's mineral specimens had been thrown in heaps to become dust-covered, with labels so displaced that the exact locations of samples were lost. Particularly in the case of copper samples exact locations were unknown and some of the most valuable samples were missing. Buckley's article on "The Mineral Resources of Texas," written during 1867 for the *Texas Almanac,* reported that copper occurred in several counties north of Fort Belknap, especially in Archer County, from which samples had been sent to New York by Governor Throckmorton.[17]

The Governor had evidently sent ore samples from the Texas Copper Mining Company to S. M. Swenson, pre-War Texas merchant and banker, who in 1867 was banking in New York. Swenson had the ore assayed by the Baltimore and Cuba Smelting and Mining Company, which found the sample to contain 60.38 per cent of copper, worth approximately $240.00 per ton. DeRyee made the 1868 Geological Report for the Texas Mining Company to the United States Department of the Interior. Joseph S. Wilson, commissioner of the General Land Office, acknowledged the DeRyee report but said that no specimen ore from the Texas Copper Mining and Manufacturing Company had reached his office. He had, however, received from M. D. Bullion, who was appointed vice-surveyor of Jack County on June 4, 1868, specimens that had proved rich in copper and interesting to mineralogists because they were pseudomorphs, having the composition of one mineral and the form of another. Bullion's letter which accompanied the ore had

[17]Texas Geological and Agricultural Survey, *A Preliminary Report of the Geological and Agricultural Survey of Texas,* By S. B. Buckley, 5, 24–25.

included the comment: " ... if this stuff is of any account, I can load up five hundred wagons without digging from a 320-acre tract." That information from Bullion, plus the report from DeRyee, with whom he had worked in Austin, were certainly of interest to the geologist assisting Commissioner Wilson, the former Texan A. R. Roessler, and Roessler seems to have returned to Texas to investigate for himself. His letter to the editors of the *Industrial Age* reports that in 1870, after traversing the Parker County area north of Weatherford and exploring in Archer, Wichita, Haskell, and Clay Counties, he concluded that "within the extent of one degree of longitude along the Little Wichita river, hardly a tract of 160 acres could be found without large accumulations of ore upon the surface."[18] One interesting aspect of this particular Roessler letter is the remarkable similarity in much of its wording to the DeRyee report which had gone to the General Land Office in 1868. Not the most edifying episode in Texas scientific history is the unseemly row which developed between geologists Buckley and Roessler. How scientific the exposition of their differences, I am not qualified to say; certainly the exchange was acrimonious. Buckley accused Roessler of plagiarizing, not DeRyee but Buckley himself. Roessler accused Buckley of fleeing Texas at the outbreak of the War, taking with him the notes of the Geological Survey and many of the specimens. Buckley countercharged that Roessler took with him to Washington maps which belonged to the state and scenes sketched by the Survey. Each accused the other of lying.[19]

At least both Buckley and Roessler agreed that there was copper in Archer County. The county had been created in 1858, but the War and the Indian menace would prevent official organization before 1880. The *Texas Almanac for 1871* had a section entitled "Descriptions of All the Counties," in which Archer County was described as one of the most valuable in the state for its minerals. A Roessler report on Texas minerals arrived too late from Washington to be included in this almanac.[20] The *Almanac for 1872,* however, did carry Roessler's "Mineral Wealth

[18]A. R. Roessler, "Texas Minerals," Dallas *Herald,* June 8, 1872, p. 1, col. 4.
[19]These exchanges appear in Buckley's *First Annual Report of the Geological and Agricultural Survey* (1874) and in A. R. Roessler, *Reply to the Charges Made by S. B. Buckley, State Geologist of Texas, in His Official Report of 1874 against Dr. B. F. Shumard and A. R. Roessler.*
[20]*Texas Almanac for 1871,* 91.

of Texas," with notes about copper and about the scientist, who on a stop in Waco had given the *Register* his account of recent explorations in areas rich in minerals even beyond his expectations. He reported that the discovery of high-grade copper in Archer County had been reported to the Academy of Natural Sciences in Philadelphia and that many persons interested in working the copper mines had made inquiries. Even with the expense of transportation, five hundred miles by wagon, the mines had proved profitable, but with the progress of the Texas Central Railroad toward the area the comparatively unknown regions might "prove to be a source of great mineral wealth."[21]

In 1871 federal officials, capitalists, diplomats, and distinguished businessmen in Washington, D.C., who organized the Texas Land and Copper Association were well aware of the accelerated railroad construction in and toward Texas. The Texas Legislature was well aware of the need for rail lines in the sprawling state, and its members were equally aware of the lobbying and pressuring activities of the railroad companies. Tom Scott, one of the Association's bigwigs, was president of the Texas and Pacific Railway, which would reach Dallas in 1872. The Galveston *Daily Civilian,* on June 20, 1872, quoted the Louisville *Ledger* as saying that Scott was interested in an extensive mining enterprise in Texas and would investigate the rich mineral resources of the state. Scott's publicity man, J. W. Forney, and the line's "official artist" were sent to tour Texas and report on its wonders along the line of the T. & P. Said Forney in his report dated from Philadelphia on July 15, 1872: "God, in his generosity, seems to have given a share of all his best gifts to Texas." Of one thing he was sure: "The copper of Texas depends on no hypothesis, but is a fact. I saw specimens of almost pure ore. Wichita, where my German friend goes with his colony of four hundred Saxons, abounds in this metal."[22] His German friend was C. Wegefarth, general superintendent of the Wichita Colonization, Agricultural, Mining, and Manufacturing Company, whose prospectus appeared in the Dallas *Herald* for July 13, 1872. The Wichita company planned to move north in August, 1872. Its route north to Wichita County intersected the western route taken by the Texas Land and Copper Association.[23]

[21]A. R. Roessler, "Mineral Resources of Texas," *Texas Almanac for 1872,* 161.
[22]John W. Forney, *What I Saw in Texas,* 21, 27.
[23]Sometime in May, 1872, Major Wegefarth visited Archer County, and G. A.

The Library of Congress reports that the Texas Land and Copper Association was not chartered by Congress or in Washington, D.C., where it was organized,[24] and whether or not it was a chartered company I have not been able to ascertain. According to Loew and Roessler, the company was not willing to depend on hearsay and so delegated an expedition of experts to study the factors of site, geology, and surroundings before the company purchased its mineral lands. The winter of 1871-72 was spent in preparation, and St. Louis was designated as the gathering place for the entourage, which was to include a small transport of approximately fifty men, under the command of Colonel McCarty, to accompany the experts.

A news item entitled "Scientific Exploration: The Mineral Resources of Texas to be Developed" appeared in *Flake's Bulletin* and was reprinted in the Dallas *Herald* on June 1, 1872:

A large and wealthy company, called the Texas Land and Copper Association, was recently organized in Washington, D.C., having for its object the development of the mineral resources and of the mining interests of Texas. The capital of the company is largely furnished abroad, and the names of Tom Scott, Admiral Porter, Jay Cook & Co., Kennedy & Son, four foreign ministers and others appear upon its roll of directors and stockholders.

This association has organized, equipped, and started forward for Texas under the military protection of the Government, a large and effective corps of topographical engineers and surveyors, by way of Missouri, Kansas and Texas Railroad. Col. W. C. McCarty commands the expedition. . . .

The expedition left St. Louis on the 15th inst. for Sherman, Texas, from whence it will proceed to Fort Richardson, Jack county.—There they will procure a government escort and proceed to business. They will explore the waters of the Big and Little Wichita rivers, Pease river, Salt and Double Mountain Fork of Brazos river, thence prospect westward across the great

---

Graham suggested to his brother that he try to locate Wegefarth's German colony in Young County. By late in the summer the colony was in Clay County, and R. G. Carter was offered pay to guide it to the Wichita area (G. A. Graham to E. S. Graham, May 29, 1872, E. S. Graham Papers; Carter, *On the Border with Mackenzie*, 329). Wegefarth was also a member of the board of directors of the Dallas and Wichita Railroad. In 1873 the Texas Legislature created Wegefarth County, but the creative act was repealed in 1876 (Dallas *Herald*, November 30, 1872; Gammel, *Laws of Texas*, VII, 619).

[24]Robert H. Land, Reference Department, Library of Congress, to L. Friend, February 23, 1965.

Staked Plain to the Rio Pecos, and ultimately, perhaps, to the Rio Grande.

It is well known that our State is rich in minerals—iron, copper and coal exist in vast deposits.—Silver, gold, sulphur, salt, mineral asphalt, etc., etc., are said to abound, and the object of this expedition is to open the mining industry and develop the existence of these deposits if possible. Attention will be especially devoted by the explorers to the geological structure of that section of country and localities of the extensive gypsum field, of marble, granite, porphyry and quarries of other useful building material are investigated.—When their labors are completed they will undoubtedly be able to give to the world a deal of valuable information concerning the hidden resources of the Lone Star State.

Flake's Bulletin was published in Galveston, home of the Expedition's commander, W. C. McCarty, who had been a bookkeeper for Hunt, Anderson, and Company before he became Galveston agent for the Erie Railroad in 1870. In 1871 he was a partner in the firm of Catlin, McCarty & Co., of 71 Broadway, New York, and Galveston. The company's advertising brochure of twenty seven pages ended with "Our Appeal" to the oppressed and homeless to flee to the virgin soil of Texas and occupy the lands lately vacated by the Comanche and the buffalo.[25] Included in land advertised by the company was acreage in Palo Pinto, Young, Archer, and Shackelford Counties, the exact area into which McCarty led the scientific expedition of 1872. The cover of McCarty's pamphlet was illustrated by the Texas seal, with its Lone Star, and below the seal were a few lines of verse:

> God has sent blessings on this favored land
> With an unsparing, yea, a bounteous hand;
> And rich, full harvest, from the upheaved soil,
> Reward the husbandman for all his toil.
> Peace fills the State with presence pure:
> Men ply their trades, contented and secure.
> Let us revere, with pride, this our adopted Land,
> Her present glory and a future grand.

Only an adopted son would have painted this idyllic picture of Texas in 1871, torn with political faction and strained social relations, suffer-

---

[25] W. C. McCarty, *A Few Practical Remarks about Texas, Her Resources, Climate and Soil, with Many Important Facts and Extracts from Reliable Sources,* 27.

ing a general breakdown of law and order, and seething with discontent under the Radical Republican administration of Edmund J. Davis. It was an administration that encouraged railroads, hoped to promote industry, and sought ways to stimulate the immigration necessary to populate and promote the state. Governor Davis himself was a director in the Texas and Southwestern Land and Immigration Company, chartered in Missouri.[26] That company and both the Texas Immigration Company and the Texas Land and Immigration Company, chartered in Texas in 1871, were created to act as agents between those who had Texas lands to dispose of and newcomers who sought homes. In 1870 Governor Davis had assured the Twelfth Legislature that "every industrious, able-bodied adult added to our population may be considered an addition of fifteen hundred dollars to the wealth of the state." To provide background for attracting immigrants, he urged the Legislature to provide for a complete geological survey, since the practical benefits of the earlier efforts at surveying had been lost. He suggested that the survey and the specimens it would collect be under the control of the General Land Office for correlation of geological knowledge with surveys of the public lands.[27] The Legislature created the Geological Bureau but made no appropriation to carry the act into effect; so in 1871 Davis again advocated a survey for the purpose of furnishing information to persons planning to immigrate to Texas or to invest capital in the state.[28] The act creating the Bureau, approved August 13, 1870, authorized the Governor to appoint a state geologist, who should appoint as assistants a chemist and a mineralogist. The man finally appointed as state geologist by Davis was John W. Glenn, who served from March 21, 1873, to March 6, 1874.[29] But the experts of the Texas Land and Copper Association earlier applied to Davis for those state positions. Before leaving for St. Louis and Texas, Dr. Oscar Loew of the College of the City of New York applied for the place of chemist in the Texas Geological Sur-

[26]Austin *Daily Republican,* March 21, 1870.
[27][Edmund J. Davis], *Message of Governor Edmund J. Davis to Twelfth Legislature, April 28, 1870.* 9–10.
[28][Edmund J. Davis], *Message of Gov. Edmund J. Davis, of the State of Texas,* 15.
[29]Robert Thomas Hill, *The Present Condition of Knowledge of the Geology of Texas* (Department of Interior, *Bulletin* of the United States Geological Survey No. 45), 38.

vey. Loew's recommendations included one from Lemuel D. Evans of the Texas Supreme Court. When Loew got to Texas he took out papers which declared his intention of becoming a Texas citizen. Francis White Johnson recommended to the Governor that Loew be the state chemist and that A. R. Roessler, already a Texan by choice, be the state geologist.[30]

Any inducement to make the frontier area of Northwest Texas attractive to immigrants was desirable, for settlement of that area was imperative if the constant Indian attacks were to be withstood. When General Randolph B. Marcy travelled from Fort Griffin to Fort Richardson in 1871 he found fewer people in that country than had been there on his last visit in 1854. Ranald S. Mackenzie wrote from Fort Richardson in 1872 that "the outrages committed by Indians had been more frequent than he had ever known before at any point where he had served."[31] Miner Kellogg had good reason for his apprehensions of Indian attack, for the Texas Land and Copper Association Expedition traversed an area included in eleven present-day Texas counties, only four of which (Grayson, Cooke, Montague, and Jack) had organized governments in 1872. Both Clay and Young Counties had been organized by 1857, but they were depopulated during the War. When Young County organization was abandoned in 1868 and its records removed to Jack County, Jacksboro became headquarters for the surveying district which embraced all of Texas north and west of Jack County. The district surveyorship was a lucrative office.[32] Because of the importance of Jacksboro both as the location of Fort Richardson and headquarters of a surveying district, the Expedition's lingering there for a full month becomes understandable. Most interesting if less understandable is Governor Davis' appointment of S. C. Plummer, one of the engineers of the Expedition, as surveyor of Young County, a county then without organization. The election register shows that Plummer was appointed, qualified, and commissioned all on the same day, May 10, 1872. A note in the register

[30]Oscar Loew to Edmund J. Davis, February 20, 1872, and April 12, 1872; L. D. Evans to Davis, April 11, 1872; F. W. Johnson to William Alexander, June 29, 1872, E. J. Davis File, Governors' Letters.

[31]Rupert Norval Richardson, *The Frontier of Northwest Texas, 1846 to 1876: Advance and Defense by the Pioneer Settlers of the Cross Timbers and Plains*, 28.

[32]W. S. Mabry, "Early West Texas and Panhandle Surveys," *Panhandle-Plains Historical Association Review*, II (1929), 24.

locates Young and Bexar Territory as being "west of Boon's District," Boon being the surveyor for Jack County.[33] Whether the "carpetbag" appointment of Plummer was accidental or contrived, it caused public dissatisfaction and created problems for deputy surveyors, who requested the Governor to clarify the areas of authority so that the legality of surveys could be established.[34]

The Expedition had to contend with problems both of rival surveyors and of rival locaters on the mineral lands. Kellogg mentions specifically an exploring group headed by Webster from Galveston and hints at other competitors. The Wegefarth Expedition did get up into the Clay and Wichita County area, although the Graham brothers had wanted to ask that group to locate near the Graham Salt Works in Young County. E. S. Graham had settled in the area of the old Peters' Colony on land purchased from the Texas Emigration and Land Company. Correspondence in the Graham Papers shows that his agent in Pennsylvania had copper ore from Texas which was "setting the people wild here." Roessler of the Texas Land and Copper Association invited Captain A. B. Gant, who had surveyed the Graham Salt Works, to accompany the "great Scientific exploring party," but Gant went instead with the Galveston group. On his return to Weatherford, he said he did not locate any mineral lands but "found plenty of copper."[35] Other areas of Texas had their attractions too. The *State Journal* of Austin, in an item entitled "Texas Mines to be Grabbed," reported that 150 wagons, with an escort of federal troops, were to rendezvous for an eighteen-month expedition to select and locate mineral lands north and west of San Antonio. In the opinion of the *Journal*, they had "located all the public lands of any value, and as they see Grant is going by the board, they are making a hasty grab at all the mineral lands."[36]

If the Texas Land and Copper Association actually established title to any of the lands in the Kiowa Peak area or near the Double Mountains,

---

[33] Election Register, 1872, Texas State Archives.

[34] F. W. Johnson to William Alexander, June 29, 1872; F. W. Johnson and J. M. Swisher to E. J. Davis, July 6, 1872; James M. Swisher to E. J. Davis, July 20, 1872, E. J. Davis File, Governors' Letters.

[35] James Dickey to E. S. Graham, May 18, May 31, and August 18, 1872; J. A. Woolfolk to E. S. Graham, May 31, 1872; G. A. Graham to E. S. Graham, June 7, July 16, and August 29, 1872, E. S. Graham Papers.

[36] Quoted in Galveston *Daily Civilian*, June 22, 1872.

the records of the Texas General Land Office do not show those titles. Reports of Roessler and McCarty in 1872 and 1873 proclaimed "plenty of copper found," but finding and mining were not the same. The Kellogg account of the trip ends on a note of disappointment and frustration; nothing was to happen to provide the writer with any bright postscripts.

The Artist-Diarist

Who was this official artist of the Texas Land and Copper Association's Expedition, who supplies the most detailed information about this Texas tour of 1872? His journal contained his name, the name and address of one brother, his child's name, one mention of his father, and practically nothing else of personal history. The diarist wrote legibly and well and he apparently had better than average educational background. Occasional comparisons of what he observed—a mountain, a mirage, or tumblebugs—with what he had seen elsewhere indicated more than a reading knowledge of far places. He was fastidious in personal habits and selective in companionship. He believed that letters were to be treasured, and his eagerness for mail denoted close family ties and complete devotion to a daughter. Human frailties and natural misfortunes—chigger bites, a queasy stomach, diarrhea, hemorrhoids, and sunstroke—beset him. He could have been philosophical about these disabilities had some of them been unavoidable; but most of these ordeals he attributed to stupid management of the Expedition. For the most part he seems to have fairly well held his tongue, but the diary did allow him to release his feelings. Still, of the man little is revealed.

The diary stands on its own merits as a contribution to Texana, to be catalogued as "Description and Travel" and subtitled "North Texas in 1872." To someone who has spent most of a lifetime in the area which Kellogg saw with an artist's eyes, the word pictures, describing the Red River banks as a "burnt sienna color" and the mass of bull thistle as "candelabra of many lights of brilliant purple on light pea green branches," evoke nostalgia and create a new awareness. But who was this artist?

Actually, autobiographical material, were it all assembled, is plentiful. Kellogg's Texas journal is but one of at least five kept by him, their entries totalling well over four hundred pages. He also left diaries covering a couple of months in 1867 and his experiences of 1843, as well as his random manuscript Notes and Memoranda, written in 1886 and 1887. These Notes consist of 67 consecutively numbered pages concerning his early years plus other memoranda and jottings to total 159 pages. Included in his literary remains are two sketch books, manuscript notebooks on "Bedouins and Camels" and on the "Sinai Peninsula," a total of 410 separate sketches and drawings, and fifty letters, chiefly from well-known personalities of his period. These items, no family letters included, are listed in a typescript prepared by Joseph S. Callery, of Sandusky, Ohio, a dealer who had the disposition of the materials after the death of Kellogg's only daughter in 1937. Other materials, particularly pictures, went to various descendants of Kellogg nieces and nephews. The manuscripts held by Callery have been widely dispersed: to private hands, to historical associations, to libraries, and to the Archives of American Art in Detroit, Michigan. Kellogg was the author of at least six pamphlet-type publications and several magazine articles, from all of which some knowledge of his activities at specific dates may be extracted. Printed material concerning him is very sparse. He receives mention briefly in several Cincinnati local history items; a few contemporaries spare him a line or two; various dictionaries of American artists give brief biographical notes which largely repeat each other. His obituary, which appeared in the Toledo *Blade* of February 18, 1889, was fairly detailed. His son-in-law, Edmund Locke, was vice president of the company which owned the *Blade,* and the biographical facts used by the paper seem to come directly from one set of Kellogg notes.

Callery, in describing the Kellogg manuscripts, deplored the fact that a collector of such unusual discernment who was an important figure in the art circles of his own day had not been the subject of a published biography. Since that plaint two articles have been devoted to Kellogg. E. P. Richardson, editor of the *Art Quarterly,* has devoted to Miner K. Kellogg the first of his studies on the Archives of American Art Records of Art Collectors and Dealers, identifying Kellogg as a painter, traveller, showman, publicist, and *marchand amateur,* "one of those clever, versatile men who can always attract notice and make their own way in the world, shifting easily from one kind of activity to another, or practicing several careers at once."[1] A display of Kellogg works in a gallery of the Cincinnati Art Museum was the occasion for a brief sketch of Kellogg by Richard J. Boyle in the *Cincinnati Art Museum Bulletin* in February, 1966.

Kellogg does merit a biography by an author possessed of considerable artistic knowledge and one who has access to all of his writings. This account, based chiefly on his manuscript Notes and Memoranda, may at least give background for some of his comments and comparisons in his Texas journal. He may seem to be a name dropper, but he had some interesting names to drop. His Notes were made when he was in his seventies, when his past was more vivid and more interesting than his present, and the names that stood out were those he recorded. A world traveller for his time, one of the early American innocents abroad, a dweller in artists' studios in Florence and Paris and London, someone who had dined with presidents and diplomats and moved in company close to princes, was something of an anomaly in the Texas Permian red-bed area in 1872.

Miner Kilbourne Kellogg was the third son of Charles Fraser and Almira Kilbourne (Harris) Kellogg. The father, a native of Connecticut, learned the trade of a tailor at Troy, New York, where he was married on December 29, 1808. The couple moved to Manlius Square, Onondaga County, New York, where an older brother, Leonard Kellogg, published the Manlius *Times*. Sheldon Ingalls was born in 1809, Charles Henry in 1812, and Miner Kilbourne on August 22, 1814, when the nation was involved in the War of 1812. The family moved to Oswego, and the father joined a dragoon company for the defense of Sackett Harbor, while the mother took care of the family business of weaving—on a Kellogg-invented loom—cotton fringes used for ornamenting window and bed curtains. The family retreated from Oswego before the town was captured by the British, who destroyed the little fringe factory and sank portions of its machinery in the Oswego River. The Kelloggs were living in Cazenovia, seven or eight miles from Manlius, when a sister named Almira Sophia was born on January 17, 1817.

Because Mrs. Kellogg was in poor health, probably tubercular, the

---

[1]E. P. Richardson, "Miner K. Kellogg," *Art Quarterly* (Spring, 1960), 271–274.

family decided to seek a less rigorous climate and proposed to move west to Nashville, Tennessee. Phineas, Jr., the youngest brother of Charles F. Kellogg, took the children and mother to stay with Grandfather Phineas at Orville, New York, until April, 1818. Then they joined the father at Geneva, New York, Uncle Phineas conveying them in a two-horse road wagon with a linen cloth cover by way of present Syracuse (then, Salt Point) to Geneva, then on to Anglica and Olean Point. No boats were available for purchase and the uncle had to return with the team while the Charles Kelloggs and a family of friends turned in to build their own boat for sailing west. It was an ark, eighteen feet long by eight feet wide. The mother often took the helm as the father plied the oars down the Allegheny to Pittsburgh, where the children saw their first strawberries and their first baker's bread. They floated on past the remains of Fort Duquesne, paid a call at Wellsville, glimpsed at Steubenville, Wheeling, and Marietta, and stopped for supplies at Limestone (present Maysville, Kentucky). On July 8, 1818, they reached Cincinnati, Ohio, the largest and most impressive town of the "Far West." There old friends persuaded them to settle, and the idea of Nashville as a future home was abandoned.

The "Queen City of the West," with some ten thousand inhabitants and not over a half dozen brick buildings, then nestled close to the river banks. The Kelloggs lived on their boat for two weeks until they secured a two-story frame house with a paling fence at the corner of Sixth and Main, their tailor shop also being on Main Street. A baby brother named Warren Converse was born on December 8, 1820; the mother died on December 15 and the baby four days later. The Kelloggs moved to Hudson's Row on Walnut Street before March of 1822, when the father married Miss Elizabeth Gazley, beloved by all the children and especially by the youngest son, who later wrote of her: "Father had been most fortunate in his selection, for every care and kindness was bestowed upon the children—economy and industry was the rule in the household, order and system reigned, and Father was made happy and prosperous."[2]

About the time of his father's second marriage Miner started to school, first under a teacher named Harrison, who used the newly intro-

[2]Miner K. Kellogg, "Notes for an Autobiography" (in Notes and Memoranda), 10.

duced Pestalozzi system, and then under seventeen-year-old Milo G. Williams, who imparted the rudiments of "Reading, Writing, and Cyphering." Business was good; domestic life was satisfactory; educational facilities were adequate; but Charles F. Kellogg, wavering between a line of personal benefits and a line of general good to humanity, was in a mental state to receive "any plausible doctrine that promised a revolution in the accepted order of things and would create an entirely new system in the organization of society for the good of the human race."[3] He was a natural to succumb to the enchanting doctrine of a new social system as propounded with calm logic and good temper by Robert Owen. Kellogg became an enthusiastic Owen proselyte, eager to start west for Owen's proposed Utopia at New Harmony, Indiana, on the Wabash River. Other Cincinnati families joined in the journey, westward by steamer on the Ohio to Mount Vernon and then fifteen miles overland to the village where the Rappites were moving from the town they had sold to Owen. The arrival was recorded by Owen's friend Donald Macdonald on Sunday, April 24, 1825: "Some families arrived from Cincinnati. Among the number were Mr. Jennings, Lawrence, & Kellogg. They reported that numerous other families were coming."[4]

As Miner Kellogg, then aged eleven, recalled the events sixty years later, he was the first member of his family to arrive in New Harmony and the last to depart. He accompanied the courier with advance notice of the new arrivals and was welcomed by Owen himself, of whom he wrote:

He was bareheaded and bald with a most benevolent aspect—bade us welcome in quiet and Fatherly tones, and reaching up for me, took me in his arms to descend—greeting me with a kiss, placed me upon the ground with the remark that I was the *first disciple of his* that had yet arrived to make a home with him in New Harmony.[5]

Kellogg devotes some fifteen pages of his manuscript Notes to the experiences in New Harmony: the factories, the military-type school, the severity of duties during a bitterly cold winter, his learning to swim, his early interest in music, his father's frustrated efforts to purchase clay for

[3]*Ibid.*, 16.
[4][Donald Macdonald], "The Diaries of Donald Macdonald, 1824–1826," *Indiana Historical Society Publication*, XIV, No. 2 (1942), 292.
[5]Kellogg, "Notes for an Autobiography" (in Notes and Memoranda), 18–19.

the manufacture of porcelain, the social life and diversions of the community, including the introduction of "bloomers" as feminine attire.

Owen was away from his New Heaven on Earth from June 6, 1825, to January, 1826. On his return he was accompanied by a "Boatload of Knowledge" in the persons of distinguished men and women who came to cast their lot in the community of equality. Kellogg did not mention all of the newcomers, but he did recall William McClure, geologist and philanthropist; Thomas Say, a zoologist and naturalist who took the lad on excursions into the woods in search of birds, insects, and reptiles; and William Phiquepal d'Arusmont, afterwards the husband of Frances Wright, who visited New Harmony and "encouraged the movement by her eloquence and engaging language and noble manners."[6] Two painters were in the group, Balthazar Obeonesser and Charles-Alexander Lesueur,[7] but if they gave Kellogg any lessons in art he omits that fact from his Notes. But he did begin to draw. At one of Owen's Town Hall lectures he rested a paper on his hand-woven straw hat and attempted a likeness of the speaker. Owen heard of the picture and asked to see it. "He smiled at it and said he thought it might be very good and added, patting me on the shoulder 'proceed my son and you will make an artist one of these days.' These words from so great a man impressed me for a very long time and were the first to give me courage to 'proceed' in making attempts of a similar character."[8]

The eldest of the Kellogg boys, Sheldon, also wrote his memoirs, or autobiography, which contains an interesting account of the contrast in the Alpha and Omega of New Harmony as far as the Kellogg family was concerned.

... We reached the vine clad hills overlooking the town on a brilliant Sunday morning. A serene and enchanting view. The clean, rosy looking, unpainted, brick dwellings and factory buildings and sparkling river beyond, the sun shining brilliantly on all. The sweet tones of the church-going bells

---

[6]*Ibid.*, 25. Thomas Say, "the father of descriptive entomology in America," arrived at New Harmony in 1825 and made it his home until his death in 1834 (see *Dictionary of American Biography*, XVI, 401–402). Frances Wright (1795–1852), a Scotch reformer and freethinker, joined Owen in editing the *New Harmony Gazette* in 1828 (see *DAB*, XX, 449–450). In August, 1965, New Harmony was designated as a National Historic Landmark.

[7]William E. Wilson, *The Angel and the Serpent*, 138–139.

[8]Kellogg, "Notes for an Autobiography" (in Notes and Memoranda), 29. Kellogg

reached our ears in Musical harmony. The whole party stopped with one accord to gloat the eye and gratify the ear. "Is this delicious spot to be our home in the future"? "How happy and united we shall be." The world we had left behind appeared unlovely in comparison. Exclamations of delight came from every side, and a supreme content dissipated our anxieties and soothingly settled upon us all. Our train slowly descended into the clean and broad Street, and each family had apportioned to it a nice brick dwelling, but a short time before having been vacated by families that had been sent off by Mr. Rapp to Economy, a town below Pittsburgh. I suppose none of our party had ever seen so cleanly, well dressed, and orderly behaved a village population before. They were all in Sunday attire, and I clearly recollect how much I was charmed by the pleasing variety of colors presented to my eyes. What a cheerful set of faces I saw, and how quietly contented they all appeared. Peace and prosperity certainly rested here amongst these cleanly and healthy looking Germans. And harmony and tranquility reigned amongst them until the very last one had left us for their more northern home. A mighty contrast was presented when the newly arrived communists had full sway of the destinies of our little village. Dissensions, bitterness, enviousness, carpings, wilful and selfish stubbornness not to be ruled by anyone brought about a general scatterment in the course of a couple of years—and our kind hearted and charitable philanthropist saw that American human nature and "circumstances" were not to be overcome to any good purpose.

The fact soon plainly shewed itself, that the great mass came there not having anything to throw into the common pool, but only to see how much they could take out. When they found that they had to labor for the common good and get only their equal share of the benefits, their selfishness produced dissatisfaction, and consequently, separation.

At about the end of a year, we found it necessary to leave, and permit the jarring elements, now so prominent, to work out their own salvation, if possible. We had lost faith in any successful result. So, three or four families with my father's—all old Cincinnati friends, agreed to go to a farm some miles from Charleston, near Jeffersonville, Indiana,—there to try the "community" principle once more.[9]

---

did an oil painting of Robert Dale Owen, son of Robert Owen and intimate of Kellogg during the New Harmony days. The painting is the property of Mrs. Aline Owen Neal, of New Harmony.

[9] Sheldon Ingalls Kellogg, "A Narrative of the Life of Sheldon Ingalls Kellogg," 32-34, TS furnished by Mrs. John Whitney Blemer.

The Kelloggs and their friends, financed by a loan of twenty dollars from Robert Owen, were but one of a number of splinter groups that departed New Harmony. Their second "community" effort was short-lived, and the penniless family eventually all got back to Cincinnati. Both Sheldon and Miner spent some time en route at Vevay, fifty miles below Cincinnati, in the home of a brother-in-law of their stepmother, one General Keen, the local postmaster and newspaper editor. Miner, the last one to be summoned home, lived for a time with the Swing family as "the other members of the family had been quartered in other places among friends who pitied our forlorn condition but never uttered a word about the 'crazy doings' that had so impoverished and humiliated us." The two years of labor and deprivation proved too much for Elizabeth Gazley Kellogg, who was soon buried beside Mrs. Almira Kellogg.

The father took a small store, attracted some of his old customers, and soon prospered sufficiently to buy a stock of clothing from Philadelphia and put out a sign at a nice shop on Fourth and Main. He was practicing a new system of cutting learned from Allen Ward of Philadelphia. It was the Ward fashion plates from which Miner began to copy in pencil and to make his first efforts at drawing the human form.[10] Young Kellogg helped his father in cleaning the shop, but he lived in the home of James W. Gazley, brother of the second Mrs. Kellogg, a former congressman and the editor of the local *Western Tiller*, where Miner was printer's devil and newsboy. As Charles F. Kellogg continued to prosper, he made his third good marriage, on February 10, 1827, Mrs. Eliza (Smith) Downes, who reared little Almira and brought up her own family of Kellogg children.

Kellogg's memories of his father include his activities as a prominent member of the Masonic order, in a period and a place of strong Anti-Masonic sentiment, and also his affiliation with the followers of Emanuel Swedenborg, after his wavering from the New England Puritanism of his parents through the Episcopal Church, Universalism, and Unitarianism. The leading Swedenborgian in Cincinnati was Adam Hurdus, a local organ builder, promoter of the Sunday school which Miner at-

[10]Kellogg, "Notes for an Autobiography" (in Notes and Memoranda), 50.

tended, often the preacher, and the donor of the first organ to the church. Interest in music was a bond between father and son. The austere grandparents had destroyed the violin which Charles F. Kellogg had made for himself, and so perhaps destroyed his ties with the family church and initiated a family tradition of liberalism and religious tolerance. When, at New Harmony, Miner had made himself a fife of cane, he wanted to play the tunes his father had learned as a fifer during the War. The father managed somehow to buy the boy a silver flute. He later reached the Keen family in Vevay with the help of that flute, by playing "Washington's March" for a little boy in exchange for directions to the road to Vevay. On the steamboat back to Cincinnati, the flute also ensured a friendship with the Negro steward, who gave Miner his first violin. The father provided a new violin and enrolled Miner as the first music pupil of Joseph Tasso—Italian by descent, Mexican by birth, and Paris trained —who became professor of music in the Cincinnati Female Academy in 1829.[11] After about a year under Tasso's tutelage Miner was chosen to play a "solo with variations," unaccompanied, at the Bazaar projected by Frances Milton Trollope, who had a millinery business in Cincinnati between 1829 and 1836.[12] A fellow music pupil, James Frederick Wood, whom Kellogg was to encounter later in Rome and who was ultimately a Roman Catholic Bishop in Cincinnati, was perhaps also one of the band of amateur musicians who often serenaded at night.

Any other spare time went to painting, sometimes at the chair factory or with carriage painters, sign painters, or anyone who would help Kellogg in grinding and mixing colors and using brushes. The brilliant color and polish of the fire engines attracted him to join Fire Company "No. 3" and run with his hose carriage and engines named "Constitution" and "Liberty." There was no pay, but freedom from city taxes and exemption from military duties constituted fringe benefits.

Both Kellogg and Hiram Powers had some art instruction from Frederick Eckstein, and Powers used his fellow student as model for a bust which is inscribed "M. K. Kellogg, Age 14 Years—The first bust by

---

[11]Henry A. and Mrs. Kate B. Ford (comps.), *History of Cincinnati, Ohio, with Illustrations and Biographical Sketches*, 248.

[12]Kellogg, "Notes for an Autobiography" (in Notes and Memoranda), 52. Mrs. Trollope did not endear herself to Cincinnati by her book on the *Domestic Manners of the Americans*.

Hiram Powers, Cincinnati, Ohio, 1828." When Abraham G. D. Tuthill, a portrait painter, arrived in Cincinnati in 1831, young Kellogg took lessons in oil painting. At the age of seventeen, he decided to abandon his job as dry-goods clerk for Patterson and Grant and establish his own studio in a single room on the third floor of a building at the corner of Fifth and Main Streets. His outstanding achievement was his always remarkable facility in copying portraits, and his copies of works by John Vanderlyn and Rembrandt Peale revealed his proficiency. Efforts at original work included a portrait of his friend Adam Hurdus. During a cholera epidemic in 1832, Kellogg worked gratis in the Cincinnati hospital, learned a bit about anatomy, and persuaded Dr. James M. Staughton to let him attend anatomical lectures at the Medical College without charge. His quest for art students was in vain, although he made up a class at the Mechanics' Institute in Mrs. Trollope's Bazaar and gave them free lessons in perspective. He also took immigrant boys as "non paying" students. His studio had to be moved four times before he got his first paying job—oil paintings of "eight colossal eyes for the college," commissioned by Dr. Staughton.[10]

Kellogg is supposed to have received some painting instruction from Frederick Franks, a Swedish artist who had a painting gallery and a museum in Cincinnati.[14] At any rate, Franks employed Kellogg to provide music for the "dissolving views" in the museum and in 1833 persuaded Kellogg to travel with him to help with exhibits on a tour supposed to end in Baltimore. With his violin and $5.00 the young artist left home —to be gone for six or seven years.

At Louisville, where also the cholera had struck, they put on an exhibit and Kellogg volunteered to play in the theater orchestra for a "cholera benefit" performance. Compensation was the opportunity to see Edwin Forrest play "Damon" and the chance to buy a better violin. As they turned east, they found that cholera had again struck at Cincinnati, and Kellogg wound up at Dayton, sick and broke. Uncle Phineas Kellogg supplied food, and the nephew painted his portrait in payment. From Dayton, Kellogg accompanied Elder Lane—one of the incorpo-

---

[13]Kellogg, "Mems" (unpaged sheets in Notes and Memoranda); Ford, *History of Cincinnati, Ohio*, 299.
[14]George C. Groce and David H. Wallace (eds.), *The New-York Historical Society's Dictionary of Artists in America, 1564–1860*, 240.

rators of the Lane Theological Seminary in Cincinnati in 1828[15]—to Cleveland by stage, to Buffalo by steam, by the Erie Canal to Troy, by rail to Albany, and then down the Hudson to New York. Samuel L. Waldo and William Jewett,[16] noted and successful portrait painters of the city, gave him "kind and good counsel." He got in a free concert at Castle Garden, but attempts to sleep in the park proved so unsuccessful that he had to take lodging near the wharf, and he arrived in Brunswick, New Jersey, with "only fifty cents in the world." He rode one of Lane's horses across New Jersey to Milford on the Delaware and literally painted his way at Everittstown, Flemington, Frenchtown, Lambertville, and in New Hope, Pennsylvania. Acquaintance with the lawyers and public officials at Flemington led him to Trenton, where life took a little turn for the better.

The New Jersey Assembly, impressed by his copy of a Gilbert Stuart portrait of Washington, commissioned him to paint a picture of Washington for the state capitol. The resulting portrait won him increased compensation, a resolution of thanks, and a recommendation from members of the state government that President Van Buren appoint the artist to West Point. The idea of the military academy had been implanted by General Robert Swartwout, New York merchant and agent for the Navy,[17] who sat for Kellogg in Trenton. When their conversations revealed Kellogg's desire to go to Italy to pursue his career as an artist, Swartwout suggested that West Point would give him the necessary foundation in science and drawing. With this idea in mind and with his sixty dollars pay for the Washington picture in his pocket, the artist left by stagecoach for Washington city, where New Jersey Senators Samuel Lewis Southard and Garret Dorset Wall introduced him to the President. Kellogg was too old to be appointed as a cadet, but perhaps special arrangements could be made. Van Buren sent him to Secretary of War Joel R. Poinsett, who, in turn, arranged interviews with all the other Cabinet members. The accumulated packet of autographed letters from the Cabinet to Academy Superintendent Richard Delafield and to indi-

---

[15]*History of Cincinnati and Hamilton County, Ohio; Their Past and Present* . . . , I, 142.

[16]Groce and Wallace, *New-York Historical Society's Dictionary of Artists,* 350, 654.

[17]*Appleton's Cyclopaedia of American Biography,* VI, 5.

THE ARTIST-DIARIST 31

vidual professors secured for Kellogg admission to the Point, promises of assistance, a free room in the bachelor home of Dennis Hart Mahan, and the prospect of board at "Mammy" Thompson's for three dollars a week.

The small sums collected in Trenton for outstanding portrait orders and the money the cadets paid him for having their pictures sketched did not provide enough income for even slight expenses, and any extra priming of the purse was welcome. That was the reason he rode horseback over icy roads to do a portrait of the dead daughter of General Leavenworth. The picture had to be made from a plaster death mask, extremely difficult to fashion in the freezing weather, and the pay amounted to less than half what he had been promised. This side job had been tossed his way by Robert Walter Weir,[18] who taught art at the Academy, befriended the cadets generally, and used his studio for student gatherings and a stage for amateur theatricals, in many of which Kellogg participated. Weir had wondered at his protégé's insistence on studying topography and architecture as well as perspective and art, but forebore opposition when the student insisted on his need to "learn how to study." In Weir's studio he designed and cast the figure for the frieze for the Point's new Art Hall, and there he gave sittings for Weir as the master prepared his painting of "The Embarkation of the Pilgrims," destined for the rotunda of the Capitol in Washington. Kellogg painted a portrait of Weir, which the teacher sent to the Academy of Design to be exhibited with the title of "Portrait of a Gentleman."[19] A press notice of the painting was gratifying, even when in error: "This we believe is by an English artist—it is rather low in tone but exceedingly clever." So wrote James Edward Freeman,[20] whom Kellogg would meet years later in Rome.

Kellogg's memories of West Point and its faculty and cadets, so many of whose names were immortalized in the years from 1861 to 1865, were nostalgic. His factual report to Secretary of War Poinsett, who had entertained him in his home and had an appreciation of his potentialities, perhaps tells best the West Point story.

[18]Robert Walter Weir (1803–1889) is listed in *Dictionary of American Biography,* as are many of Kellogg's acquaintances.
[19]*New York National Academy of Design Exhibition Record, 1826–1860,* I, 273
[20]James Edward Freeman (1808-1884) receives mention in *DAB.*

West Point, N.Y. Dec. 31, 1838

To the Hon J. R. Poinsett
Respected Sir

Being here through your favor, is all the apology I can offer for thus intruding upon your time.

It pleases me to be able to say that the many benefits I proposed to myself by a season in study at this institution, I am daily realizing. I have been here 3 months. Mr. Mahan has furnished me with room, bed, and fuel in his own house. Dr. Bliss is my instructor in Geometry & Lt. Alden in French. My *Pencil* is directed by Prof. Weir through whose kindness I receive valuable information in the art. His copious library is freely opened to me, for which I cannot be too thankful.

Such a combination of benefits, so cheerfully conferred fills me with the most grateful feelings towards all concerned.

To you, Sir, in particular am I indebted for opening the way to these incalculable advantages—on the proper use of which, depend my future usefulness in the pursuit of the Art.

My stay will probably be until June next.

Upon your disinterested kindness in my behalf I often reflect with great delight; it shall be my duty and desire to prove myself worthy of it.[21]

When June next came, Kellogg was irresistibly drawn home to family and friends, but he had been away too long and had changed too much; he "could not go home again." Welcomes were warm, and he was elected to membership in the Third New Jerusalem Society, so associating himself with his father in Swedenborgianism, but the associates of his youth had disappeared or changed; old playgrounds were built over; old streets were unrecognizable. He became so unnerved that only seclusion in the home of a friend and a diet limited to fresh milk effected a cure. Whatever the cause, the ulcer or depression or ennui disappeared when the Jacksonian Democrats in Cincinnati made up a purse and dispatched him to the Hermitage to paint a portrait of Old Hickory. Andrew Jackson, now three years removed from the Presidency, was worn from financial problems of his family and the political problems of his friends, but he remained the idol of the nation.

President Jackson, Andrew Jackson Donelson, and Kellogg made up the Hermitage household for over six weeks in 1840, while Kellogg's

[21]Miner K. Kellogg to Joel R. Poinsett, December 31, 1838, Joel R. Poinsett Papers.

studio, adjoining his bedroom, was close to the Jackson apartment so that the General would have no stairs to climb. There was healing for Kellogg in the quietness of the surroundings and in new vistas opened as the old General chatted on about the fight over the National Bank, the battle of New Orleans, the violence of political antipathies, injustice to his beloved Rachel, and the problems of orphan kittens. Especially therapeutic was the approval of the completed picture when Jackson invited his friends to view it. Among the guests were Major Robert Armstrong, Major Donelson, and Governor James K. Polk of Tennessee. As they were leaving, the Governor asked that the portrait be displayed in the State House at Nashville, Kellogg to be a guest at the Polk home for the occasion. Jackson's own carriage conveyed the artist to Nashville, complete with the picture and his souvenirs, a lock of Jackson's hair, and three canes grown at the Hermitage. In Nashville he "made a trio at the table" with the Polks while he painted the Governor's portrait[22] and copied the Jackson picture for him "half the size of the original, surrounding the head and bust by an oval border upon which was inscribed a sentence taken from one of his public speeches: 'Without virtue and intelligence in the people, no free government can stand'."

Back in Cincinnati, Kellogg framed the Jackson picture and delivered it to the committee, who held a brief public exhibit in his studio and agreed that it should be taken to Washington for exhibition, with a stopover exhibit in Pittsburgh. In Washington a room in the Capitol was set aside for the viewing, and President Van Buren and various Cabinet members ordered copies for their departments. Poinsett commissioned his own portrait, as did the President, for it was an election year and Van Buren could use a new picture. Kellogg wrote Jackson that he spent the "entire time of the presidential battle in placing upon canvas the features of the firm and unflinching defender of the rights of the People."[23] Van Buren had been sure of the Democratic nomination at Baltimore, but William Henry Harrison defeated him in the November election, and that unwelcome news reached the presidential ear during his last sitting for the portrait. Kellogg, however, had a place in another exhibit;

[22]James K. Polk, *The Diary of James K. Polk during His Presidency, 1845 to 1849,* III, 225, 395.
[23]Kellogg to Andrew Jackson, December 30, 1840. Papers of Andrew Jackson, 1st Series, Vol. 104, Microfilm Reel 53. See also Martin Van Buren to Jackson, May

the Pennsylvania Academy of Fine Arts in 1840 listed his "Portrait of an Artist" as sale item No. 65 for the Artist's Fund Society.[24]

In Washington, Kellogg was accredited by the President as a courier for the State Department, and early in January, 1841, he sailed from Boston on the sloop-of-war *Preble* under Captain Vorhees. Their first destination was Lisbon, to deliver the United States minister to Portugal. For two weeks they were delayed in a fog in the Tagus. In a period of strained relations with England, Gibraltar was closed to them; so the next stop was the United States' Mediterranean station at Port Mahon, to deliver letters to Commodore Isaac Hull, letters bearing on English troubles: the Oregon question, the quarrel over the northeastern boundary, and problems holding over from the Canadian rebellion in 1837.[25] There was no United States vessel on which Kellogg could proceed on his mission to Naples; so with Hull's reluctant consent, he finished his trip on an Irish yacht, only to find Naples under a nine-day quarantine. His sketches made en route, were labelled "Racy Bits by the Wayside" and were dated "Naples, 26 March, 1841."[26] The communications he bore for Ex-Governor Enos Thompson Throop, then serving as chargé d'affaires to the Kingdom of the two Sicilies, had to be lifted by tongs from a box held out by Kellogg. The artist used his period of quarantine to make water-color sketches of distant Vesuvius, and on his final release he joined Ashur Brown Durand, another American artist making the customary pilgrimage to European art centers.[27] They visited Vesuvius and the Pompeii Museum before going on to Rome, where Durand finished his portrait of artist Samuel B. Waugh. Then they were off to Florence, where Kellogg renewed acquaintance with his old friend Hiram Powers.[28] The men had had similar boyhoods with jobs as clerks

---

15, 1841, in John Spencer Bassett (ed.), *Correspondence of Andrew Jackson*, VI, 112.

[24]Anna Wells Rutledge (comp. and ed.), *Cumulative Record of Exhibition Catalogues. The Pennsylvania Academy of Fine Arts, 1807–1870. The Society of Artists, 1800–1814. The Artists's Fund Society, 1835–1845*, 113.

[25]For the career of Isaac Hull (1773-1843), commodore until July, 1841, see *DAB*, IX, 360–361.

[26]Joseph S. Callery, "A Short Biography of Miner Kilbourne Kellogg," 4.

[27]Groce and Wallace, *New-York Historical Society's Dictionary of Artists*, 196–197.

[28]Miner Kilbourne Kellogg, *Mr. Miner K. Kellogg to His Friends*, 6. For a discussion of Hiram Powers, an important sculptor of the time, *DAB*, XV, 158–160.

COURTESY CINCINNATI ART MUSEUM

M. K. Kellogg in oriental dress. Oil portrait by Marling, 1846. Cincinnati Art Museum, gift of Paul G. Pennoyer, New York.

COURTESY HERMAN DREW NICHOLS,
PIEDMONT, CALIFORNIA

Alvina Kilbourne Harris Kellogg. Oil portrait by her son Miner K. Kellogg.

COURTESY HERMAN DREW NICHOLS,
PIEDMONT, CALIFORNIA

Charles Fraser Kellogg. Oil portrait by his son Miner K. Kellogg.

COURTESY CINCINNATI ART MUSEUM

Sheldon Ingalls Kellogg. Oil portrait by his brother, Miner K. Kellogg. Cincinnati Art Museum, gift of Paul G. Pennoyer, New York.

COURTESY CINCINNATI ART MUSEUM

Catherine Raynor Edmonds Kellogg, wife of Sheldon Ingalls Kellogg. Oil portrait by her brother-in-law Miner K. Kellogg. Cincinnati Art Museum, gift of Paul G. Pennoyer, New York.

COURTESY CINCINNATI ART MUSEUM

Kellogg's "caravan" outside the walls of Jerusalem preparing to leave the city. Oil painting by Miner K. Kellogg. Cincinnati Art Museum, gift of Paul G. Pennoyer, New York.

Bust of Kellogg by Hiram Powers, 1828. Cincinnati Art Museum, gift of Paul G. Pennoyer, New York.

COURTESY MRS. JOHN WHITNEY
BLEMER, DIABLO, CALIFORNIA

Landscape, overlooking the Arno Valley, Italy. Oil painting by Miner K. Kellogg, c. 1861–1865.

and errand boys. Powers had been apprenticed to a clockmaker before he so successfully designed and animated the wax figures in the Cincinnati Western Museum.[29] The outstanding local citizen and art patron, Nicholas Longworth, had befriended Powers, given him valuable introductions to prominent men in Washington for whom he did portrait busts, and in 1837 had made it possible for Powers to go to Florence, where he was to spend the rest of his life. Both Kellogg and Powers were Swedenborgians; both had experienced the artistic ferment of their Ohio home town.

In May, 1841, Kellogg wrote to his patron, Poinsett, to report on the adventures of his voyage and the advantages he was anticipating in Florence. Poinsett's reply ran: "You are perfectly right to give up the principal part of your time to copy nature. It is certainly the most proper study of the artist." He urged his protégé to study the works of the masters, and in reply to Kellogg's proffer of services in Florence answered·

We want nothing from there except news of your success and that of your brother artists. I wish you would all take part in promoting the views of the Founders of the National Institution at Washington. It is a matter that concerns both your interests & patriotism. A flourishing state of the arts at the seat of government would be felt in the remotest parts of our country and would induce governments, states and individuals to foster and patronize them.[30]

Kellogg visited Bologna, Venice, and other cities of northern Italy before settling in Florence for a prolonged study of the old masters. His remarkable gift for copying paintings with exactness secured from the director of the Pitti Palace permission to copy a Raphael canvas, a copy produced in less than six weeks and sold subsequently to P. M. Suydam, of New York, who became Kellogg's long-time friend. Copying of other paintings in the Pitti Palace and of representative works in the Uffizi followed. A bachelor artist friend, Seymour Kirkup, helped with advice and with books from his library. Officials of the galleries and the grand duke congratulated Kellogg on the expert facsimiles of works by Titian,

---

[29]Ford, *History of Cincinnati, Ohio*, 235; Edward H. Dwight, "Art in Early Cincinnati," The Cincinnati Art Museum Bulletin (August, 1953), 7.

[30]Poinsett to Kellogg, September 17, 1841, Miner K. Kellogg Papers.

Guido, and others. William Woodburn, expert for the National Gallery in London, was also impressed when he visited Kellogg's studio, and he gave the artist letters of introduction to acquaintances in Constantinople.

In December, 1843, Kellogg departed Florence for Egypt. At Malta he made accurate drawings of the ruins of Krendi; his journal entry of January 29, 1844, described the colorings in the Egyptian tomb discovered by the archaeologist Giovanni Belzoni in the Valley of the Kings, not far from Thebes. Despite pain from rheumatism, Kellogg explored the Pyramids and Cairo. He hired camels to take him to the Holy Land because an epidemic of the plague prevented his going by boat from Alexandria; the alternative proved a fortunate substitute, for the dry desert air dispelled the rheumatism. Henceforth Kellogg was impressed with the possibilities of using camels in arid areas. In early March, 1844, he was with friends at a convent at Mount Sinai and, accompanied by A. B. Ackworth, of London, went to sketch the holy mountain. His study of the topography of the area convinced him that traditional Mount Sinai, not Mount Horeb as some authorities had announced, was truly the scene of Moses' promulgation of the Law to the wandering Israelites.[31] From Sinai he proceeded to Hebron and after another nine-day quarantine entered Jerusalem. There he attended a general meeting of missionaries to the Holy Land before he continued sketching his way to Damascus. The return trip was by Beirut and Smyrna (another quarantine there) and then to Leghorn and Florence. He left Italy again in December, 1844, this time for Constantinople to visit Dabney Smith Carr, the American minister to the Sublime Porte. Of course he sketched all the way—Leghorn to Naples to Malta to Smyrna and up the Hellespont to take up residence in the foreign quarter at Pera. A letter to the Cincinnati homefolk, February 27, 1845, revealed him as an interesting raconteur with an observing eye. The editor of Cist's *Miscellany,* in which the letter was printed, informed his readers that it had been "pierced with incisions and fumigated with various odors as a preventive

---

[31] When Kellogg was in the United States some four years later he contributed to the *Literary World,* II (February 19, 1848) an article entitled "The Position of Mount Sinai Examined," in which he described the topography of the area to justify his differences in opinion from the holdings of some noted Biblical scholars. His article was quoted, with commendation, by John Kitto in an 1850 book called *Scripture Lands; Described in a Series of Historical, Geographical, and Topographical Sketches,* 66–72.

to transmitting the plague. Among these that of vinegar predominates."[32]

Kellogg and Carr kept bachelor quarters and entertained and were entertained even though Carr's annual salary of three thousand dollars precluded his giving diplomatic receptions. There were interesting people to meet, especially the members of the various embassies and the occasional foreign visitors, including British and American salesmen, and the English missionary Joseph Wolff, an Anglican priest who was a Jew converted to Protestantism by way of Catholicism.[33]

Kellogg's studio was a room in a Greek home. There he painted British Consul General Cartwright and finished a group portrait of the three daughters of Sir Stratford Canning, the British ambassador, in oriental costume. More challenging and interesting was the arrangement to do a portrait of an important Turkish official, especially since the Moslem faith forbade the representation of living persons. The way had been paved in 1840, however, when Sultan Abdul Madjid allowed Sir David Wilke to paint his picture.[34] It would be nice diplomatic balancing for an American to paint the second man in the Turkish hierarchy. This was the grand seraskier, Riza Pasha.[35] Carr asked the permission, and Kellogg took his canvas to the Riza's palace on the Bosporus, where a black eunuch from the harem acted as a guard during the sittings. After a formal reception with members of Riza's official escort present for the viewing of the framed portrait, an aide presented Kellogg with a red Morocco case in which was a gold filigree holder and a coffee cup studded with diamonds. The picture had been previously taken into the harem for viewing by the ladies; they also approved.

Riza Pasha, opponent of reform and protégé of the Russian ambassador, had as his chief political antagonist the grand vizier, Reschid Pasha,

[32]Charles Cist (comp.), *The Cincinnati Miscellany; or Antiquities of the West and Pioneer History and General and Local Statistics*, 243.

[33]Wolff was on his return trip to England after an experience described in his book, *Narrative of a Mission to Bokhara, in the Years 1843–1845, to Ascertain the Fate of Colonel Stoddart and Captain Conolly*, 347.

[34]Sir David Wilkie (1785-1841) is recognized in *Dictionary of National Biography*, Vol. 61, pp. 253-258.

[35]For Riza Pasha (Riza Hasán Bajá, 1809–1859), grand marshal of Turkey and distinguished for services in the Crimean War, see *Enciclopedia Universal Ilustrada*, Vol. 51, p. 919. For Reschid Pasha (Mustafá Mehemed) see *ibid.*, Vol. 50, pp. 1099-2000.

leader of the Reform Party and object of assiduous cultivation by Stratford Canning, who used young Austen Henry Layard of his staff as his agent in dealing with the Grand Vizier. Layard and Kellogg became fast friends. With Layard, Kellogg would ride about Constantinople searching for subjects: a Hebrew bride in her wedding costume or a blind Bulgarian with a black bear. They dined with the Spanish ambassador and with Baron de Baer, Belgian minister and noted coin collector. Meals were followed by "pipes and narghile" or the hookah. Dinner at the Cannings would be accompanied by conversation and music, with Layard on the flute and Count Perponcher on the violin.

One evening at the Cannings' an exciting and interesting discussion developed about Andrew Jackson's action in the execution of Alexander Arbuthnot and Robert Ambrister during the Florida War, with Kellogg ardently defending his hero, unaware that Canning at the time had been British minister in Washington and had used every possible means to have Jackson punished for his treatment of those two British subjects. Soon after the dinner party came the news of Jackson's death. Although Kellogg and his host held differing opinions about Jackson, on his next dinner invitation to Kellogg, Canning added a gracious postscript: "Allow me to condole with you on the loss of your illustrious fellow countryman & friend."[36] At the time of Kellogg's departure from Constantinople Stratford Canning presented to the artist a gift accompanied by the following note, dated Pera, August 7, 1845: "Dear Sir, The tiny snuff box which I venture to send with this, is intended to aid your recollection of one who wishes you well and hopes your talent will in due season find a proper theater for its display."[37]

When Layard heard of some discoveries of ancient ruins at Aezani in Asia Minor, he suggested that Kellogg and Perponcher, secretary to the Prussian legation, accompany him to the site. Layard described the group as a "very merry party" because his companions were good travellers, were amusing, agreeable, and well informed, and were "ready to meet with good humour the privations and difficulties of Turkish traveling."[38] In July, 1845, they went by steamer to Iznik and by horseback across Anatolia to present Bursa—then called Broussa—where Layard

[36]Stratford Canning to Kellogg, August 5, 1845, Miner K. Kellogg Papers.
[37]Canning to Kellogg, August 7, 1845, *ibid*.
[38]Layard Papers, Add. ms. 38913, Memoirs, I, 330.

was ill with sunstroke for five days. On his recovery they climbed Olimpio de Bitnia and sampled mint juleps made with the snow found eternally on its crest. At the ruins Layard explored and copied inscriptions and Kellogg sketched the scenery and made careful drawings of the ruins of temples, bridges, and amphitheaters. As he recalled, "we worked like beavers to be *the first* to make known the details and value of ruins until this time only hinted at by some former travellers." Their return trip, with Kellogg sketches of course, was by way of ancient Nicomedia. Back in Constantinople, Layard announced that he planned to try his luck in opening some of the tumuli on the Euphrates in search of the ruins of Nineveh. If he was not successful he would join Kellogg in Italy and together they would go to America to the Oregon country. Layard's first letter to Kellogg reported success in the project which was to result in his becoming known as "Layard of Nineveh." And Kellogg would never get further west than Texas.

Colonel Carr and Kellogg left for Florence together, as the artist had promised the minister to show him the Italian wonders. Because of that he had to refuse Sir Stratford's invitation to travel by the ambassador's steamer as escort for Lady Canning and her daughters on their way to Venice.

When Kellogg resumed life in the artist colony in Florence, he shared with Hiram Powers the Layard reports on the Nineveh discoveries. Layard wrote in July, 1846, that "Mr. Powers, the sculptor, has been kind enough to send me the fullest instructions for taking moulds and then casting." To Kellogg he described more personal experiences than the technical problems of preserving of his archaeological discoveries.

> The morals of the ladies of this country are exceedingly lax . . . There is, however little beauty in Mosul, but at Bagdad there are some remarkably pretty women. In Mosul, providing your dwelling is convenient, the ladies make no difficulty in walking in, not only when you want them, but uninvited, and at Bagdad the same good custom prevails.[39]

Meantime Kellogg worked in another trip, this time on the *U.S.S. Saranac.* He sketched Etna in eruption, visited Tunis and was presented to the Bey, and visited the ruins of ancient Carthage. Soon afterwards,

---

[39]Gordon Waterfield, *Layard of Nineveh,* 145, 127.

Bayard Taylor met Kellogg at the Powers home and wrote to his brother:

> I met Kellogg, an American painter of very great talent, who has been traveling in Greece, Egypt, Syria, Asia Minor, and Turkey. I have been to his studio, and looked over some hundreds of sketches which he brought back. He was at Thebes, was thirty days on and around Mount Sinai, and spent nine months in Constantinople ... He showed me a splendid diamond cup, given him by Riza Pacha, Grand Visier to the Sultan, for painting his portrait, and a snuff-box of gold and agate, a present from Sir Stratford Canning. He paints splendidly.[40]

Taylor embellished one of his many travel books with an account of a delightful evening in Florence spent in the company of gifted and likeminded Americans, some eight or ten painters and sculptors who he thought would rank high among living artists. Besides the outstanding Powers, he mentioned Henry Kirke Brown and George L. Brown, Horatio Greenough, Chauncey B. Ives, and Kellogg "whose sketches are of great interest and value, and their results will give him an enviable reputation."[41] This was about the time that at least one canvas went back to New York to keep Kellogg's reputation alive there. "The Straw Braider" was Item 149 in the 1845 Exhibition at the National Academy of Design.[42]

Although Powers was able to make Taylor a loan of fifty dollars to start him and his knapsack on the way to Paris, the sculptor was in a financial plight himself and began to accept loans from Kellogg. He also persuaded Kellogg, "as being his only reliable friend," to undertake a voyage to America to display in his native country Powers' statue "The Greek Slave" in the hope of enhancing his prestige as an artist as well as supplying his pressing financial necessities.[43] The touring exhibit did mean both money and prestige for Powers; for Kellogg it ultimately turned out disastrously; the men quarrelled, and finally, at least so Kel-

---

[40]Bayard Taylor to Franklin Taylor, October 26, 1846, Horace E. Scudder and Marie Hansen-Taylor (eds.), *Life and Letters of Bayard Taylor*, I, 57.

[41]Bayard Taylor, *Views A-Foot; or Europe Seen with Knapsack and Staff*, 383.

[42]*New York National Academy of Design Exhibition Record 1826–1860*, I, 273.

[43]Kellogg, *To His Friends*, 8, 25; Kellogg, "Powers" (in Notes and Memoranda), 3.

logg thought, the continued dispute between the former friends prevented Powers from ever returning to America.

The statue, that of "a young and beautiful Greek girl deprived of her clothing and exposed for sale to some wealthy eastern barbarians," was considered Powers' masterpiece and became "the most celebrated statue of the day." The work reached America at a time when Americans had a deep sympathy for Greece; the subject was appealing; there was national pride in Powers; Kellogg was astute and diligent in his display. Changing tastes have meant that the "Slave" is now recognized not as a masterpiece but as a milestone in the artistic development of the United States, a development to which Kellogg contributed.

The story of Kellogg's relation to the statue and to Powers is told with bitterness in the several pages of his Notes and Memoranda labelled "Powers" and chiefly in two pamphlets by Kellogg: *Justice to Hiram Powers. Addressed to the Citizens of New Orleans,* printed in Cincinnati in 1848, when he was Powers' agent and best friend; and *Mr. Miner K. Kellogg to His Friends,* printed in Paris a decade later to reveal what he considered Powers' perfidy.

The model for the "Slave" was finished in 1842, and in 1844 Powers completed his first copy in marble and sold it to one Captain John Grant of the English Navy, who placed it on exhibition in London. Lord Ward engaged a second copy, and soon copies were commissioned by Sir Charles Coote and by a New Orleans banker named James Robb. Because he was anxious to have the work seen in America, Powers, in December, 1846, requested Robb to allow his purchase to be exhibited in various cities as it was being conveyed from the eastern seaboard to New Orleans. Robb consented on condition that his name not be mentioned. To expedite matters, and probably to get speedier monetary returns from the exhibitions, the copy destined for Robb being yet unfinished, Powers secured the Ward statue (Ward to wait for another) and delivered it to Kellogg, who was to supervise the showings and then deliver the work to Robb. Kellogg also had Robb's commission for one of his own paintings, the "Circassian," which he planned to deliver along with the statue. All was well until the fall of 1847, when Sir Charles Coote decided that he could not afford the copy he had ordered. Powers then decided to send the Coote statue directly to Robb and let the Ward statue continue on its triumphal tour. His justification to Robb was that the Coote statue would have no identification with having been exhibited and that also it was particularly fine because of the spotless marble of which it was made. Robb decided that he had been the victim of substitution and a "trading spirit" and demanded delivery. After being threatened with a lawsuit, Kellogg sent the statue on to New Orleans from Philadelphia in June, 1848. The Coote copy had arrived in the United States in May and had attracted crowds of viewers in New York, Boston, and other cities. Interest was enhanced by discussions of the "morality" of the nude, and in Cincinnati, home town of both Powers and Kellogg, the matter was solemnly referred to a committee of clergymen, who finally gave the statue their approval. It was from home in Cincinnati that Kellogg addressed his pamphlet to the citizens of New Orleans. In the Crescent City, Robb was displaying his purchase in a rival and unexpected exhibition with much emphasis on his great liberality to Powers. The artist friends believed the liberality on the other side.

Unfortunately for auld lang syne, the Kellogg-Powers story did not end on this compatible note of one artist's rising to the defense of another because "the reputation of an artist becomes the precious jewel of his life."[44] According to his second pamphlet, Kellogg not only had received no security for moneys loaned Powers but had further incurred expense in paying his way to the United States and bearing all the costs of advertising and of renting exhibition halls, as well as the donation of his time. The total advance amounted to some four hundred pounds. The gamble paid off in that the exhibition was a success, that Powers was now successful and famous, and that for almost three years Kellogg continued in charge of Powers' affairs. Although Kellogg returned to Florence in July, 1851, a complete adjustment of finances was never made; nevertheless no apparent difference in friendship or any indication of loss of confidence emerged until late in 1853, when third parties became involved. Powers admitted orally to making misstatements about his friend and agent but said that he would make no written retraction because "he did not wish to acknowledge his indebtedness for his success in any way to Mr. Kellogg."[45] Repeated efforts by Kellogg to retrieve

[44]Miner K. Kellogg, *Justice to Hiram Powers. Addressed to the Citizens of New Orleans*, 2.
[45]Kellogg, *To His Friends*, 10.

his correspondence and statements of accounts failed to get letters, papers, or receipts. Kellogg's deepest wound came not from the loss of what he admitted was a relatively small amount of money owed him but from reports that he had defrauded Powers by profiting sufficiently from the proceeds of the exhibition to be able to purchase a valuable collection of paintings. He resented the implication that he had given up his profession to become a dealer, and he feared the financial losses which might result from damage to his professional reputation and might even force him to part with his treasures accumulated over a long period of time. Kellogg's statement *To His Friends* was printed in Paris on April 21, 1858. On October 3, 1858, Powers wrote his long-time patron Nicholas Longworth:

> My Dear Friend—My last to you was in relation to Mr. Kellogg's pamphlet. I thought it best to put you in possession of the facts in the case, and on your guard against the plausible style of this attack.
>
> Mr. K. must have been at considerable expense with his pamphlet; scores of them have been sent to many places. A man here by the name of Gould, has been distributing them about, but I do not find that any impression has been made, except that Mr. K. and his friend Gould have got their labour for their pains. The idea prevails that the pamphlet is a card or an advertisement of Mr. Kellogg's Picture Gallery at "19, bis rue Fountain, Saint Georges, Paris."
>
> I do not find that there is occasion to notice the Pamphlet in a public manner, and Mr. K. is welcome to all the good it will do him or the harm it may do me.[46]

On Kellogg's behalf, it might be said that nothing in the pamphlet justifies the snide remark on its being an advertising medium. Furthermore, Powers has been described as dogmatic, overbearing, conceited, opinionated, and scathing in his comments on the work of other artists. Nathaniel Hawthorne, who was living in Florence in the summer of 1858 and was an admirer of Powers, had no illusions about some of his less admirable traits. On one occasion Hawthorne wrote that Powers was "no exception to the rule that an artist is not apt to speak in a very laudatory style of a brother artist." On being told that Powers had had

---

[46]Hiram Powers, "Letters of Hiram Powers to Nicholas Longworth, Esq., 1856–1858", *The Quarterly Publication of the Historical and Philosophical Society of Ohio*, I (April–June, 1906), 57.

many difficulties on professional grounds with other artists, Hawthorne's comment was: "No wonder! He has said enough in my hearing to put him at sword's points with sculptors of every epoch and every degree between the two inclusive extremes of Phidias and Clark Mills." When another sculptor visited Hawthorne and conversationally paid Powers off for his trenchant criticisms by decrying Powers' multiple sales of the "Greek Slave" and for offering a statue to private persons for a fifth of what he asked for it from the United States Congress, Hawthorne wrote that he repeated the conversation "only as another instance of how invariably every sculptor uses his chisel and mallet to smash and deface the marble work of every other."[47]

But what of the personal fortunes of Miner Kellogg during those four years between 1847 and 1851, when he was shepherding one or the other of the statues of the "Slave"? Certainly he touched down in New York, Boston, Washington, Baltimore, and Philadelphia. Bayard Taylor wrote to him in New York to introduce him to Mrs. Caroline Matilda Kirkland, authoress and editor, who as a lover of art, sought an opportunity to see the "Slave," which she later described in her *Union Magazine*.[48] One wonders if he attended the spectacle provided by the Model Artists of 1847 at Palmo's Opera House in New York. Because the entire town was paying to see the statue, one Dr. Collyer decided to bring the marble to life and so introduced a new movement in the fine arts by exhibiting "living men and women in almost the same state in which Gabriel saw them in the Garden of Eden on the first morning of creation." Kellogg was probably not artistically appreciative when taverns, hotels, and saloons were exhibiting *tableaux vivants* in every form and shape.[49] His taste ran in other directions.

While in New York he read to the New York Ethnological Society some letters he had received from Henry Layard and then wrote to Layard that he had been elected to membership in that organization for there "is a deep interest in your discoveries."[50] Layard, on January 16,

[47]Nathaniel Hawthorne, *Passages from the French and Italian Notebooks (The Complete Works of Nathaniel Hawthorne)* 272, 306, 482–483.

[48]J. Bayard Taylor to Kellogg, August 25, 1847, Miner K. Kellogg Papers; Margaret Farrand Thorp, *The Literary Sculptors*, 119.

[49]Meade Minnigerode, *The Fabulous Forties, 1840–1850. A Presentation of Private Life*, 141–142.

[50]Waterfield, *Layard of Nineveh*, 178–179.

1848, wrote to Kellogg of his preparation of a sketch history of Nineveh and opined: "I think the book will be attractive particularly in America, where there are so many scripture readers."[51] Just a month later Kellogg was in Washington and made his own contribution to the scripture readers when he sent his "Position of Mount Sinai Examined" for publication in the New York *Literary World* of February, 1848. He had been in Washington to call on President Polk in November of 1847, when they reminisced of his painting the Polk portrait at Nashville in 1840, and the President had agreed to pose for another picture. The artist was busy at the White House in late March and early April, when both the President and Mrs. Polk sat for him.[52] Sometime in 1848 he and Rufus Wilmot Griswold attended a New York seance held by female mediums named Fish and Fox. The men planned to have the women make a return visit to Kellogg's studio in a boarding house on Broadway opposite Bond Street, but Kellogg was called to Hartford, Connecticut by Colonel Samuel Colt, to take a cast of the face of his father Christopher Colt, who had just died. Griswold took over the entertaining of the mediums in what Kellogg thought the first meeting of "spirit rappers" ever given in New York, with a guest list which included William Cullen Bryant, Nat P. Willis, James Fenimore Cooper, and H. T. Tuckerman. Kellogg's own comment: "I have never heard of their benefitting anyone but *those mediums* who gain a living by their operations on believers."[53] The "Greek Slave" and Kellogg were both in Cincinnati in 1848 when he issued the pamphlet in defense of Powers. Sometime during the American stay he did a portrait of Chief Justice Roger B. Taney for the Baltimore Bar as well as pictures of those current heroes of the Mexican War, Generals William Jenkins Worth and Winfield Scott. Mrs. Scott invited him to one of her "at homes" in Washington.[54] The Kellogg address was 663 Broadway in New York in 1851, when he had two pictures exhibited at the National Academy of Design. Item 12 was the Scott

---

[51]*Ibid.*, 182.

[52]Polk, *The Diary of James K. Polk during His Presidency*, III, 224, 395, 419.

[53]Kellogg, "Fish and Fox Meetings" (in Notes and Memoranda). Rufus W. Griswold (1815–1857), journalist and anthologist, was literary executor and editor of Edgar Allan Poe (see *DAB,* VIII, 10–12).

[54]Mrs. Winfield Scott [signed "Mrs. General Scott"] to Kellogg, November 21, 1849, Miner K. Kellogg Papers.

portrait, commissioned by the city of New York; item 377 was "The Greek Girl," the property of George W. Riggs of Washington.[55]

Kellogg returned to Europe in 1851, a fifty-two-day trip via sailing vessel to Marseilles and then to Florence. He resumed his painting and his travels—to Genoa, Palermo, and to Africa. James Augustus Suydam, a landscape painter and one of his pupils, is said to have accompanied him on a tour of Greece and Asia Minor, probably in the mid-fifties.[56] The continued months of painting and travel were punctuated by requests of Powers to make some financial settlement, and in 1854 Kellogg tried again fruitlessly to retrieve his correspondence. His pictures continued to be seen in American exhibits. At the National Academy of Design Show in 1854, No. 364 was "Maltese," the property of James A. Suydam. His brother, Peter Mesier Suydam, displayed "Circassian" as No. 367.[57] This second picture bore the same title as the one Kellogg had sold earlier to James A. Robb and which was loaned by Robb for an exhibit at the Pennsylvania Academy of Fine Arts in 1855.[58]

It must have been the coolness of his relations with Powers, an urge for new surroundings and fresh inspiration, or the new need to do special research in the Louvre that caused Kellogg to leave Florence. In 1855 he leased for a term of years a studio and galleries built especially for his use in Paris and there transferred his art collection and materials. He was pleased to be exhibited at the Royal Academy of Arts in London, when Item 232 in the 1857 showing was his "An American Gentleman in the Costume of a Bedouin Sheik—Mount Sinai in the Background." In 1858 a Kellogg painting, which could have been the same or a similar canvas, owned by Edwin King, was shown at the Pennsylvania Academy of Fine Arts with the title "Portrait of a Traveller as an Arab Sheik —Mount Sinai in the Distance." Kellogg was still the Orientalist in 1859, when he painted from life a full-length portrait of Ferûkh Khan of Persia, who, with Carrol Spence, had just signed a special treaty between Persia and the United States.[59] In 1859 also John Young Mason,

[55]*New York National Academy of Design Exhibition Record, 1826–1860*, I, 273. The "Greek Girl" subsequently became the property of the Maryland Historical Society.
[56]Groce and Wallace, *New-York Historical Society's Dictionary of Artists*, 615.
[57]*New York National Academy of Design Exhibition Record, 1826–1860*, I, 273.
[58]Rutledge, *Cumulative Records of Exhibition Catalogues*, 113.
[59]S. G. W. Benjamin, *Persia and the Persians*, 145.

President Buchanan's minister to France, requested Kellogg to approach Horace Vernet about accepting a commission to paint a battle piece for the rotunda of the Capitol in Washington. Perhaps Vernet was already too busy with his commission from Louis Philippe to paint the historical galleries at Versailles.[60]

In 1855 Kellogg purchased a painting entitled "La Belle Jardinière," a picture of the Virgin, the Infant Jesus, and St. John, attributed to Raphael of Urbino. His spare time went into tracing the history of the picture and comparing it with a painting in the Louvre, similar in name and subject, to determine whether the painting in his possession was the original or "primary concept" by Raphael. The painstaking research into the history and tradition concerning Raphael and the painting was to be incorporated into a thirty-four–page pamphlet finally published in London in 1860. In it Kellogg expressed the hope that the publication would bring to light additional information regarding the painting. Lord Ashburton was sufficiently impressed to purchase "La Belle Jardinière" for his collection in June, 1862.

The sale of the picture must have been opportune, for Kellogg had given up his bachelor status for new responsibilities. On February 17, 1858, four days after he dated the pamphlet exposing Powers, he married Celia Logan. The Kellogg genealogy by Timothy Hopkins, *The Kelloggs in the Old World and the New*, states that Celia Logan was the sister of Eliza and Olive Logan and the daughter of Cornelius A. Logan. The father, Sister Olive, and Brother Cornelius Ambrose, Jr., all have sketches in the *Dictionary of American Biography*. The only printed account of Celia Logan, outside of mention in books on the theater, seems to be a sketch in Frances E. Willard's *A Woman of the Century*, which, despite its name, concerns a number of women, chiefly those with a feminist tinge. In his biographical notes, Kellogg deliberately excludes mention of his wife. One can only conjecture as to the meeting and marriage of the American exiles in Paris, both of whom had once lived in Cincinnati. Kellogg was forty-four years old and had lived abroad for most of the last seventeen years. His bride was twenty-one.

Born on December 17, 1837, probably in Philadelphia, Celia was the

---

[60]Kellogg, "Mems" (in Notes and Memoranda), unnumbered page. A prominent artist, Jean Emile Horace Vernet (1789–1863) is listed in *Encyclopedia Americana*

second daughter of Cornelius A. and Eliza (Ackley) Logan. Her father had studied for the priesthood but became an actor, dramatist, and theatrical manager. The eldest daughter, Eliza, became prominent on the stage and is frequently mentioned in writings of the youngest daughter, Olive, who was three times married and was identified as actress, journalist, lecturer, and author. The Logan family travelled about the Midwest as the father conducted his theatrical company, but after 1840 Cincinnati seems to have become more or less the home base. According to her death notice in a New York newspaper of January 20, 1904, Celia Logan went on the stage, first in Cincinnati and then as leading juvenile at the Walnut Theatre in Philadelphia. T. Allston Brown states that her first stage appearance was March 9, 1852, as Herminie in *Love's Sacrifice* for the benefit of her sister Eliza at the Chestnut Street Theatre, Philadelphia.[61] In December, 1852, Celia married Conrad B. Clarke, when she was barely fifteen years old. According to Brown, she was divorced from Clarke; according to her obituary, Clarke soon died of consumption. Her father died in February, 1853. The sketch in *A Woman of the Century,* ignoring husbands as much as possible, states that Celia went to London "at the age of maturity" and began the reading of manuscripts for a London publishing house.[62] If "maturity" was twenty-one, then the trip to London and marriage came the same year.

As Kellogg recalled, it was late 1859 or early 1860 before he "removed to London and settled in a fine studio and exhibited my collection of old masters to the aristocracy and experts of Europe." His studio was No. 10a Cunningham Place, St. John's Wood Road, N.W. and the home address was No. 3, New Burlington Street.[63] In London, Kellogg renewed his acquaintance with the Cannings and went with Lady Canning to the British Museum to see the treasures from Nineveh being sent there by their mutual friend Henry Layard. Layard also introduced the Kelloggs to Charles Somers (Viscount Eastnor) and his lovely wife, the former Virginia Pattle.[64] Virginia Somers Kellogg was born on April

---

[61]T. Allston Brown, *History of the American Stage,* 222.

[62]Frances E. Willard and Mary A. Livermore (eds.), *A Woman of the Century...,* 470.

[63]Miner K. Kellogg, *Researches into the History of a Painting by Raphael of Urbino, Entitled "La Belle Jardinière," ("Première Idée du Peintre"),* i.

[64]Waterfield, *Layard of Nineveh,* 182.

25, 1860, and Lady Virginia acted as one of the godmothers for her namesake when the baby was baptized by Minister J. Bayley on March 11, 1861, at the New Jerusalem Church in Argyle Square.[65] Two letters to Kellogg from Lady Somers indicate business relationships as well as the friendship of the families. One letter ended, "Will you do me a favor and in giving my love to her & my little God child deliver the enclosed to Mrs. Kellogg as a little remembrance from me."[66]

Family ties were strengthened when Sheldon Ingalls Kellogg and his family toured in Europe and included a visit to the new cousin. Miner Kellogg painted a portrait of Sheldon I. Kellogg, Jr., in London about 1861.[67] With or without his family, the artist was in Belgium and Switzerland in 1862, and he hastened to Lausanne when he had word from his brother that one Dr. Frederic Nessler, formerly a member of the household of Count Bentzel Sternau, was living there. In 1855 Kellogg had purchased from an amateur art dealer two pictures that had once been a part of the art collection of Count Sternau at his villa, Mariahalden, on Lake Zurich. Now, seven years later, Kellogg had an opportunity to find out something of the collection from which his paintings came and perhaps to verify their authenticity. His wife probably remained in London, where she was correspondent for the Boston *Saturday Evening Gazette* and the *Golden Era*. She was also trying her hand at fiction and under the pseudonym of L. Fairfax wrote a novel entitled *The Elopement: A Tale of the Confederate States of America*, printed in London in 1863. The Library of Congress copy of this book has laid in it a letter from Kellogg which supplies several biographical bits.

26 Mch 1863

Dear Taylor

I send this under cover of a little work written by my wife under a *nom de plume* which is *necessary* if not politic to assume just at this unhappy moment of civil war in our country. As it is my wife's first attempt at book writing I am sure that you will look up[on] it with friendly lenience.

We should be delighted if you could be the means of having it noticed in the *Times* in as favorable a manner as you may think it entitled. I am sure

---

[65] Baptismal Record, Miner K. Kellogg Papers.
[66] Lady Somers to Kellogg, no date, *ibid*.
[67] The portrait is the property of Mrs. Henry Drew Nichols, granddaughter of Sheldon and grandniece of Miner Kellogg.

you will do so in a friendly spirit, since you are somewhat acquainted with our many years struggles with illness and poverty in a strange land, and how necessary it is that works however good in themselves must find some friendly hand to bring them to the public favor.

I am sure you will be glad to know that Lord Ashburton has purchased the "Raphael" I brought with me to London—especially after he had brought to bear upon its merits and authenticity the best judges in Europe.

We leave tomorrow for Switzerland—Vevay—and may spend several months there and in Italy—our health and that of the little girl require a change of climate and scene.[68] The Leonardo I have left at my solicitors C. N. Bevan Esq 6 Old Jewry where you or friends can see it if desired.

With sincere regards to Mrs. Taylor, and my best wishes to yourself.

                                          Believe me
                                          ever yours
                                          M. K. Kellogg

P.S. Please withhold for the present the name of the authoress of the *Elopement*.

On advice of his doctor, the Kelloggs left for the Continent, passed through France, remained for the summer among the mountains and lakes of Switzerland and went over the Simplon by private carriage to take leisurely tours of Milan and Verona before spending the winter in Venice. Mrs. Kellogg may have found it necessary to augment the family income or she may have wished to pursue her separate career. One story is that the Milanese press turned to her for aid in securing news of the American Civil War. There were language difficulties; so she would translate the War news into Latin, which the journalists then turned into Italian.[69] Kellogg spent his time in furthering his knowledge of art history and he continued research on his painting called "Herodias," supposed to be unique in that it bore Leonardo da Vinci's signature as well as the date, 1494. The American landscape painter Sanford R. Gifford had visited Kellogg's gallery in Paris in May, 1855, and wrote:

He has a gallery of Old Masters that he has been collecting a good many years. There are several fine pictures among them. One little sea-scape, attributed to Claude, which seems to be genuine—and a Herodias which he says is

---

[68] Kellogg's Notes identify his illness as erysipilas. One wonders if he chose to go to Vevay in remembrance of the months spent at a Swiss-American village of the same name on his way home from New Harmony to Cincinnati.

[69] Willard and Livermore, *A Woman of the Century*, 470.

the original of the one in Florence that was copied from Da Vinci by his pupil Luine ... It is not always an easy thing to determine the authenticity of an "Old Master"; I find generally that those who know most about them are the most cautious in giving a decided opinion.[70]

Kellogg believed firmly in the authenticity of the Leonardo signature and when he got back to London in 1864 he published the results of his research in *Documents relating to A Picture by Leonardo da Vinci, entitled "Herodias," (From the Mariahalden Gallery)* by Miner K. Kellogg.

By 1865 Kellogg had been an expatriate for almost a quarter of a century. In that year his father died; in that year the Civil War ended; he decided the time had come to bring his family home. They planned first to be in Washington, D.C., and there he and his daughter did take up residence. He and his wife were separated in December, 1865. So little that is purely personal is contained in his Notes and Memoranda that a page commenting on his family tragedy seems almost an accidental inclusion. One paragraph reads:

After the War of Secession in America, I returned to my country equipped with enough material to make a useful member of the fraternity of Art. But unfortunately as soon as I landed in Baltimore—with all this material in cases on shipboard, domestic treachery exploded upon me—and everything was rendered useless and closed to my sight for twenty years—my little fortune in money expended in courts in defense of my character and for that of my only child, in other words, my hopes were destroyed and after that nothing but incessant removals from place to place in a vain search of safety and a livelihood for myself and only child.

In the summer of 1868 Celia Logan Kellogg returned to London and renewed her theatrical career, appearing as Lady Anne in *Richard the Third*. She was thirty-one and was said to be possessed of the "face and form which Shakespeare idealized."[71] Kellogg resumed his acquaintance with the American art world, and Henry Tuckerman's *American Artist Life,* which appeared in 1867, was complimentary. He described Kellogg as an intelligent collector and a "careful and interesting artist who had painted a well executed series of portraits such as the Circassian, the Greek and the Jewish and Moorish." One picture exhibited and sold

---

[70]Quoted in Richardson, "Miner K. Kellogg," *Art Quarterly* (Spring, 1960), 273.
[71]Brown, *History of the American Stage,* 222.

by Kellogg was, according to Tuckerman, "remarkable for its flesh tints and perhaps objectionable for its nude motif—representing an eastern beauty reposing after her bath."[72] The paintings Kellogg executed in 1867 were not of Eastern beauties but of contemporary American personalities: a Winchester, Virginia, Civil War heroine for the Winchester *Evening Times,* and John Surratt, sketched at his trial.[73] A new and rewarding friendship was that with Vinnie Ream, who, at the age of fifteen, had received a congressional commission to do a full-length statue of Lincoln for the Capitol. In correspondence dated 1868 and 1869 Vinnie expressed her solicitude for Kellogg's health, requested his advice, inquired about "sweet little Somers," and returned curtains, which she may have borrowed for background while working on a bust in clay of "Mr. Brownlow." Her letters were signed: "Your little friend, Vinnie Ream."[74]

In December, 1869, Kellogg read a paper entitled "Fine Arts in the United States" before the American Academy of Literature, Science, and Art in Washington. His talk, intended to suggest for the consideration of members of the Department of Fine Arts "the propriety of applying to the Government of the United States for aid in founding an institution for the diffusion of knowledge in the Arts of Design," was published in 1870. It was a well-argued brief for the education of Americans in the "refining arts of polished life," pointing out the paucity of museums and art galleries in the United States, and embodying the philosophy of the relationship of government and the arts as expressed in Kellogg's appreciation for the opportunities given him at West Point and by Poinsett's feeling of governmental obligation to encourage artistic endeavor. A year later, Kellogg may have been visiting Peter M. and Henry Suydam in New York. Both were members of the American Geographical Society, before which on December 20, 1879, Kellogg read a paper on "The Geography of Mount Sinai." The paper as published in the Society's *Annual Report for 1870–71* was a considerably expanded version of his contribution on the same subject to the *Literary World* in 1848.[75]

[72]Henry Tuckerman, *American Artist Life,* 423.
[73]Callery, "A Short Biography of Miner Kilbourne Kellogg," 4, 11.
[74]Vinnie Ream to Kellogg, two undated letters and letters of December 17, 1868, March 18, 1869, and March 24, 1869, Miner K. Kellogg Papers.
[75]Miner Kilbourne Kellogg, "The Geography of Mount Sinai," *Annual Report*

THE ARTIST-DIARIST 53

Kellogg's motive in joining the Texas Land and Copper Association's Expedition to Texas in 1872 is not specified in comments about him or in his account of the Expedition. No doubt he wanted the compensation as artist, and he may have hoped for financial reward in later investment in the venture. His finances were not going well. A letter of February 28, 1871, from the office of his solicitors in London indicates that interest from his slight investment there would be negligible and it also hints at efforts of reconciliation with his wife.[76] In 1872 Celia Logan Clarke Kellogg was in Boston to write up the World's Jubilee and there married James H. Connelly. The father thought that at last Somers belonged completely to him.

Who arranged for his participation in the Expedition is not clear, although the diary suggests that his employment came through L. H. Chandler. The diary does not mention the use of camels in Texas, a Kellogg proposal back in 1847. The suggestion was realized to some extent around the late 1850's, but by 1872 the interest was in train tracks westward.

From May to September of 1872 the Kellogg record is in his Texas journals. The disappointing Texas days behind him, he spent some time in Washington and then joined Peter Suydam in New York, possibly in the Suydam home at 163 West Fifty-seventh Street. Memorable occasions during that New York stay were evenings with General Richard Delafield and his older brother Dr. Edward Delafield. They often reminisced of the days of 1839 when Delafield was superintendent of the Academy at West Point, and of the gallant and friendly companions of those days before "Dreadful Civil War broke the chain which linked our memories together."

Whether it was an attempt by her mother to get possession of Somers or a court suit of some type, Kellogg was impelled to leave New York. He sent his daughter to California to visit Uncle Sheldon, who had recently moved to San Francisco, and he went to Cleveland to visit his half-brother Horace, whom he had not seen in fifteen years.[77] Eventually Somers also joined the Horace Kellogg family while her father attempt-

---

of the *American Geographical Society of New York for the Years 1870–71*, II, 55; III, 615; XII, 379–400.

[76]William B—— to M. K. Kellogg, February 28, 1871, Miner K. Kellogg Papers.
[77]Lovell Horace Kellogg, son of Charles Fraser and Mrs. Eliza Smith Downes

ed to make his living as an artist. In 1879 he wrote to Mr. Samuel H. Russell of Boston:

> For many years my art treasures have made me at once a recluse and a Cerberus—and I can support such an existence no longer. Besides, my motherless daughter just coming into womanhood must be provided for, and should I be taken away, the only support she could rely upon would be from my artistic property which, disposed of in haste among this ignorant people, would certainly be sacrificed and leave her penniless.[78]

Probably in an effort to dispose of one valuable piece, in 1879 he had his "Observations on Herodias" reprinted and signed the pamphlet from No. 92 Broadway. The Metropolitan Museum's file on Kellogg shows that at least four canvases from the Kellogg Collection were on loan to the Museum from around 1880 to May, 1886. In 1885 Kellogg disposed of his "works of art, books and curios" to L. E. Holden of Cleveland, Ohio. Their agreement was that Holden buy the Collection in return for an income of $100.00 per month to be paid to Kellogg for the remainder of his natural life. In turn, Kellogg was to serve as an expert to buy and restore works of art and supervise building a gallery for the Collection. In that gallery the Kellogg items were to remain intact and to be "collectively known and designated always as the 'Kellogg collection'." Nearly thirty years after Kellogg's death the Holden pictures were given to the Cleveland Museum, and both agreement and artist were forgotten; the catalogue of the paintings presented by Mrs. Holden to the Museum did not mention Kellogg at all. A catalogue of the Kellogg pieces in his Paris gallery in 1858, now in the Museum, indicates that five of the paintings which he treasured are included in the Holden Collection: "Salome with the Head of St. John," which Kellogg called the Herodias; Cigoli, "Head of a Member of the Medici Family as St. Peter Martyr"; "Annunciation," which Kellogg called Allori; G. B. Tiepolo, "Sketch for a Ceiling"; and a Venetian sixteenth-century painting entitled "Woman Taken in Adultery."[79] How much work as an expert Kellogg was able to do for Holden is not known.

Kellogg, was born in Cincinnati in 1835 (Timothy Hopkins, *The Kelloggs in the Old World and the New*, I, 479).

[78]Quoted by E. P. Richardson, "Miner K. Kellogg," *Art Quarterly* (Spring, 1960), 273–274.

[79]*Ibid.*, 274.

It was during the stay in Cleveland that the artist made the notes for his autobiography. In a few cases they were repetitious. Only the pages which dealt with his youth were numbered consecutively. Apparently he jotted down his recollections on various occasions as some situation was recalled to him. He reacted with a note when he had a little local publicity in a Cleveland periodical:

Mr. Kellogg is well known as an expert in regard to the old masters, of whose work he has quite an extensive and valuable collection, which are now in the hands of Mr. L. E. Holden of Cleveland, who contemplates building a gallery for their reception at no distant day. Mr. Kellogg is about seventy-five years of age and really deserves great credit for his work among pioneers of art in Ohio, in a day when there was in this country far less appreciation of art than now.[80]

Kellogg was distressed by what he considered the general ineptness revealed in the entire article. On a page headed "Mems" in his Notes and Memoranda he wrote:

"Monthly Magazine of Western History"—June 1886—Cleveland O. Article on Art in Ohio. Strikingly inaccurate from ignorance of the character of the artists of Cincinnati—scarcely any personal knowledge of them—mere gossip at its source. Nothing authentic and reliable, and greatly to be deprecated in a Journal supposed to contain the most exact data to be obtained at the time published. It only proves how little attention or interest the history of the Fine Arts or their followers have received since the early settlement of the Western Country. Up to this time certainly there had not been sufficient advance in the production of good works of art in the West to call for or merit any searching analysis into the subject. *Little—very* little progress has yet been made in the dissemination of education in the principles of Art anywhere *West* of the Alleghany Mountains—and even *East* of them such an education is only being attempted. No Institution public or private has yet been founded wherein a pupil can be given even the most *elementary* knowledge necessary for the professional pursuit of Art. It is not yet made a part of the studies in a common school, and entirely ignored in what are called academies—colleges and Universities! There is consequently an excellent excuse for all the ignorance displayed even by writers who make the subject a special theme upon which to attract attention of readers!

[80]"Miner K. Kellogg," *Magazine of Western History*, IV (June, 1886), 165–166.

While Kellogg reminisced and worked in Cleveland, his daughter had married and moved to Toledo. Her first husband was Edmund Locke,[81] son of David Ross Locke, owner of the controlling interest in the Toledo *Blade* and well known as Petroleum V. Nasby. Somers Kellogg Locke's only child, a son, died the day of his birth. In September, 1888, her father moved to Toledo to be with Mrs. Locke, and he died there after a five-month illness on February 18, 1889.

[81]After her divorce from Edmund Locke, Virginia Kellogg Locke married Dr. Walter H. Snyder of Toledo. Mrs. Snyder died in 1937 (Toledo *Daily Blade,* May 25, 1937).

THE JOURNAL

M. K. Kellogg's Mems: Exploring Expedition to Texas, 1872

"Expedition to N.W. Texas" as artist to survey—explore & locate lands for a company of eastern Capitalists. My expenses paid by it.

Leave S LOUIS—MAY 18 '72 5:40 p.m. from Southern Hotel: via Missouri Pacific RR to *Sedalia*—thence by Missouri Kansas & Texas RR. Sup at Franklin—the freshest and best food I have had at any hotel for many years. Brilliant moon & chilly over this beginning of the great plains. Ther 62°. The most fertile region I have ever seen. Arrive at *Sedalia* 1 o.c. am.

19TH MAY '72. Good bed and breakfast at hotel Ives. Not a particle of dust after copious rains—making travelling delightful. Dine at Schell city.[1] After passing Fort Scott—see doves, prairie chickens and rabbits scared up by our Iron horse. Conglomerate stone now appears to vary the rich green tint of the vast prairie dotted over with grazing cattle, which are with difficulty driven from our path by the steam whistle. We have now entered Kansas. Plovers & whip'rwills. At Schell city a copper lode very rich was struck last week. Reach *Chetopa* at 6:43 the last station in Kansas 3 miles from the boundary of the Indian Terry.[2] This looks like a *new* New Engd

---

[1]Named for New York bankers Augustus and Richard Schell (V. V. Masterson, *The Katy Railroad and the Last Frontier*, 83 n).

[2]The Katy had reached Chetopa on June 6, 1870, and the road's general manager wired: "We have struck the Territory line and are going like hell." By winning the

village with its white church spires—and from here are fine 4 horse omnibuses going into Southern Kansas—We await here the arrival of the up train until 7:30 P.M. At sundown clouds are gathering across the zenith through which the brilliant moon rides steadily on its course. Owing to a land slide after heavy rains, the RR was broken—occasioning delay in our arrival until 5 o.c. am.

INDIAN TERRITORY

MONDAY 20 MAY '72. At the RR terminus near S. Canadian River—where our party were encamped among the tents and cars of the workmen of the road, a company of U.S. Cavalry, Colored are protecting this station from outlaws[3]—Quite a village has been improvised, with frame shanties, tents &c in streets—with significant signs upon them—Tobacco-Feed store-Barber shop-Pioneer Dining Car-General stage office-Occidental Hotel-Board & Lodging &c. Exciting and amusing scenes, in shoeing wild obstreperous mules—catching & slaughtering Bulls by dogs and Butcher on horse back shooting, then racing through the woods—everything indicating the vicinity of frontier life—rough & ready.

TUESDAY 21 MAY '72. Rain hard last night. This morning arrived Mr. Harper & wife. He is editor "Banner" Mt. Vernon, O. Gave him many items of our Exped.[4] Mrs. Ream—Vinnie's mother

---

race to the Indian Territory border, the road had won the sole right to build south through the land of the Five Civilized Nations to Red River and Texas (*Ibid.*, 70, 75). The Katy raced for passengers also. In the fall of 1871, G. A. Graham wrote to his brother from Fort Gibson in Indian Territory: "If you come this route get tickets only to St. Louis, where you can get through tickets to Sherman for $50. I am informed by a gentleman today that within 10 days they will have arrangements made to ticket through to any part of Texas" (G. A. Graham to E. S. Graham, October 8, 1871. E. S. Graham Papers).

[3]Secretary of the Interior J. D. Cox had visited Indian Territory at the time of the opening of the railroad bridge across the North Canadian in April, 1872, and had experienced life in the rough at the terminus town. As a result, he telegraphed Washington that neither life nor property was safe in the Territory. The 10th Cavalry was immediately sent for active service in the area (Masterson, *The Katy Railroad and the Last Frontier*, 157).

[4]News of the Expedition was spread generally. Austin's *Tri-Weekly Gazette* of May 27, 1872, reported: "An exploring party has been organized in Washington, of scientific men, for the purpose of visiting Texas and making thorough search for mineral deposits, including the Big and Little Wachita rivers, the Salt and Double

arrived from the south with her daughter in law & son.[5] Her son owns a farm 6 miles below here where we make our next camp. He married a Choctaw girl very pretty & sweet and well educated. Mrs. Ream left for the north and the daughter & child returned to her farm in P M train. P.M. raining hard—thunder & lightning. Rainbow—N wind. Sleep very well for first time since leaving St. Louis.

WEDY. 22 MAY '72. Col McCarty & Peters[6] arrived this morning and with several of our party leave for arranging camp 6 m. from here en route. Make acquaintance of Lieut Lee[7]—U.S. Cavalry Colored company from Ft. Sill, who informs me that he has received order from Sec. War to remove all the whites from this place who have no permit from Indian Agent. This has become essential to preservation of peace and Indian rights. Arrive at the *Terminus extreme* of M.K.&T. R.R. 6 m.s. of "South Canadian" River is our *first* camping ground where we go regularly into camp about 200 yds w. of RR track. On the land of Mr. Ream (Brother of Vinnie), whose log farm house stands near us on the slope of the range of hills which overlook an extensive and magnificent valley rich with the natural verdure of the prairie.

Mountains, and the upper waters of the Brazos river." Weatherford knew directly of the approaching Expedition, for Roessler had invited A. B. Gant, a member of the Twelfth Texas Legislature, to accompany the party (J. A. Woolfolk to E. S. Graham, May 31, 1872, E. S. Graham Papers). For Gant, see H. Smythe, *Historical Sketch of Parker County*, 385–386.

[5]Mrs. Robert Lee (Lavinia McDonald) Ream, mother of the sculptress Vinnie Ream. The son, Robert Ream, married Anna Guy, sister of Governor William Guy of the Chickasaw Nation. Their child, Robert L. Ream, was born at Ream Station, Choctaw Nation, in 1871. Colonel Elias C. Boudinot named Vinita (a diminutive of Vinnie), Oklahoma, for Vinnie Ream, whom he greatly admired. Not long before her death, Vinnie Ream Hoxie was commissioned to do the statue of Sequoyah to represent Oklahoma in Statuary Hill in Washington (*Dictionary of American Biography*, IX, 317–318; H. F. O'Beirne, *Leaders and Leading Men of the Indian Territory*, 242).

[6]*Flake's Bulletin*, quoted in Dallas *Herald* for June 1, 1872, lists D. Peters as a member of the Expedition. Loew and Roessler, in "Erforschung des Nordwesttheiles von Texas im Jahre 1872," identify Richard Peters as assistant to Chandler, the general manager.

[7]Phillip Ludwell Lee, born in Virginia, served in the New York Cavalry from August, 1862, to April, 1865. He was mustered out in October of 1865 and re-enlisted in the 10th Cavalry as first lieutenant in July, 1866. He commanded Company F (color gray), organized June 21, 1867 (E. L. N. Glass [ed.], *The History of the Tenth Cavalry, 1866–1921*, 13; Francis B. Heitman, *Historical Register and*

THURSDAY 23D MAY '72. Unpacking boxes, arranging goods & traps—organizing messes, distributing arms and practicing with them on doves, quails and other small game. Col. McCarty, a splendid marksman ranges the forest hills, seeing wild turkeys, deer and bear & panther tracks & trails. We learn there are numbers of these nice companions among these unexplored forests. Col. sees an enormous rattlesnake which so frightened his horse that he could not get a shot at the reptile. Photograph the camp and party as I had arranged them. Lieut Ward[8] of Ft. Sill dines with us—carrying prisoners to Leavenworth.

FRIDAY 24TH MAY '72. Rainy and dreary all night. Rifle practice— boxing and ball amusement in morn. Stampede of mules at night. Loose 4 mules & 1 horse.

SAT. 25 MAY '72. Airing tents and luggage. Photogd views around camp.[9] Irish Lord on Infall 7. The mountain above camp is called "Succhi"—the valley "*Coal Creek*," and is 5 m. by [illegible]. Dine with Mrs. Ream. Camp fire amusements.

SUNDAY. 26 MAY '72. Fine breezy day. Unwell—too much pork— no other meat. Bad cookg. Chandler[10] arrives. Dr. Loew[11] on lizards & bugs.

Dictionary of the United States Army, from Its Organization, September 29, 1789, to March 2, 1903, I, 625).

[8]Charles Richard Ward, of Pennsylvania, who graduated from the United States Military Academy in the class of 1871 and was commissioned second lieutenant of the 10th Cavalry, served at Fort Sill and Fort Richardson. He became first lieutenant on May 17, 1876. Ward was dismissed from the service on January 17, 1888, for "drunkenness on duty" (*Ibid.*, I, 1000).

[9]When Callery originally offered the Kellogg journal for sale it was accompanied by eighteen photographs, which seem subsequently to have disappeared.

[10]Lucius H. Chandler, son of Dr. Chauncey C. Chandler, was born in Belfast, Maine, in 1817. He became a resident of Norfolk, Virginia, in 1850, but with the outbreak of the Civil War, moved to Washington in 1861. He was in the U.S. Consular Service from 1861 to 1863, when he returned to Norfolk, where he was U.S. district attorney until 1868. Elected to Congress from the Norfolk district in 1865, he was refused his seat because the area was a portion of seceded Virginia. Chandler was away from Norfolk between 1868 and May, 1875, when he was appointed U.S. pension agent. His death was by drowning, possibly suicide (Norfolk *Landmark*, April 18, 1876).

[11]Dr. Oscar (Karl Benedict) Loew, chemist and mineralogist, was born April 2, 1844, in Germany and was educated at Leipzig and Munich. After his trip to Texas for the Texas Land and Copper Association, he was chemist of George M. Wheeler's expeditions to New Mexico, Colorado, and Southern California. He was professor of

MONDAY 27TH. Heavy rain squall—nearly taking away tent. Airing duds. Dined Mrs. Ream & Lina Hill.

TUESDAY 28TH MAY '72. Cleaning & arranging tents after yesterday's rain. Still awaiting goods from S. Canadian station, where Chandler has just purchased ambulance.

WEDNESDAY 29TH MAY '72. Photog. from hill side of valley. Also sketch. Lovely day—breezy & hot promising another rain, the thing which has created the worst roads ever known in this region. We hear from all travellers that we cannot travel with our heavy teams—that we would be mired in the holes, wear out our animals—and not make Sherman in a months time.

Matters in camp still disorganized—or rather in disorder—entire lack of discipline—boding no good to the Expedition. I feel discouraged—still hoping that on arriving in Sherman better discipline and capability will be manifested. Thus far there is little seriousness, or comprehension of the importance of the duties we have undertaken—rather a pleasure than a laborious party. The position of our camp is unfortunately 600 ft from water—and that is from a mere rivulet from the mountain—so warm as to be very unrefreshing—& as no special detail is made for bringing it to camp, no one feels disposed to so do for anothers use. The consequence is that there is at times not a drop to drink; and as to ablutions they occur seldom, even for face & hands. Nights are spent with none about camp: in case of sickness or accident we might suffer greatly.

29TH MAY '72. Green flies & buffaloe nats are now tormenting us and bleeding animals. The latter suffer extremely and of course [are] very unruly, requiring constant watching and care.

This P.M. the 10the Mtn howitzer was tried for first time—range 500 yds—Ammunition and fuses bad—will require remaking for any certain effect. Evening most vivid & constant lightning & grumbling thunder—wind from south & then none at all. Prepare for heavy rain squall. All hands staying tents with extra guys. Prepare to catch rain water by hanging tin buckets to tent flies; yet all night passes without

---

chemical botany in Tokyo, Japan, between 1893 and 1925, except for two years with the United States Department of Agriculture, 1898–1900 (Samuel Wood Geiser, "Men of Science in Texas, 1820–1880," *Field and Laboratory*, XXVII [1959], 127–128).

a drop falling to refresh us. So much the better for the road if not for comfort. Kegs are brought along to carry water across the great dry plains. Not used as yet, and drying up in sun. I recommend they be filled and kept so—no attention paid to suggestion—so that probably when they are most needed they will be useless. At night tents filled with flies & insects. Tonight seize upon a tarantula who is after them on the inner wall of tent. Dr. Loew, our Entomologist is called in to aid in his capture and is charmed to procure so fine a specimen. He adds this to his already swelling collection of bugs & insects. He got his first snake today ensconced in some wrapping paper in our tent—so that we begin to realize the presence of wild companions in our path —more valuable than agreeable.

THURSDAY 30TH MAY '72. Day opens with a clear sky and warm sun—which increases in brilliancy and heat—driving everything but nats and green flies to shelter. I went to the woods to sketch, but it was so sultry and the nats so tormenting that I hastened back to tent, where with flaps up, and flys spread in extention to allow a nice breeze to pass through from the prairie I am allowed to make these notes in some comfort, and as only Chandler is present, and he asleep, all is quiet except the occasional puff, puff of the Locomotive in the near distance. Our flag flies gaily in a northern breeze, and bedding & blankets are spread upon the guard lines and grass getting a good & needed airing. Therm. 92° at 1:30 P.M. Thunder, lightning & rain in night.

FRIDAY 31 MAY '72. Indian Territory. This morning strike tents and take up new camping ground 1½ m. south—under trees and near cool excellent water. Write to Sheldon sending wild sensitive plant of prairie to Somers.[12] Mosquitoes troublesome. Jiggers also. Cold towards morning of

SATURDAY 1ST MAY '72. Sketch log cabin of stage stand near camp. Stage running to Sherman. Still delayed for lack of extra wagon for transport. Have too many things for rapid movement. *Undoubtedly.* Capt. Plummer[13] arrives from Sherman with news of expedition ahead

[12]Kellogg's twelve-year-old daughter. Her parents had been separated for some seven years; 1872 was the year of her mother's remarriage.

[13]Satterlee Clark Plummer, son of Brigadier General Joseph B. Plummer, was born in Wisconsin, graduated from the United States Military Academy in 1865, and received his captaincy in 1868. He was stationed at Galveston from April to Novem-

of us for same object and urges haste. Says we are not likely to get escort from Ft. Richardson. Gen McKensie[14] being interested in some similar expedition.

SATURDAY 2D JUNE '72. Strike tents after leaving out much unnecessary luggage with Mr. Ream and repacking wagons. Move off at 5:25 o.c. P.M. a hot yet lovely day & fine breeze. I ride ahead in ambulance which is loaded down with luggage and six persons. Peters inside too unwell to go on horse. White[15] left this morning for Sherman in Plummers wagon to have surgeons skill on a very bad right thumb—a dangerous looking felon.

Arrived at camp at 7:15 P.M. detained by several bad holes, 4¾ miles. Mules working unexpectedly well, and the first day's travel is very encouraging for progress. Put up tent fly & bunk on carpet. Delightful weather with Jupiter as evening star and the firmament resplendent with lesser lights as a canopy. I sleep indifferently—the ground so uneven that my ribs & back would not fit in. All is silence—strange to say not even a frog concert which we have enjoyed up to this time. Course *South* - - - cross a high-bent & rickety bridge over the Cold [Coal] creek—cross also R.R. track of M.K.T. which is here but temporary and runs nearly parallel to our course. Distance calculated by odometer. *Camp No. 3* is on the road to Sherman—close by a small tributary of Cold creek which affords good water—it is only 3 feet wide by 6 in deep, running N.W. & S.E. a fine circular prairie—environed by closely wooded forests, its northern border enclosed by a high, level line of hills unbroken in outline and untrodden by civilized man. The same range that overhung Camp "Departure."

---

ber, 1866, and at San Antonio, Austin, and other Texas posts from December, 1866, to June, 1868. He left the Army at his own request on December 15, 1870, returned as second lieutenant of the 4th Infantry in May, 1876, and was dismissed from the service in July, 1877 (Heitman, *Historical Register and Dictionary of the United States Army*, I, 795; George W. Cullum, *Biographical Register of the Officers and Graduates of the U.S. Military Academy at West Point, N.Y., from Its Establishment in 1802, to 1890* . . ., III, 60).

[14]Ranald Slidell Mackenzie (1840–1889) was in command at Fort Richardson in 1872. (*DAB*), XII, 95–96. R. G. Carter, *On the Border with Mackenzie* . . ., details the Mackenzie campaigns to eliminate the Texas Indian menace between 1871 and 1876.

[15]C. K. White was wagon master (Dallas *Herald*, June 1, 1872).

MONDAY 3D JUNE '72. Aroused at 4 am. strike tents, get coffee & bread by sunrise. A charming breeze and almost cloudless sky. Our white cook is not on hand. This is one of the inevitable results of *private* expeditions where hired men leave at pleasure. Leave camp 6:30 am. South. Arrive at McAlester station[16] 5 miles at 8.15. A frame house & grocery and stables for the "Overland Transportation Co."[17] Remain 15 minutes & move on to a small Indian village of Perryville[18] which we reach at noon, & await the wagons which slowly follow the ambulance out of sight. Two small stores of goods & groceries - - - barber shop—black smith shop, and other cabins for convenience of neighborhood. Choctaws are lazing silently about the shop porches - - - a very dark race, listening to speeches from candidates for legislature—a singular & picturesque group of the civilized Indians. I took crackers and cheese at shop counter. See for first time in this region angora goats, they are Choctaw bred—large and white and beautiful. Very sandy roads, and scrub oak timber. Without awaiting teams depart *enroute* at 1 pm descending cross a pretty brook of clear water, and pass through forest—see one cleared place fenced in and a comfortable house with a garden where we buy a couple dozen green onions for 50 cts; the first green vegetables we have yet obtained. It is yet a mystery what the Indians live on—certainly we can buy but little food of any kind and are living on bacon and the few doves we shoot on the way. For myself I am in bad condition as to bowels, for lack of fresh meat and good cold bread. I apprehend that disease will catch our men with such food. One mile and half south of Perryville cross a clean little stream, Perry creek, and soon find camping ground about 1½ o.c. P.M. The teams stuck somewhere behind with one broken pole which has to be mended. Green flies beset & bleed our horses freely, but we are not troubled by insects. Snooze away the hot afternoon until the teams arrive at 5 P.M. when the poor jaded men and

---

[16]J. J. McAlester built a pioneer store in the coal-rich region at the crossroads where the California Trail from Fort Smith crossed the Texas Road (Masterson, *The Katy Railroad and the Last Frontier*, 161).

[17]The Overland Transportation Company, a heavy freighter outfit organized by the Katy general manager, had the contract for hauling government supplies to Forts Richardson, Griffin, and Sill (*Ibid.*, 126).

[18]Perryville, a supply base for General Stand Watie's Confederate forces, was burned by Union troops in 1863. In 1872 it was a vanishing village (*Ibid.*, 167).

animals obtain rest & refreshment after a very hard day's work. Col. McCarty goes back to Perryville in ambulance to see about repairs to teams whilst we make ready our flys for a short repose—intending to move on by midnight so as to pass a prairie infested by the green fly before daylight.

We have seen no evidence anywhere in the Territory of its being inhabited, the Indians are located back from the road in the seclusion of the wooded hills—Yet no traveller could imagine these fine green valleys and apparent meadows stretched upon the faces of the hills to be anything but the magnificent parks of a nobility whose castles and mansions he is sure to get a peep at soon.

All our horses & mules stampeded at 6 P.M. and were hunted all night, the last one being brought in at daylight. It rained a little last night. Distance by odometer 13 m.

TUESDAY 4TH JUNE '72. 10:15 A.M. Leave camp, course south passing up the northern face of watershed of the "Green fly" Prairie, stop to water at a small stream within a mile of ridge 5.15 miles from camp. This is a grand open & treeless prairie, bounded on all sides by long low ranges of hills 500 ft high. I suppose the extent to be 30 miles E & W & 12 miles N & S. After passing the ridge and on descent, stopped to sketch appearance of entrance to *Limestone Gap.* Then after passing around the Eastern base of wooded hill enter woods and halting near small stream "Thompson's" and encamp & refresh at 1:45 P.M. Distance eleven miles. An Indian hewed log cabin and another of an Irish family engaged on R.R. near by are near spring. I get a pint of excellent fresh milk of the Indian which seemed delicious. Oh! for a piece of well baked bread. We were not so much annoyed by Green flies as yesterday—and consider ourselves very fortunate indeed—for they are terrible surgeons, more than ½ inch long. In camp we build fires and smoke them away from the poor animals who are powerless for defence. A delightful breeze springs up at 2 o.c. adding charm to a landscape fertile & beautiful and a tender blue sky abounding in grand cumuli of fantastic forms & dazzling brilliancy. The absence of birds and insects is very remarkable considering the richness of the foliage & the denseness of the forest covering the hills. I hear quails & female crows calling their mates. A track of a large bear was seen near our yesterday's camp. Ther. at noon about 93°. Peters & Winchebauch[19] remained behind to avoid the green flies, intending to follow this evening. At night I frequently hear the singular song of the "Chuck Will's Widow" which is simply a reiteration of its name—the female emitting only the latter two syllables. The howl of wolves is now heard during the night. The white and the pink prairie rose now more plenty assuming larger clusters, likewise the lovely crimson pink flower of the sensitive plant. Small yellow butterflies are flickering over the prairie and forktailed hawks and buzzards hover high in the clear heavens.

Ammunition wagon stalled in midst of stream whilst we were behind taking photog of entrance to Gap. We did not get into camp until 8 o.c. P.M. a lovely situation near stream and oak trees. Soon camp fires were blazing and we get something to eat at 10 P.M. I get a tolerably comfortable sleep in the ambulance, standing amid grass up to its body—excellent food for the animals - - - distance made today 20 miles.

WEDNESDAY 5TH JUNE '72. Leave camp 1½ miles north of "Limestone Gap" at 6:45 - - - reach toll gate at 7:10 A.M. and the "Gap." Here a fine stream breaks through a ridge of limestone 100 ft high, scantily spotted with scrubby oak amid the rocks cropping out everywhere on the Eastern face of ridge sometimes nearly perpendicular then sloping away into a verdant & flowery valley a mile wide running N & S through which our road runs nearly parallel with the R R here just being graded. On the Eastern border of plain, lovely broken ridges of hills dome down with rounded summits covered densely with native forests. One of the most charming & picturesque retreats yet encountered. Workmen are blasting through the ridge at the "Gap" for R.R. For some hours we pass several similar valleys, with same Western wall of limestone reminding one of parts of Palestine about Hebron. At 12 o.c. come upon Stringtown consisting of a Bakery and a grocery store and a single dwelling in which appear white female faces. We get a palatable lunch at the bakery—*good* bread, butter and beef—

---

[19]Enno F. Wenckebach, born in Hanover, Germany, was commissioned first lieutenant in the U.S. Army in 1862 and was promoted to captain in 1867. He was honorably mustered out on January 1, 1871, and returned to the Army as second lieutenant in the 6th Infantry on March 18, 1881, from which he resigned July 31, 1881. He died in January, 1882 (Heitman, *Historical Register and Dictionary of the United States Army*, I, 1018).

which all our folks relish amazingly judging from the rapid manner in which the counter was cleared. The Engineer's office of the MKT RR is here in a snug frame house—I suppose the station is the result of its progress. This being the great Road from Texas & Mexico,[20] we frequently pass long lines of 10 ox teams laden with freight—many of the animals bearing Mexican brands. After an hours stop, we start on —but unhappily our front team falls into a bog on the road—and all hands get to work to heave it out. Axes are soon at business in the woods cutting trees for levers which relieve the vehicle in a half hour and on we go. A fine breeze and sky obscured by clouds. No flies—and all comfortable. Here is evidence of cultivation in a 10 acre enclosed fence extending across the narrow valley.

I find that about ½ m. further is the *real Stringtown* where is a blacksmith shop and a depot for workmen of R R and a few huts. At ——— we cross a boggy place through woods—10 days ago must have been impassible. We crossed the N. Boggy river—steep banks and boggy. A team sticks here. Whilst we continue our route into a magnificent rising plain some three miles wide enclosed by graceful, dome shaped ridges—some entirely of grass like a wheat field—others dense forest. On the Eastern ridge we find a spring some 100 ft above plains, and a family of a workman on R R. The wife washes a few pieces of linen for me whilst I wash myself in the cool spring water. By this time our teams appear and stop at the base of hill beneath the spring. Peters & Winchebaugh here overtake us. We decide to remain here encamped for the night. From the spring is a very extensive view of a grand prairie two miles from E to W & 4 miles N & S, almost without a tree. I presume it to be the watershed between North & Middle Boggy and the summit of the R R was being cut through it. I make a slight outline of it looking W by N. in front of this book. Distance today 15 miles.

[20]Grant Foreman reports the road as having an expanse of several hundred yards. Over it the government shipped supplies by ox-drawn wagons to Fort Sill and Fort Cobb and to the frontier posts in Texas. As the railroad was extended south, 1870–1872, supplies were unloaded at each temporary terminus to be reloaded into the freighters' wagons. Cattle headed north from Texas made way for lines of emigrant wagons headed south and west (Grant Foreman, *Down the Texas Road: Historic Places Along Highway 69 Through Oklahoma* [Historic Oklahoma Series, No. 2], 36–37).

THURSDAY 6TH JUNE '72. Leave camp at "Caddo Mounds" or Choctaw Potatoe Hills at 6 o.c. A.M. of a lovely cool morning—long lines of windy clouds moving west over the western hills. The hills derive their name from their forms—a ridge running N & S with a succession of semi circular bosoms clearly & smoothly defined against the sky, smoothly covered by grass and destitute of either bush tree or rock—as a reclining human form. The western border of the plains is wooded and less elevated—and a nearly level outline. This vast amphitheatre is without a single sign of human habitation, or of civilization if we take away the temporary tents of the R.R. laborers, and the straight line of yellow which here and there interrupts the verdant carpet of the plains—a line very soon to be passed over by the smoke of the locomotive and the long dark cars filled by strangers and the living cattle and other riches of this most wonderful portion of the continent. Cross "Middle Boggy" a rapid stream within high banks, with good bridge—7 o.c. Toll $300—for our party. A Few good frame buildings & Hotel in a locust grove—and behold! a Photographic gallery—under a tent. Our photographer descends & makes acquaintance with his brother "artist"—Cross Boggy River at 12. Toll. good milk & corn bread. Cross *"Rockford"* at 2 o.c. P.M. a nice stream over immense beds of rock of conglomerate & smooth rounded surfaces in which appear strata of red granite & kneiss [gneiss]—take a specimen to Dr. Loew. The road from 11 till 2 P.M. has been of deep fine sand, making travelling slow—and road disagreeable from roots & stones exposed in the path. Day hot & clear—in passing rolling prairies we see great distances, making land into ocean lines at horizon blue & misty.

At 2:20 P.M. arrive at campground on right of road on border of woods. See first herds of Texas cattle on their way north. Distance 19 m. Wind brisk from north straightening out our colors from the upper branches of a scraggy oak. All going on healthy and cheerfully. In spreading my blanket on the high bushes I caught a pink cricket, a specimen so rare that neither Loew nor myself had ever seen one before. Dr. Loew has today ridden a Choctaw poney just purchased—the first time he ever rode a horse. They seem fitted to each other and he is as delighted as a boy with his first watch. *"Choctaw"* is his name —I mean the poney's.

Thus far we have gained no information from an inhabitant of the Territory if I except Dr. Harris at South Canadian. They are either ignorant or reticent. We know they are opposed to the inroad the whites are making by R Roads & whiskey & ruffians—and treat strangers with decided coldness and silence. I find many whites have married squaws & settled. The rich "Irish Brogue" is familiar to many and the "sweet German accent" to others—and they seem to have become as patriotic and ignorant and indolent as the native & noble Indian with whom their progeny are to divide the happy Territory. A safe and quiet hiding place for many a fellow who has left his country for his country's good—a rich hunting ground no doubt for a N York detective. Nearly all hands go for a bath in the Rockford creek—the Dr. bringing back fine specimens of granite, gneiss &c—new to him.

This day has been more like a *real* campaigning one than any before. Order begins to grow from previous anarchy, and every one is finding his place and duty. Coming to camp at an early hour gives the cook time to make a decent biscuit and the men a chance to bath themselves and clean up their towels & linen. Two or three cases of slight sun stroke warns us of the necessity of better protection for the heads. Our people are reckless in this regard—How different the Oriental. The one imagines that the lighter and thinner the covering the better—the other wraps his head in great quantities of woolen and silken shawls, or heavy felt caps. Several of our animals have lost their shoes. This fact, and the want of other repairs will retard our march another day. No flies.

FRIDAY 7TH JUNE '72. Last night threatened rain. Bright sheet lightning—not no thunder—some tents were raised as precautionary—but no rain came—the morning opening cool & somewhat overcast but promising an agreeable day. Sweet breeze from the south. I *guess* the degree of heat to be 65°. For some days past the Doctors thermometer has been packed away—and there being none other in the party I am reduced to guesswork, which from long practice is pretty good. Having left my watch in Washington I am dependent upon others for the time, which varies with every watch so I might almost as well *guess* at that too. Last night about 8 oc a wonderful meteor shot across the southern horizon from the East causing quite a commotion in camp. I got only a glimpse of it through the trees of the grove under which we reposed.

We slept well as no mosquitoes appeared. The Doctor skinned a good specimen of a ——— snake. Some few bugs & beetles crawl & flit around, but nothing venomous frightens us. At our last camp we got a young tarantula and bottled him. They are numerous on the mounds about there. We notice abundant clusters of the beautiful pink rose sometimes bushes 12 feet in diameter. Did their fragrance equal their color they would be lovely indeed. But they are made to tickle only one of our senses, being entirely destitute of odor.

This morning not a particle of dew—which sometimes amounts to a shower in effect. I have noticed before that after an evening of thunder & lightning and clouds threatening rain the morning follows with dry herbage and cool atmosphere. Quail salute us by their cheerful calling of "Bob White" and some of our wits imagine that White is a very extensive family in this district. We hear however nothing more from Wolves—whip poor Wills, crickets, rain-crows nor frogs—so "Bobby" has the entire floor to himself, and makes the most of it. Our camp has been greatly annoyed for some days by hogs which are gaunt and fierce looking—often making battle and defeating our dogs—pointer, hounds, and poodle—little poodle being the pluckiest of all—but so small that the little grunters run over him at will—sending him head over heels and back to camp in a forlorn condition of mind. A nice loaf of bread which cook was good enough to save *cold* for me, was appropriated by piggy and carried off triumphantly to the woods. May he enjoy it since I cannot. No one else of us luxuriates in any other than hot bread—and if they can stand it so much the better for them. Thunder lightning & hard rain during night from N.W.

SATURDAY 8TH JUNE '72. Off on route at $5°$ A.M. Heavy sandy road. S. At 5:50 observe a mound on left close to road. Investigate and find a parallelogram, clearly built & sloped & regular. Earth work of 300 ft by 60 wide & 15 high. Covered—possibly composed [of] a small limestone—destitute of trees—rounded ends & running north & south —large trees grow close around below on all sides. Passing on S a few rods a hill rises gradually from road on the right opposite the mound. Go up, investigate, find a headland with plateau perfectly made, composed of limestones of fantastic shapes—& many entirely perforated by circular holes, as though flints had been once contained therein—but no flints could be found. This headland projects northerly into the valley through which we have travelled and from a most extensive panorama is seen probably 30 miles or more to E & N & W.

INDIAN TERRITORY 8 JUNE '72

This elevated plateau presents a broken, steep surface to the East as we pass on the road beneath it and horizontal layers of white limestone crumbled & falling upon its side. I conclude this to have been the quarry which supplied stones for the earthwork near by just described—the stones of which were carried in sacks or otherwise—*all* being so small as to admit of easy transport. Our road gradually ascends around the head through rough loose stones until it issues upon a grand plateau reaching almost treeless, as far South and E & W as the eye can reach—in the misty distances appears a magnificent river winding through the grandest valley ever beheld. But it is not a river—it is only the effect of the differences of color between the light green of the prairie grass and the darker lines of forests surrounding them. A nice hewed log farm house with porch stands back a hundred feet from road on our right and an excellent fence encloses cultivated acres to great extent—principally corn 3 or 4 feet high—certainly the most progressive looking place yet seen in the Indian Territory—a nice new Red Cultivator standing in the field speaks of Yankee assistance in the flourishing appearance of things. I saluated two men seated under the porch apparently awaiting breakfast. They answered my questions like educated persons & courteously. The "headland" is called "Buffalo head," because buffalo used to make the trees which once shaded it their resting place. There were two or three of the artificial mounds in the neighborhood. The owner of the farm was "Leflore."[21]

We now seem to descend the grand plains before us. The earth is black, rich sandy loam—herds of cattle of fine blood & various colors graze upon the luxurious natural table the Lord has set before them and the lark sings praises to him in the silent wilderness.

I am glad my curiosity succeeded in stopping the ambulance to explore the mound and its environs—which has probably been passed by the stagecoach for many years with[out] exciting any particular investigation of its character. This may have been one of the important forts

---

[21]Charles Le Flore. See O'Beirne, *Leaders and Leading Men of the Indian Territory*, 88-89.

of the ancient Mexicans or Aztecs in their advance northward against an inferior & savage though numerous enemy. And connected with those in Ohio and other western states. A time when the present adage was reversed and "*Eastward* the march of Empire takes its way" was the joyful cry of an enterprizing and courageous & belligerent people.[22]

8:40 A.M. cross a small rivulet the boundary of the descent of the grand prairie we are passing. It runs through a stretch of good timber. A few minutes brings us to a fine country house of the left and a good wooden bridge over a nice stream with high banks called the "Bigblue." 10 A.M. reach Mt. Vernon—a frame building store & grocery on the right and cattle pens & immense fields of fine corn 4 ft high giving one an idea of the reality of the tales of thousands of acres cultivated by a single owner. Eggs & string beans 1st time. At 2:30 P.M. come to "Carriage Point" got cheese & crackers to refresh us after submitting to a fearful hurricane & rain during an hour ensconced in the woods as the least dangerous position—fearful all the time of falling trees. Passed on 5 miles and encamped in the prairie near good water and a few small trees and bushes, with magnificent grass for animals. Distance today notwithstanding storm & bad road 23 miles at 4:15 P.M.

SUNDAY 9TH JUNE '72. At 7 oc AM *Enroute* - - - Cloudy after a nights steady rain and a sunset of unsurpassed splendor of form & tints. Wind N.W. & light, roads heavy at starting. I now appreciate what a boundless prairie means - - - such a sight is now presented, with a few lonely trees & bushes scattered about as sentinels and guides.

RED RIVER

Reach Red River at 11 oc AM 9TH JUNE '72. Sun comes out bright and the river muddy, its banks and soil in vicinity of burnt sienna color. Sketch view of river at ford by Rope—also two Photos. Took boat across Red River & buy raisins and crackers at a store on Texas side— a sign saying "First chance"—on reverse "Last chance." meaning "Whiskey for sale," a thing not allowed in the I.T.

Wall Rock Creek. Arrive here at 3 o.c. P.M. Go into camp on high

---

[22]For a discussion of mound builders see Joseph B. Thoburn, "The Tropical and Subtropical Origin of Mound-Builder Cultures," *Chronicles of Oklahoma*, XVI (1918), 97–117.

S bank of the stream in small opening in woods. Photo of stream. Distance 14 miles. Visited by Col. Johnson[23] & Mr. Cowan from Sherman. Johnson an old Texan of "Lone star wars" even older laborer & settler than Sam Houston. Gives me some important traits of Indian nature. Col McCarty accompanies them in their ambulance back to Sherman & we follow tomorrow.

MONDAY 10TH JUNE '72. TEXAS. 8 miles north of *Sherman.* After a good wash in running stream we start off *en route.* A perfectly clear sky & fine breeze. Ther 70° about at 9:05 A.M. Reach Sherman 12 o.c. M - - - enter the little town of 800 inh. in good military order and are stared upon by the silent crowds about the corners and public market square who have so long anxiously awaited our coming as children do a menagerie. We halt in the square in front of the Hotel and court house get lager and some of us a "square meal" at the Hotel—a thing I have not had since at St. Louis—the bad bread & bacon not at all agreeing with my stomach—and we could get neither vegetables nor meat nor eggs in the I. Territory.[24] We have chats with Prof. Roessler & Col. Johnson and our scouts who have so long awaited us and then started for our tenting ground, arriving there at 3 o.c. P.M. A beautiful plain 2 miles south of town. In the afternoon several of us went back to town and Capt. Humphreys[25] consented to act as artilleryman in firing 50 guns in honor of the nomination of Grant at Phila. The gun

---

[23]Francis White Johnson (1799–1884) was a well-known figure in Texas in the days of Anglo-American colonization and the Texas War for Independence. In 1872 he was engaged in the land business in Austin and Round Rock. He collected voluminous notes for a "History of Texas," notes edited after his death as the historical introduction for Johnson's *Texas and Texans.* Unfortunately, those notes contained nothing on his participation in this Expedition.

[24]Loew commented that the principal nourishment of the country people consisted of bread, coffee, and—"who would believe it in such a warm climate"—bacon (Oskar Loew and A. R. Roessler, "Erforschung des Nordwesttheiles von Texas im Jahre 1872," *Petermanns mitteilungen aus Justus Perthes' geographischer anstalt,* XIX, 453).

[25]John B. Charlton described Ballard S. Humphrey as "the finest drill master in the army" and a "man fit to tie to" ([John B. Charlton], *The Old Sergeant's Story: Winning the West from the Indians and Bad Men in 1870 to 1876,* 64). Humphrey was honorably mustered out of the U.S. Army on January 1, 1871, and re-enlisted in the 9th Cavalry on December 12, 1872. (Thomas Holdup Stevens Hamersly [comp.], *Complete Regular Army Register of the United States: For One Hundred Years (1779 to 1879),* 528).

was our Howitzer which the mayor had asked of us for the purpose.[26] The evening was enlivened also by speeches in the square pro & con Grant. Returned to camp at 9 P.M. Shooting affray in town.

TUESDAY 11TH JUNE 1872. Yesterday surprized in reading N.Y. Herald of 29 June[27] regarding the divorce case—could not possibly be true but annoys me greatly as I cannot learn the facts for a long time to come. Most of our party in town after business. Several visitors in camp talking exploration chances and Indian opposition. My ears suppurating from cold. Sores from jiggers. Sleeping on ground among many kinds of bugs, horned toads, fleas and spiders. Air delightful—few flies—no musquitoes. Cool nights & dewy. Clean up rusty guns after the late hard rains which penetrated wagons. Howitzer left in town for repairs.

WED. 12 JUNE '72. Cornfields show a splendid prospect—dark green leaves 4 ft long & 5 inches wide. Soil several feet deep of Vandyke brown color. Certainly as rich as I could imagine of any soil. Said to be the richest in the state. Roasting ears expected in 3 weeks time. Went to town to buy little things and talk with Roessler & Johnson. Returned to camp to dine. Several townsmen & rangers dine with us. Jiggers tell hard upon me. Touch them with sweet oil and carbolic acid giving me relief.

THURSDAY 13TH JUNE '72. Lovely sunrise of prismatic effect. After sewing up rips & on buttons and making convenient bags for little things I went to town to see Judge Parsons[28]—but found that it was his brother who I do not know—and did not find him. Return at 6 o.c. and prepare for rain—which came upon us from N.W. at 12 night. Therm. at 2 P.M. 92° rather sultry.

FRIDAY 14TH JUNE '72. Therm at 8 o.c. A.M. 85° - - - Sultry &

[26]The mayor of Sherman in 1872 was L. W. Williams (Sherman *Democrat*, September 19, 1948, p. 6). The Galveston *Civilian* for June 12, 1872, carried a note from the Sherman *Land Journal*: "The exploring expedition under the command of Col. W. C. McCarty arrived in our city on Monday last en route for the frontier. It is a fine expedition and has a complete corps of engineers, geologists, chemists, photographers, etc. They go well prepared for Indians."

[27]Evidently an error in date. Whether Kellogg means his own divorce I have not been able to ascertain. The New York *Herald* for *May* 29, 1872, afforded no light on the subject.

[28]Kellogg may mean Judge Levi Parsons, president of the Missouri, Kansas, and Texas Railroad.

cloudy. Mark Blankets—fit up smaller tent for 6 of us. Roessler on violin & Loew on zitta [zither?] accompanied by several voices give us some nice music in the quiet moonlight. Our cots having arrived from S. Canadian where we left them we have a nice nights sleep off the ground. Cold night heavy dew. North wind. Cooks still unable to cook biscuits well enough for me—heavy hot dough is worse than nothing for me and I make meals of coffee—crusts of biscuit if it may so be called and poorly boiled potatoes. Astonishing waste of food about camp. Some of other necessaries—no one having special duty to enforce care and economy. By the time we reach Ft Richardson there will be less to regret in this regard as there will be so much less to care for. Harmony, confidence & unity of purpose are not yet manifested.

SAT 15 JUNE '72. Mark the wagons & tents with stencil in Vermillion—TL&C Co. (Texas Land & Copper Co.) - - - mend clothes. Go to town, get a good healthy meal. Return at 5 P.M. Ears painful, swelled and hard of hearing. Night misty & slight shower.

SUND. 16TH JUNE '72. Take account of articles issued by Assn. pistols, blankets, saddles &c. Matters assuming a little more order. Our list of men now numbers 43 but still unfilled. Cloudy morning. My pistol "Colts Navy" numbered 197558. Inspection of horses & arms—all hands in line. Wind S.S.E. Tif bt. M^c & P.

MOND 17TH JUNE '72. Sunrise cool & brisk breeze from S. Am going to town this A.M. for clothes and to order Bath tub 2 ft sq. 6 in deep for Peters. After getting my *dirty* washed clothes and a Restaurant dinner return.

TUESDAY. 18TH JUNE. In tent arranging traps for more *en route* in a day or so. Turpentine bottle leaked over water colors and played the deuce with many things giving me 4 hours labor in cleaning & repairing damage. We are still delayed by purchasing more wagons and other things—we have already in my opinion three times as much stuff as necessary for the trip—and still it comes. What is to result from this accumulation & loss & delay it is not difficult to divine. I can scarcely describe the confusion and negligence and extravagance of this company. Such a suggestion as order & economy coming from me is so slighted or opposed by some of the leading spirits that I am now quite silent, and let things have their way—as I find myself becoming a wet blanket on the hopes of a frolicsome & easy journey entertained by some of the party. But still I feel that there is *danger* ahead which is not to be successfully overcome by the present want of organization, discipline and forethought, and fear that I may yet feel obliged to leave the Expedition—there being no reason why I should risk reputation—money—and likely life also, for the mere chance of success now offered. There has been so much blowing and publishing as to our intentions that Texans everywhere are beginning to be incredulous and sarcastic—a feeling likely to grow into a determined opposition to our movements. Of course the Indians are by this time thoroughly acquainted with our force and designs, and must be ready to frustrate them if they wish. From the moment I entered the party I have earnestly recommended secrecy & celerity of movement, giving nothing to the public until we have finished our labors and accomplished something honorable. But I am considered an old fogy—and my counsel in this regard unheeded by some of the more heedless and inexperienced of those in authority, who I regret to see still manage to exercise considerable control over our actions. Enthusiasm & hilarity are good if subjected to experience and forethought—but very alarming without them on so perilous an Expedition as this before us. Ther 90°—nice breeze.

WED 19 JUNE '72. Weather still lovely - - - sunrise 75° and lively southern breeze. Cactus seen 1st time 2 o.c. P.M. Therm 93 - - - sultry.

THURS 20TH JUNE '72. Letter to Sheldon with Photos of our camps & Red River to Somers. Packing up to start out from vicinity of Sherman. Leave camp near Sherman—at 12 noon. Course N.W. Wind N.E. & clouding up and rain clouds passing north of us. Pass over a lovely farming country—rolling prairies and vast views—distance blue as the sea. Little wood—but splendid grass enriched by flowers of thistle yellow and pink with white. Clumps of ———— dot the ground.

Coming to a line of wood stretching through the prairie ahead of us, and over a deep dry ditch where a team sticks fast in the clayey soil very tough and dark, we enter another treeless stretch and come to a halt for the night. Time 4:20 P.M. Distance 9 miles. Herds of cattle & horses are upon our route. Prairie chickens—doves & rabbits. McCarty, Chandler, Winchebauch, & Roessler went to Sherman from camp and have not yet caught up with us. They took Davis and leave him, an invalid. Switcher[29] & ———— have gone ahead to ———— to await us. Therm 96 at 1 P.M. I go on guard at 7—relieved at 1.

FRIDAY 21ST JUNE '72. DEVER CREEK.[30] Strike tents at 5 A.M. Start at 6:30 am. Course W. Light breeze from N. Herds of cattle more numerous over the beautiful & rolling prairie—grass very high & thick and pink flowers abundant and lovely against the clear green ground. Pass through Whitesboro at 11:30 am. Village. Fine farms with rich corn, oats, & wheat in shocks on all sides. Excellent hard road and arrived at camp going into corral at 1:30 P.M. Distance 12½ m. Therm 88°. Sultry—slight shower from E. with thunder & lightning at 6:30 P.M. Our only delay today was a team sticking in a deep sandy bluff crossing a dry brook, "Big Mineral Creek." The Expedition in close and military order looked like business today for the first time—and all went off smoothly—inspiring hope. One mile beyd. "Big Mineral Creek" camp.

SAT 22 JUNE '72.[31] Cloudy & unsettled. March at 6:30 o.c. A.M. Course W. Cheap chickens 1$ pr doz - - - butter 12½ cts pr pd. Sweet & buttermilk plentiful at farm houses 60 cts for all that 12 of us could drink—corn bread included. Nightingales—lark—jack rabbit—1st

[29]That Kellogg here means James Monroe Swisher is indicated by his later identification of the man as a former member of Hays' Rangers. Swisher had served in Company A, Texas Mounted Rifles, during the Mexican War. In 1871 he commanded a group of rangers in Coleman County (Henry W. Barton to L. Friend, January 20, 1965, citing Compiled Service Records of Texans in the Mexican War). The E. J. Davis correspondence in the Governors' Letters, Texas State Archives, contains several letters from Swisher concerning the Expedition.

[30]I was not able to locate this creek on the Roessler map of 1872. The map was advertised by E. H. Cushing of Houston in the Dallas *Herald* for May 4, and August 3, 1872. The names of various metals were printed on the 1872 map, and on his 1874 version Roessler used symbols to designate metals. On both maps copper was indicated in Wichita, Archer, and Haskell Counties. Of the second map, R. T. Hill said: "A. R. Roessler was the original topographer of the Shumard survey, and thus acquired a fund of geographical knowledge with which he has favored the public through the medium of several maps. One of these, printed in 1874, is by far the best contribution to a knowledge of the general surface features of the state" (Robert Thomas Hill, *The Present Condition of Knowledge of the Geology of Texas* [Department of Interior, *Bulletin* of the U.S. Geological Survey, No. 45], 45). See also Keith Young, "The Roessler Maps," *Texas Journal of Science*, XVII (1965), 28–45.

[31]Kellogg seems to slight Gainesville. This is the day that some members of the party paid their respects to the Cooke County seat. The Gainesville *Gazette* of June 29, 1872, noted: "The exploring party from Washington, D.C., passed through our town on Saturday last, en route for the mining regions of Western Texas" (quoted in Dallas *Herald*, July 6, 1872).

drove of cattle 400 going East. Corn & grain every where luxuriant—Cotton small & healthy. Great spaces covered with yellow flowers of arnica family—*Compositea*—interspersed with the lilac horsemint—very harmonious specked with the pink "Sabatea Gratelis." Harvesting splendid wheat. Orchards of peach trees too thickly packed—small fruit, green. Wild grape vines plentiful in woods—grapes unripe—but blackberries large, ripe, and delicious. Watering animals with dirty rainwater in pools—very picturesque groups indeed. Texas Vultures or Carrion crows almost covering dead trees.

12:30 Encamp at "Clear creek" - - - Therm 87° at 1:30 P.M. Go regularly into corral with rope exterior—prepared for worst—all hands prepare & sleep on arms—rumors of Indians near us doing their thieving raids.[32] Dist. 15½ m.

SUNDAY 23D JUNE '72. Fine cool morning at sunrise. Ther 63° about the lowest of the month. Leave camp at 5:40. Course W. The same display of acres of the brilliant yellow Compositea & pink sabatea—like carpets spread in the morning air. The yellow flowers with rich brown centres all turned to the sun are like bright and living eyes gazing steadily upon yours as you pass. We are now about 160 m. from S. Canadian whence we entered upon our camping life. The prairies are grandly displayed over immense distances rolling and of a uniform pea green tint with slight lines and small masses or clumps of dark green trees to break the monotonous scene. Just now, here & there appear fields of yellow grain ready for the harvest and cozy cottages lodged amid groups of peach and plum trees. I see no appletrees and but few vegetables in gardens except cabbage. Watermelons & tobacco are visible this morning. Am surprized to notice the Jamestown weed [Jimsonweed] so frequently along the route. It seems to mark the deserted spots of former habitations. The Texas thistle bears a flower of same color as the Canada, but much larger, and is very beautiful in itself but when covering acres in an unbroken mass is splendid, especially beside an adjoining mass of the bright eyed golden compositea. Cockleburs line the road which is hard and good on a bed of cretaceous formation. 9:25

[32]On June 9, 1872, White Horse, a Kiowa chief, led a raid on the Abel Lee dwelling on the Clear Fork of the Brazos, sixteen miles from Fort Griffin. Lee, his wife, and a daughter were killed, and three captured children were taken to the Indian Reservation as slaves (Wilbur Sturtevant Nye, *Carbine and Lance: The Story of Old Fort Sill*, 197–199).

Water at Big Clear Creek which is really clear and 4 feet across—after having splendid lunch of Butter & sweet milk & cornbread at a farm restaurant nearby. One wagon stuck in crossing—but Charley's "Susy Darling" and "Dolly Varden" wheel mules came to the rescue as usual and pulled it through—gratifying to the laudable pride of the Darkey. Marching slowly over rolling unbroken, deserted prairie with scarce a tree or bush visible until 11 o.c. when a wagon sticks in a dry slough—with the aid of a Jackscrew and extra mules it is released. Distance 12⅓ m.

At 3:15 P.M. Reach *"Head of Elm"*—situated within view of the valley of Red River—Bluffs of considerable height with summits flat and resembling a fortress of stone. Sandy roads. Camp near by the dirty village and lazy roguish people.[33] We make a long march today to reach beyond the deep sandy road tomorrow. Distance 21½ m. Sketch of "The Elms" at the headwaters of the Trinity River from our camp, the valley of the Red River in the distance. A fine and singular scene in the evening sun. Preaching in the log meeting house. Hamlet of 5 or 6 log houses—principally grog shops—called "Saloons."

MOND 24 JUNE '72. At 6:33 A.M. Start en route—lovely morning passing & ascending gradually magnificent rolling lands with fortress like crests & nearly denuded of bushes & trees—and arrive 8:30 at the grand acropolis overlooking the great *"Crosstimbers"* and as extensive a view as I ever beheld on the W & N. through this region courses the Red River though invisible in the midst of the forests.

This celebrated wooded belt of "Crosstimbers" extends as far as the vision, varying in width from 5 to 30 m, running from NE to SW, consisting principally of scrub oak—bordering on creeks are Elma—and pecan, hackberry, bur oak—post oak—Blk Jack—scrub hickory are to be found.

[33] According to Loew, Head of Elm, the easternmost point in Montague County, consisted of six houses, two of which were drinking halls, with a third being used monthly as a house of prayer when the Methodist minister came through on his circuit. Now called Saint Jo, and once designated as the "Gateway to the West," Head of Elm was the oldest town in the county. Of the seven stores in 1871, five sold whiskey; there was also a post office and a blacksmith shop. The village was a watering point for cattle going up the trail and for ox wagons of merchants hauling from East Texas and Louisiana. The first permanent building, constructed in 1872, was the Stonewall Saloon of Captain I. H. Boggess (Jess S. Henderson [ed.], *100 Years in Montague County, Texas* [unpaged]).

On descending into this shady forest on foot I met a farmer in his wagon who expressed an anxiety that we should stop & examine a mineral deposit about 4 miles back in the timbers at the base of the bluffs I sketched yesterday evening. Minerals crop plentifully out of the hills which some call silver and other names but no one seems to know what it is—and there is a substance which burns like oil—5000 tons of it may be picked up on the surface. I think it may be asphaltum.

The road now becomes deep in sand—hard pulling through the timbers—we overtake a line of ox teams on ascending ground—causing us some delay. A farmer has here opened up a little farm on a little prairie and in six months has a field of fine healthy corn growing and fenced in with brush. Indians can easily gobble him.

Montague, Texas

After a tedious drive through sandy roads without finding water we come to *Montague* at 12:30 P.M. A miserable hamlet only a little better than "The Elms" though one or two respectable private houses are in the vicinity and some fields of corn. A jail is of squared logs and square and about 20 feet high—one small iron barred window. Steps outside to 2d floor. Lower floor for criminals and upper for debtors. The county town. Soil thin—white sand. No game or birds seen today nor insects nor flies. D. gets a horned frog. The other day he was presented with a Spanish wasp—in showing his prize it attempted to climb out of the box—the brave doctor pushed him back with his thumb which was instantly stung—and the Doctor swore in his decided way and german accent, to the merriment of all bystanders. Go into camp 1 mile from Montague at 1 P.M. in the timbers. It is peculiar that there is no underbrush in the forests—nothing but fine grass—even musquite grass, large & luscious to animals. Dist. 13 4/10. Therm 83½°. Last evening we have news of prowling Indians between us & Jacksburg [Jacksboro]—how true they are we cannot know, but prepared for any emergency. The truth is that so many of the loafers & spies in these parts are anxious to be employed by us that they are very likely to originate these rumors for their own benefit. Other parties are already formed and active to get ahead of us—one at Sherman—and everything that can delay us is to their interests. We are now in the midst of enemies—*not* Indians. We hope to circumvent and overcome both but should have been here a month ago—*quietly*.

TUES. 25 JUNE '72. Last night *dewless*. Light breeze from S. This morning pleasant. South breeze. In the ravine near camp where a pond waters cattle is a singular geological formation—conglomerate of small hard stones of agate hardness. In sandstone foundation, the cretaceous having ceased. No fossils—get many specimens—possibly rich deposit for lapidaries. Our camp is a mile N. of Montague near a road running N & S. Last night the notorious horse thief "Missouri Bill" ["Buffalo" crossed out] on whose head the Govt. offers a reward sent a friend to camp to seek admittance for him to our party. He wishes to get out of this country. I suggested this morning that we might add considerably to the *honor* of the Expedition by granting his request! We march without his company. There are other thieves visiting us—not horse, but *land* thieves—giving us their serviceable suggestions and offering their aid in securing good lands. Our camp is on the Henrietta road.[34] We retrace this morning, our road south to *Montague* starting at 6:15 A.M. going slowly through deep sandy roads & timber till 10 A.M. enter open prairie with "Victoria peak"[35] 2 miles ahead on our route—conspicuous pointed loose rocks and 4 or 5 stunted trees on summit. Roessler mounts horse & accompanied by 2 men and goes for it hammer in hand. The train proceeding SW and around the base where is a ranch fenced in for cattle which are driven in for claimants who assist each other, and take thence their own according to brand. 5 or 6 small log cabins, some protected by stockades, and high worm fences for cattle pens make up this exposed post liable to Indian depredation. We have just passed the same train of oxen we did yesterday. At 10:30 A.M. turn to S. The same conglomerate & sandstone make up the stony foundation of the soil as it did yesterday at the ravine I described, and probably from the Victoria Peak, a very interesting geological study.

[34]Loew and Roessler noted that Henrietta, founded about 1862 by Dr. Eldridge, of Montague, had been deserted as a result of Indian forays in which farm homes were burned and several citizens were scalped.

[35]Victoria Peak, usually known as Queen's Peak, is in western Montague County about four miles north of Bowie. In 1866–1868 it was the site of a settlement, which was the closest community to the government camp at Buffalo Springs in Clay County (W. C. Kimbrough, "The Frontier Background of Clay County," *West Texas Historical Association Year Book*, XVIII [1942], 123).

About 3 m W of road & 5 SW of peak rises a hill of similar height partially covered with timber. It reminds me forcibly of Mt. Tabor surrounded by the plains of Esdraelon. Outline segment of circle. "Brushy Mtn." ascending bare prairie & get very extended view to the N. The sandy road is so uneven from some cause unseen that I can scarcely make a note. 12:20 P.M. again enter woods after watering mules at a ditch in prairie, too dirty for us though we greatly need a drink, having been without since morning. Fault of commissary or wagoner in not filling casks at starting. Some conglomerate cropping out—causing the picturesque notes herewith. 2:30 P.M. arrive at deserted farm house, the owner Cooly having left it because of Indian depredations & stealing all his stock—large fields of splendid corn in tassel awaiting the reapers hand. We got stuck here sometime in the deep bed of a dry brook—all sand. No birds or flowers today to cheer the weary traveller. Monotonous. Jolting, dusty & hot—with breeze from S. not cool. No flies nor insects. A wilderness indeed—though hog & deer tracks were seen—also 4 deer. At 3 we got some water to drink in Sandy Creek. Therm 96.

Camp at 3:30 near a farm house—harvest of wheat 50 bus per acre! Sod—Timber surrounding. Roessler & men return & report two herders on Vict. Peak entrenched with winchester rifles—pickets of herders over their 5000 cattle in the surrounding prairie. Some 25 Indians having passed a week ago doing mischief. On guard tonight. Dist 20 m.

Texas

WEDY 26 JUNE '72. Whilst on guard last night at about 9 oc Three shots in rapid succession were heard close to camp. The reports aroused the camp to arms. Knowing that Maddox had gone out to hunt his horse that had strayed or been stolen from camp we fired a shot to get a response, also yelled his name and he responded and came into camp with his left hand shot by his own revolver—the first shot was at some man asking him "if he had brought one," Maddox taking him or them for horse thieves blazed away at them - - - one shot his revolver hitching on the next attempt he tried to turn the chambers with the left when two other barrels exploded & wounded him. This little incident has aroused an opinion of the necessity of stricter attention to discipline in the face of enemies and probably end the card playing by the light of a lantern

After a long silence of birds they again greet us. The nightingales, Chuck W. Widow, larks & quails. Col. McCarty killed doves for breakfast this m. Wild turkeys are about but he gets none. The farmer here, Marlett,[36] gives much information regarding the neighborhood, having been here 8 years. He always goes armed and never leaves his house without a man left to guard it. In ploughing he fastens his gun on the plough. His sons have killed Indians, but he has never done so. This year he says is more dangerous than any previous on account of the establishment of Fort Sill[37]—which has proved only a protection to the savage and not to the white settler. His cabin is partially stockaded— he now intends to complete it as times are getting more dangerous. Hogs are fat and numerous in the woods and of some good stock. The dry creek bounding our camp is a foot deep in fine sand. Start en route at 7:10 A.M. *26th June.* Rather cloudy & no breeze—may be precursor to change of weather. Crossing several small prairies of poor grass, with very rough stony roads—conglomerate—through parks of scrub oak, sharp look out for Indians—the bones of one hanging to a musquite tree killed last fall by a neighboring young farmer who gives us all the particulars after we camp near his ranch at 11 A.M. Ther 93 at 2 o.c. P.M. Distance 10 miles.

THURSD 27 JUNE 1872. Temp 80 at 7 A.M. Wind light from S. Cloudy night but clearer this morning. Yesty many went hunting & fishing with no reward. One saw a cougar and another a coon and another Deer tracks—but Dr. Loew beat them all—"He fished 4 hours & caught three little sun fish and a cat—of one ounce each." He went to the fire & cooked them and divided with his comrades. Applause. Since yesterday morn I have suffered from Diarhae. Somewhat better this morn. If we ever camped on picturesque spots I could exercise the brush—but all is monotony—Some green plains—& scrub oak parks

[36]The 1870 Census of Montague County lists Charley Marlett, aged forty-nine, a farmer born in South Carolina. He had three grown sons: Joseph, William, and Franklin.

[37]Fort Sill, near the eastern base of the Wichita Mountains, established on January 7, 1869, to serve as a base of operations against the Cheyenne and Kiowa Indians, became the center for the control of the southern plains Indians. For the history of Fort Sill see W. S. Nye, *Carbine and Lance: The Story of Old Fort Sill.*

alternately—nothing to force a tired out man from reposing. Quails call this morning. The train of ox teams camped near us and are off over the hill this morning.—and as we are to rest our mules today, it will reach Fort Richardson before us. Some 500 cattle are grazing nearby. Dewless night. 12 m overcast & sultry & dusty. A Sketch of camp. 3 P.M. Temp 93°. Many men are out hunting—others taking needed rest. Flies a little troublesome—no musquitoes—grasshoppers & spiders and tumblebugs plentiful. We have stationed mounted pickets on the summit of a neighboring bare hill whence they can view the country for many miles. This being on the direct path of Indian raids is a dangerous place & demands the above precaution. It is truly a wilderness—no signs of human beings in any direction—it is indeed the limit line of civilization—where the scattered farmers labor with arms in their hands & others are killed or scalped or driven off—their females massacred or carried into captivity. This sad tale I hear from many who have once had homes upon this border—which is less inhabited than 20 years ago. Is it a humane policy to protect the savage & feed & arm him, whilst such atrocities are of common occurrence? The hardy bold settler thinks not; and the question he will soon settle for himself. "Pleasant Cooley" the young farmer here is now sitting by me and giving me notes. His father was killed last year by a white boy—and he was killed by some men on the farm as revenge. Cooley opened this farm last winter and the corn crop is finer than anything he ever saw. Corn is worth $2 per bushel at his door. It was he who killed the Indian whose bones graced the tree we passed yesty. He - - - Cooley - - - had lost a mare & colt and in hunting the thieves came upon a body of Indians with the horses, among which he recognized his own. A fire commenced between the parties which resulted in the killing of two Indians and capture of two horses. Cooley scalped one—the other was dragged off by his fellows. The scalp was of long black hair, the scalp lock braided in with the beautiful locks of a white woman reaching to the waist. He took the scalp to ——— as proof that Indians were really killed in this region, a thing doubted by legislators. The horses Cooley got were not his own and soon disappeared—by theft or otherwise. So that he is left without a single horse or mule—only the pig is capable of holding his own against the Indians—it gets fat on mast which is most excellent here. The bear is seen here in winter.

Today we got a dinner of yearling—a rare feast to get fresh meat and I put in a little to strengthen a weak stomach. Bacon had few admirers today. Boils may become fewer hereafter. The Drs. Loew & Brown[38] & Peters have "fine specimens" under their right arms & elsewhere. Diarrhea troubles many. Water is generally bad—alkaline—warm or dead pools of rain.

Today water is good from a spring. We generally suffer from negligence in supplying water for night because of camping some distance from it, and everyone shirking the heavy duty of bringing it by hand. The ambulance is sometimes used to cart it in kegs. At present our clothes need it as much as we, though I managed to wash a shirt & drawers in a basinfull this morning and await their drying without inconvenience with the therm. at 93. Tomorrow I shall luxuriate! We have fortunately passed the *jigger* district and their bites are healing. I wish I knew what was the real word—chigger or jigger—our boys pronounce it the latter. It is so small as to be almost invisible but soon builds a large bloody house about him which itches extremely and if scratched is inflamed into a large running sore. Many cannot resist bringing them to this—though I have. But such a scratching goes on in tents as to annoy those who otherwise could sleep. Today & yesterday more regularity & discipline prevails—danger breeds precaution in the most careless mind. Things are now in some order before dark—animals picketed and within the enclosure of wagon & tents. No stray ones to be hunted up in the morning—causing delay.

FRIDAY 28TH JUNE '72. Light rain from 9 to 11 last night and this morning still overcast and no breeze. Diarhea still troubling me & several others; pretty soon our force will be forceless, for want of proper food. I got a little milk & bread this morn by kindness of Cooley the farmer. Yesterday eve many were complaining of the beans being smoked or of the veal—something that had upset them. This morn no sugar for coffee—5 days rations gone in 2. Our eating & cookstove close to, within 3 ft. of the stinking carcass of a beef neither beautiful nor appetizing. It could have been removed but no orders given to that end. No dew this morn. I notice that there is none after a rainy evening.

[38] I am not able to identify Dr. Brown. The Dallas *Herald,* June 1, 1872, named a Dr. Johnson, but he does not appear in the Kellogg account of the Expedition. J. S. Brown is named as the commissary in the *Herald.*

Leave at 6 A.M. One horse disabled in hind leg & cannot follow. Course W. At 7 o.c. we find mowers of grass for Fort Richardson,[39] with teams. Change of rock to limestone—with some conglomerate. All the ridges are similar form—like earthworks. Stop to water in a branch running amid the bare ridges. Some live oaks form nice groups and the musquite tree is becoming numerous—and large purple convolvulus.[40] Evolution practice. Horse gets his legs & follows up horsemen and teams. Broken lines of postoaks cross our path, juttings from the great mass of Cross timbers. 7:20 pass watershed and descend grand open prairie commanding an immense view to SW of lines of hills of rounded summits as their western terminus—running into vast plains on their eastern. At 9 A.M. pass through woods & rough rocky road and find better soil & liveoak dense forest on the left. No bird insects or game. Roads sandy—last nights rain laid the dust and as it is cool & cloudy we make say 3 m pr hour. 9:40 cross an important branch of Trinity (W. fork) - - - Water muddy—15 feet across and running with visible force over a rocky bed. Musquite trees abundant, the whole land covered as we pass over the creek—like a nursery of locust trees. Arrive at Jacksboro at 1:00 P.M. threatening shower - - - slight sprinkle. A halt for a few minutes in the straggling village of frame & log houses, dreadfully dilapidated and propped up. A two story stone house is the courthouse of this county seat of Jack Co.[41] Dist 15½ m.

JACKSBORO

1:30 P.M. pitch tents in a secure nook on the left bank of Jacksboro Creek, surrounded by a ridge of limestone like a wall about us much crumbled and 15 feet high except an open space on the S.W. across which we place the wagons, guarded on the outside by our tents which

---

[39]Fort Richardson, located on the south bank of Lost Creek near the village of Jacksboro, was the first of the new United States frontier posts built south of Red River in the post-bellum period. The nearest settlement was Weatherford, forty-two miles to the southeast. The post was occupied in 1866, abandoned in 1867, and reoccupied in 1868 (Carl Coke Rister, *The Southwestern Frontier, 1865–1881*, 50–52).

[40]Loew must be responsible for the botanical terms. The natives of North Texas would have understood "morning-glory."

[41]A sandstone courthouse, constructed by D. W. Patton, was built in 1871 and was the scene of the trial of Satanta and Big Tree in July of that year (Ida Lasater Huckabay, *Ninety-Four Years in Jack County, 1854–1948*, 139)

look upon the open prairie. The deep water of the creek gives good bathing places under the dense shade of its brushy banks. Soldiers from the fort are now amusing themselves in it and our men will soon replace them. Turtles float about in quiet pools. Threatening clouds. Go into the fort and meet Capt. Jackson—Dr. Wolf. And after a talk return to camp toward dark and try to secure tent for coming storm but tent pins are so scarce that we risk much in neglecting to make them fast. Turn in—at 1 in the morning the storm has blown my end of the tent over me—and I wake my comrades Peters & Troutman[42]—and go to work in rain and dark and erect tent again taut enough to make a cover from the storm till morning. Chandler had fortunately accepted quarters in the Headquarters of Genl. Buell[43] in the fort, and nicely escaped a drenching. Letter from Sheldon, 13th inst. just arrived.

SAT 29TH JUNE '72. Still windy & showery from S. Visit Headquarters on invitation of Genl & Mrs. Buell—have a fine breakfast—Chandler, McCarty & Peters. Cucumbers, Chicken & Beef—& coffee as *was* coffee. Not being free yet from Diarhea cannot do justice to the set out. We sat out the morning in pleasant converse on the front veranda. The Genl. was from Lawrenceburg Ind. His father owned much land there where he settled from Ithaca N.Y. in 1818, descending the Ohio in flatboat—doubtless father knew him. Mrs. B. is from Nashville —daughter of Judge Bryan. A charming couple. The Genl. offers me an escort of cavalry to "Brushy Mtn" just visible from the fort 20 m N. that I may sketch one of the loveliest of panoramas. I accept & expect to get a most interesting series of birdeye views of this unknown land. Col. McKinsey, commander of the Post is off with several companies to drive the Indians back upon "the reservation," and Buell cannot assist us with escort without orders from Gen. Augur[44] at San Antonio, but being desirous of so doing sends off a courier immediately to Corsicana where he will telegram to Augur to know "if he will order an

---

[42]Loew and Roessler give this photographer as G. Troutman; the name listed in the Dallas *Herald* is A. C. Troutman. Eastman Kodak Company has not been able to identify him.

[43]General George P. Buell of the 11th Infantry (Hamersly, *Complete Regular Army Register of the United States*, 330).

[44]General Christopher Columbus Augur (1821–1898), a graduate of West Point, was promoted to brigadier general in 1869. He retired from the Regular Army in 1885 (*DAB*, I, 427–428).

escort or leave Buell to exercise his own judgement." An answer will not arrive for 8 or 10 days. We propose to await it in this vicinity as it seems certain that with the present hostility of "Indians on the warpath" we shall lose all our animals if not our scalps if left to our own force. Several parties are now before us making locations near our objective point.—our *blowing* has aroused a fever in all Texas—and if we dont move on more rapidly the plums may have been picked on our arrival. We are too heavy a body & too slow. A few well appointed experienced rangers can get through with less danger and more rapidity. This is my view. Rain comes in heavy showers and I work in it securing tent and ditching till soaked, but we have a more comfortable abode for the night. Spiders and ants are nothing when you get used to sleeping with them as we do. We got a wonderful 1000 legged worm for Loew today. It was 6 in long ½ in diam. and when in a vial of alcohol in co. with a huge tarantula did the heart of our Chemist rejoice at the sight. Mrs. Buell gives me several texas diamonds and other stones to send to Somers by mail and a beautiful cactus.

SUND 30 JUNE '72. After some rain last night this morning is sunny with flying clouds and high wind from S. Some of our party are seated under the trees at cards—others in town or Fort to see the monthly review for Paymaster—I remain in camp sewing, washing duds and making these notes. Col. Johnson suggests that 10 or 15 men with packmules be sent forward to *locate* what mineral lands they know to be valuable and we follow on to survey them—so as to head off other parties. I agree to and urge the same—and when Col. McCarty returns to camp will counsel over the matter. Very strong steady wind from S called trade winds, which prevail during summer. Sunday passed without interest or incident. Men in groups under trees—gaming—telling stories—talking horse races—spirit rapping & gassing. All of no value whatever—Loew is sleeping under my tent after a night watch—so is Troutman—neither of whom should be called on for such duty except on perilous occasions. It unfits the artistic & scientific corps for their legitimate duties. Dissatisfaction increases with such arrangement and with the continued bad food—little else than heavy bread and bacon. Today for luxury we had beef, string beans & squash. The vegetables cooked in bacon grease nauseate me & I merely taste them. There is no good reason why we should be fed like pigs in this place, the Hotels giving a variety of nice food. Men get so little of their salary that they do without many comforts and naturally complain.

Blue cranes or Indian cranes now appear & killdees. Sheldon's letter relieves my spirits of a terrible anxiety—My dear daughter is safe—and well & happy.

MOND 1ST JULY '72. Move camp—m. nearer to spring & grass & 500 yds S.E. of Fort on a fine open plain. The best water we have yet found. I wish such a man as Barnum had charge of this motley company of volunteers—there would be fewer drones—and all would be made to do some regular duty—Some are utterly useless & how they come to be here is a mystery. No care seems to have been taken to know the character & fitness of many who are engaged on a salary. They have no interest in the honor & success of the expedition—mere adventurers & mercenaries. We have got rid of some. I hope more will soon be missing. We have say 15 excellent practical, conscientious men—who had they the power could accomplish all we desire—and at half the present outlay. But divisions & indecisions of counsel paralyze action and here we are on the jumping off place without unity of purpose & easy Exchequer—& demoralization apparent. This evening Count Crenneville[45] a young Austrian of blood joins us—of no visible use as I see even as ornament. He and Genl Buell are in our tent taking part in the concert we have improvised in the midst of heavy rain. The Genl plays an old fashioned tune on the fiddle and the count screams out fancy songs from operas &c in different languages, and with theatric gestures and divine looks screams as only little men can equal. Our little tent is crowded with listeners, keeping me from needed rest. The rain is unusual for the reason but will prove of vast benefit to use—

---

[45]Loew and Roessler identify this man as Ferner von Crenneville, from Vienna, assistant geologist to the Expedition. R. G. Carter, writing almost thirty years later, called him Victor de Creeneville and identified him as a son of a member of Emperor Franz Joseph's staff. The young Austro-Hungarian count was attached to the Austrian legation in Washington when he joined the Expedition. Carter entertained him at Fort Richardson and furnished him a horse for a buffalo hunt. Both the Count and McCarty went with Carter to Dallas in September, 1872. Despite the Count's plan or promise to write a description of his Texas adventures, Carter said he never heard of such a book. Von Crenneville, or De Creeneville, may have been the son of Franz Graf Folliot de Crenneville (1815–1888), who was adjutant general for Emperor Franz Joseph I in 1867 (*Österreichisches Biographisches Lexikon, 1815–1950*, I, 335).

for water & grass. To the farmer it is precious & from all sides the story is that this part of Texas *never* before exhibited such abundant crops of grain of all kinds—they are simply *enormous*. Today I met Judge Baldwin, the U.S. Dist. Atty and had a pleasant talk. Regret not having time for more extended memos of much I desire to recall. But these are a fair outline thus far of the moving picture, and I shall, for their security dispatch them to Sheldon by mail—they might get lost in our progress—and then there would be very little to be relied on from the scanty, hasty notes others may have made.

TUESD 2 JULY '72. Hard steady rain all night still continuing from S. after magnificent rainbows yesty. The skies in Texas & Ind. Ter. have been a constant study & delight to me—Yest. a thin, gauzy screen of cloud passed rapidly from N. and above it great flakes of denser forms swept as rapidly from S. a wonderful display of opposite currents of air.

WEDNESDAY   Raining at times - - - 3D JULY '72. Letter to Sheldon. Night heavy storm—flooding out of our tent 3 in deep. Breakfast in town squarely. Prepare to move en route—as soon as floods allow. Sky yet dingy & threatening - - - Cowan & Bullion[46] have joined us and our number of scouts is complete. Our project now is to leave tomorrow 4th July, leaving Peters & one or two here, awaiting dispatches from Gen Augur. If he gives us escort it can follow on and join us in 2 or 3 days. But what will turn up is doubtful. I think the experienced & best men will *insist* on certain changes in the administration & guidance of affairs which will give us more security among the Indians. As the Buffalo are now far north on Red River they will be without support for great numbers in our destined course. So that we apprehend small bodies only to dispute our passage and steal & stampede our stock. So the worst may only be to leave us on foot to trudge back again. The chances are however that some life will be lost before we get back.

I now trust these notes to Sheldon through mail.

---

[46]This is M. D. Bullion, a surveyor, who had sent samples of copper ore to Washington for Roessler's assay at the General Land Office.

Expedition to Texas—1872 cont.
Book No. 2
Left St. Louis for Texas May 18—72.

JACKSBORO, TEXAS

THURSDAY JULY 4, 1872. Salute the day with Howitzer—responded by same from Ft. Richardson. Wind squall. Fort officers visit us to see a match of Rifle shooting btn 30 of us for 15$ first and 5$ 2d prize. Distance 250 yds off hand. High wind on backs. The target was 4 ft diam. 3 shots each 90 in all. 13 shots hit target—the 2 best near bullseye. 1st Walters—2d Robins[47]—of the 13 that hit the target I hit it twice—making the best shots after the prize winners. As I had never yet discharged a piece since in the Expedition, it surprized every one—no one thinking such amusement was in me. It surprized me more as I had not fired a gun for 25 years. Yesterday mailed my note book to date to Sheldon—also a letter. Swimming—in too long—got a horned toad & boxed him up. He is scratching away incessantly for release. McCarty was presented by Mrs. Buell with a young cub—with a sore back. Nice Pet! Have *bears* enough already—but we must bear another in camp—a barefaced nuisance. Afternoon amusing games in Fort. Foot races of soldiers—also in sacs—hunting the bottle. Rockets. Evening with Capt. Webb—Cards & claret punch. Back to camp at midnight—my

[47]Samuel Marshall Robbins, born in New York, served as captain in the 1st Colorado Cavalry from November 30, 1861, until he was honorably mustered out on

first evening out of camp—suffered with hemoroides from over bathing. Temp. 94.

JULY 5 '72. Quite knocked over by hemorrhoids—alone in tent. No conveniences for nursing—bathing or rest at night & suffer much in back, hips & ribs from hard ground. Temp. 94.

SAT 6 JULY. No news yet from Augur regarding escort. Wonderful sky & heavy rain at night. Still in tent; may go to Fort Hospital for care & treatment. McCarty & some others believe this delaying will lose much of the very land intended for location—others being ahead of us in the Double Mtns.[48] where our treasures are to be sought. Our principal men are now *really* fearful of failure in their labors to find their El Dorado.

SUND 7TH JULY '72. All quiet in camp. Several Engineers & officers & Peters in town—consulting as to where & when to move. As there appears no prospect of getting escort, and a misunderstanding as to the powers we hold to locate as against the resident surveyors of Districts— a knotty legal question is to be discussed if not decided. The usual want of order—& unity & harmony still prevails. Chandler in tent arranging old accounts. Troutman trimming photos. I on back looking on. Distant grumbling thunder. What we have always needed we still need—a good, prompt executive officer who will enforce his orders and command respect. Everyone is now an officer unto himself. Ammunition & stores wasted and destroyed which we ought to save *carefully* for use when out of reach of succor & supply. Our guards are scanty from shirking—& sleep at times on post. Such old soldiers as Col. *Johnson*—& brave scouts as *Switcher* of Hays old corps—express indignation at such things—& predict at least the loss of our animals when out among the Indians. I still try to hope for a change before evil befalls us. But there is division in counsel & conflict I *think* of interests which it seems unlikely will be accommodated until too late. Many men have left us for various reasons, and a spirit of demoralization exists. Blasphemy is almost universal and

---

October 26, 1865. He became first lieutenant of the 7th Cavalry in July, 1866, made his captaincy in 1868, and resigned on March 1, 1872. Robbins died September 25, 1878 (Heitman, *Historical Register and Dictionary of the United States Army*, I, 834).

[48]Double Mountain (or Double Mountains) is located in southwestern Stonewall County. The county was not created until 1876, and the first actual settlement was not made until the early 1880's.

shameless and Sunday utterly disregarded. The vicinity of villages is dangerous—affording liquor to intoxicate a poorly fed company of complaining men. It is not difficult to divine a sad result for such a combination of evils. This evening finds Peters, Winchebach and Plummer at a Hotel in town making merry—the camp & its duties ought to bind them at this moment of threatening dissolution—as examples of earnest endeavor for success. But they are to "make a night of it" whilst the camp is inefficiently guarded. Switcher says he will leave us tomorrow.

MOND 8TH JULY '72. We are to get no Escort. Not being at the Fort on receipt of news from Augur I know no details. Switcher left this morning for Austin to join another party more likely to reach our goal than we are, & we may meet him there he says! Should not wonder if others follow his example. Our cook wants to leave—also a negro teamster. Chandler is in trouble evidently at these *signs*.

Mailed minerals and live toad to Sheldon. Still on my back with hemoroides. 5 o.c. P.M. The negro driver is tied to a wagon wheel. He wishes to leave, and started—but McCarty stopped him and had men tie him up. 6:00 P.M. Wagon Master White returns to camp and tells McC that the driver better be released as the tying will have a bad effect with the men. McC says he wouldn't stand his Jaw & intended keeping him tied till our departure, but that he might be released. Which White did & the negro went to town. Robins then advised McC to tell White to follow the negro to town and take him to Chandler to get his wages or an attachment might give the company trouble. My opinion is that he *can do so any how*, as the civil courts are open and the military ready to support them at hand. This act of injustice & illegality pains me more than I can express and it may detain the whole expedition. 8 P.M. Capt Bullion has come from town—says that Geo White the negro went to Lawyer Ball[49] to sue out a writ against McCarty but Bullion being present talked him out of it, advising him to get his back pay & let the thing rest, as Ball says if the negro does not give bail to appear on trial he can be locked up until that time. The negro then takes his wages but don't say he will let the matter drop so. Temp 93 2 o.c.

[49]Thomas Ball, a Virginian, was admitted to the bar in 1858. He served in the Senate of the Fifteenth Texas Legislature. In 1871 he was attorney for the defense in the trial of Satanta and Big Tree (Smythe, *Historical Sketch of Parker County and Weatherford, Texas*, 265; H. L. Bentley and Thomas Pilgrim, *The Texas Legal Directory for 1876-77*, 45).

Chandler stops in town tonight ill. Peters has not been in camp since Sat nor Winchebach. Troutman is taking views on creek. Weather hot —but fine cool breeze. No musquitoes, few flies. No climate can much exceed this in comfortable summers—the nights being always cooling & invigorating. As to skies—in all my studies of them in various parts of the world—none have equalled these in variety and beauty & changefulness of cloud forms—they alone repay the time—if not the discomforts of the journey. I learn that Genl Augur answers "*No*" to Buell's dispatch as to giving us a Escort.

TUESDAY 9TH JULY '72. Breezy morn, clear hot. Shooting cumuli clouds from all points of horizon intensely white against a tender blue firmament. Quiet in camp—tents full of sleepers & idlers—the leaders away in town, concocting maps and most feasible route to gain lands yet unlocated by the more rapid rival parties ahead of us. A mortifying result to the sanguine promises & *blowings* at the beginning! I am confined to tent yet by illness—but manage to sew and mend a little. Temp 96. Several men have left us today. The negro teamster—fellow of the one tied, has engaged to Buell in Fort. Lusk with his 2 mule teams leaves and one of the cooks. These make a total of 17 of our party who have left us since being in St. Louis. We hire new ones instead—but have little heed as to their character & fitness. Mrs. Buell very kindly sends me pot of excellent tea, and a plate of dipped toast and some delicious jelly—a most acceptable present indeed—so different from the miserable food I take in camp. It has served me for dinner & supper too. Many of our men get their meals in town—so tired are they of camp fodder; but I am physically unable to "go & do likewise."

WED 10TH JULY '72. Splendid as usual—hot & breezy from S. - - - magnificent display of snowy bright cumuli around the entire horizon —I am gradually improving, but keep to tent & repose. Troutman gets some cloud negatives excellently—the camp seems deserted—not a soul nor beast visible—if we except the grasshoppers rattling their yellow wings from place to place impatiently seeking what they may devour—no certainty when we move on—the heads of Departments still joyously busy over their maps & papers at the Surveyor's office in the town. Cards & champagne & song enliven their weary evenings! Temp 89.

THURS 11TH JULY '72. Still finest of weather—clear & breezy but

I cannot be out to work - - - remain in tent reading & putting sketching materials in some order. Troutman hard at work printing some splendid cloud negatives taken yesterday. Brown has lost his horse & White is out after him—negligence of herders—White returned at dusk unsuccessful after a 40 m ride. A wild Texas horse—has doubtless gone back to Sherman where we bought him. Ther 90°. No word positive as to our starting - - - Pudding from Mrs. Buell.

FRIDAY 12TH JULY '72. White & five men sent out for Brown's horse. Brown & Bullion run away with in 2 horse buggy & hurt. Buggy badly shocked & laid up for repairs. I go to town to get some decent food & see if there be not really a letter from Somers, not having had a line from her since I left Washington—now 2 months. But she is free & yet mine. *This* I know. The morning is a little cloudy & portending thunder shower—quite hot & close. Temp 96. Dine at Thompson Hotel[50] on chicken—water melon—and a glass of Bordeau for 50 cts and was satisfied—returned to camp - - - "our folks" in town saying they had finished their work and are ready to start tomorrow—which I don't believe they will. This P.M. Peters sends me an invite to dine at 7 at Thompsons with Buell & others, which I decline on account of illness. Learn that 8 persons just came to town after a fight of several hours with 35 Indians 70 m distant from here—one of the men strayed during the fight and was scalped. Of course they could not tell whether any Indians was killed, as if so—he would as usual be dragged off by his fellow savages. What a commentary on the system of *military* protection in these parts. McKinsey out with 5 companies of cavalry to drive the Indians back to their reservation—and being flanked by parties who get in his rear and murder the innocent herders & settlers—and when pay day comes return to their wigwams to receive kind words—and blankets and powder & arms from the liberal hands of their "Great Father" in Washington! *Allow* the *Texans* to protect their borders and we should soon hear of peace and the settlement of one of the most prolific & healthy portions of the U. States. Yet, only think of it, here is a military post more powerful than any other on this frontier—costing a

---

[50]The first building used for a hotel in Jacksboro was a residence built by Henry Thompson. When Mrs. H. H. McConnell became manager in the early seventies the name was changed to Southern Hotel (Huckabay, *Ninety-Four Years in Jack County*, 297).

million dollars per annum, utterly unable from some cause to protect *its own vicinity* from the thieving & murderous savages within *its own jurisdiction!!*

White & the 5 men returned without Brown's horse. So he is lost altogether. Troutman & I still have our tent to ourselves—I taking the cot of Chandler instead of the hard ground as my illness forces me to do. We are annoyed by the noise of some creeping things and determined to oust all Peter's things which are strewed every where in the tent and give the poor tarantulas, crickets, spiders, centipedes—maybe snakes, a fair chance for their lives. Here these splendid & useless toggeries of a vain schoolboy have lain about in our way without *airing the ground* beneath them for 10 days past altho their owner has engaged a lad—*orderly* we call him, to look out and care for them in his jolly absence in the town. The boy knows how to shirk his duties as well as does his master and the encumbrances still annoy us, but we clean them out today *certainly.*

SAT. 13TH JULY '72. Another lovely morning—hot but with cooling Southern air and splendid fleecy clouds which Troutman is seizing ere they pass. 6 o.c. walk to town to post letter to Sheldon & book of flowers & photogs. In the evening Capt. Webb[51] was good enough to send the Post Band to our camp to give us a parting serenade.[52] It came with lanterns and surrounded by our boys enchanted us all with the charming choice of pieces Webb had selected. Nothing could exceed the poetry of the scene—with a half moon now & then eclipsed by dark clouds passing over the clear starry vault of bluish grey—whilst in the south were

[51]William W. Webb, of New York, was assigned to the 4th Cavalry in August, 1861. He became first lieutenant in 1862 and captain in 1866 (Heitman, *Historical Register and Dictionary,* I, 1012).

[52]A former soldier who had been stationed at Griffin, Richardson, and Buffalo Springs had memories of the bands:

"Each of these regimental headquarters had magnificent bands, and when the evening gun boomed out, the garrison flag fluttered majestically to the ground, and the stirring strains of martial music floated out over the beautiful Texas landscape on the still night air. It formed a picture that the old resident may be pardoned for looking back on with reminiscent regret for the 'good old days' gone by forever.

"The bands of the post each had a subordinate and private organization, known as a string band or orchestra, and when balls or parties were given in Jacksboro the citizens always engaged their services, and no such music has been heard here since then." (H. H. McConnell, *Five Years a Cavalryman: or, Sketches of Regular Army Life on the Texas Frontier Twenty Odd Years Ago,* 163).

Pencil sketch of the Expedition's encampment near Caddo, Oklahoma, from Kellogg's 1872 notebook.

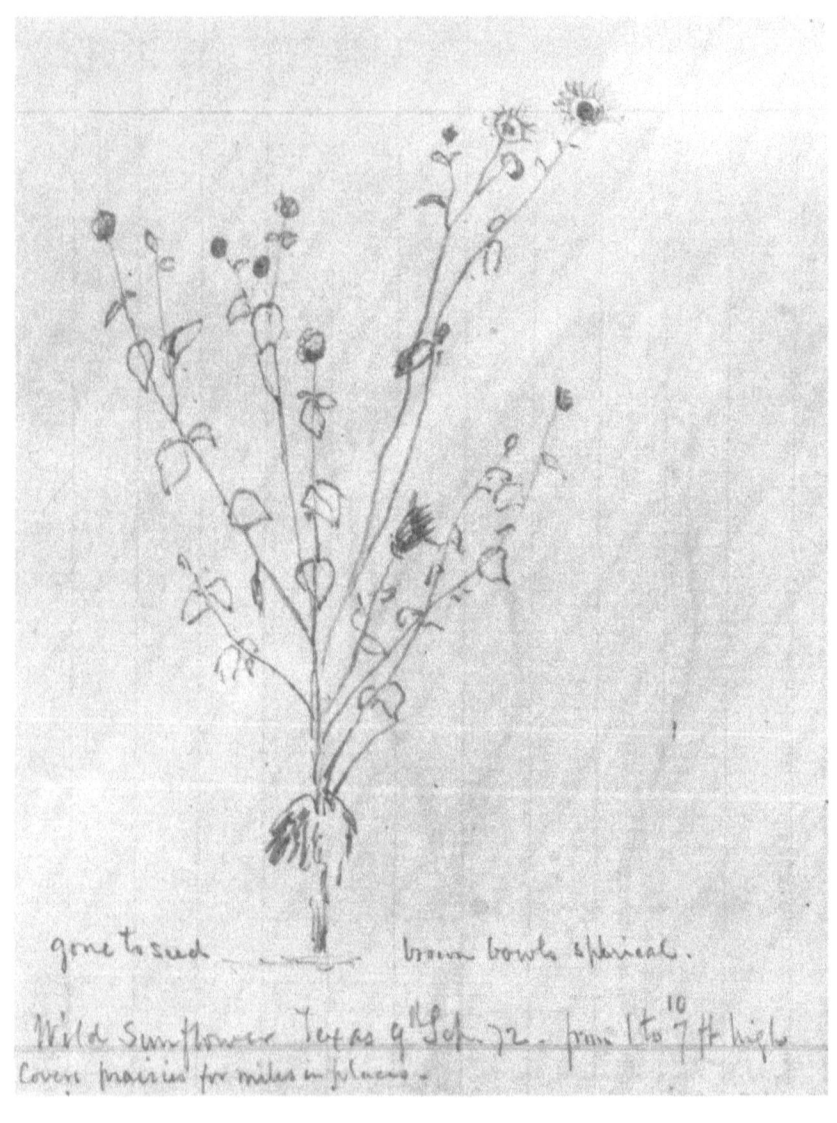

Sketch of dried sunflower from Kellogg's notebook, the pencil record of his trip to Texas, 1872.

Sketch of mesquite trees, "the skeletons by day & the bogies by night which spread themselves thinly over the ground in all directions," from Kellogg's 1872 notebook.

Page from Kellogg's notebook, showing an account of an Indian massacre and a sketch of the monument to the seven men killed on the "open treeless prairie—noted for Indian massacres—the most dangerous place in this region."

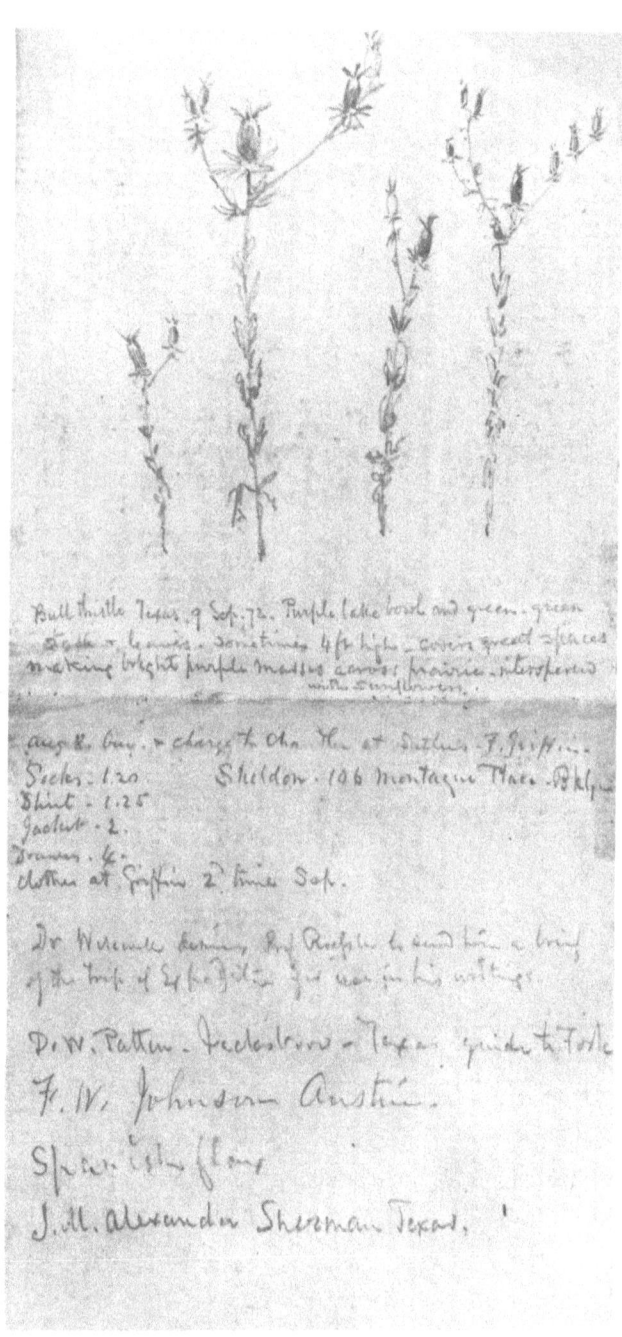

Last page of Kellogg's 1872 notebook.

ARCHIVES COLLECTION, THE UNIVERSITY OF

The 1872 map of Texas by A. R. Roessler noting regions of mineral deposits and compl and proposed railway lines.

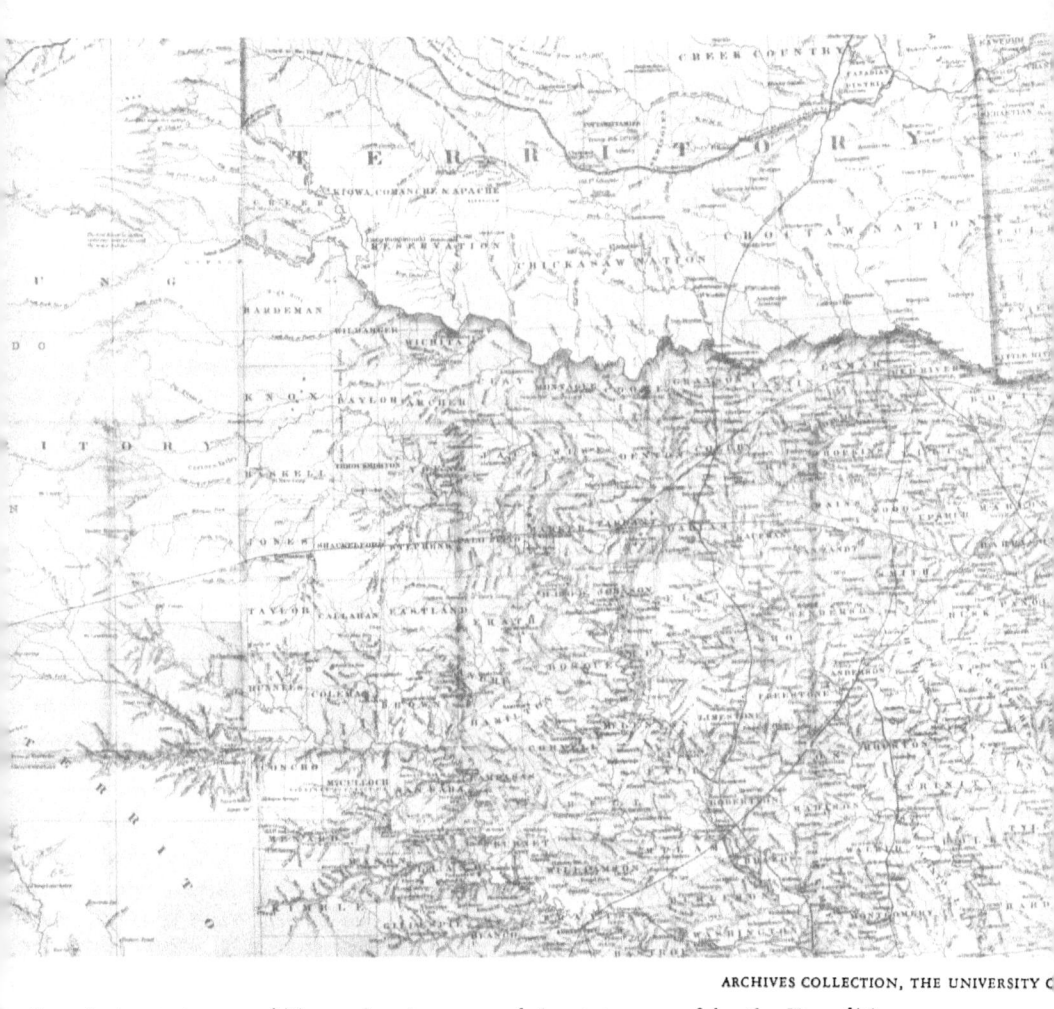

Roessler's 1872 map of Texas showing area of the state crossed by the Expedition.

REAUGH COLLECTION, THE UNIVERSITY OF TEXA

Double Mountains from the Salt Fork. Pastel by Frank Reaugh.

pictured three grand & graceful cumuli in close company charged with electricity and frequently emitting lambent flames defining their exquisite forms overlaying each other as do scenes in a theatre. Then, as it seemed, at the very moment when a vivid flash would add vigor to the bugle's blast, it came. Equally opportune came the blinding circular & angular & perpendicular sharp & cutting lines of fluid, as variation to the hilarious passages of the most noted and popular of operatic music.

What a telling chapter could be made of the quiet scene presented in camp. The group of Post and Expedition officers surrounding the flag staff in front of the Headquarters tent, with the lanterns illuminating the circle of musicians stationed a short distance in front. The irregular line of tents in an outer line completed by the wagons and animals attached to the picket rope—startled & struggling against the first blows of the great drum & the shrill horn in the opening strains of the serenade. The straggling groups of men prone on the ground near their respective tents—smoking and passing along the Indian cruelties of the day—yet with spirits of animosity assuaged by the peaceful music, and the changeful moon's rays—and the knowledge that we had a brave company just ready for action and its reward—the sleepers in isolated spots upon the sward, oblivious to music but possibly not to the contents of loving letters from home—these & other noticeable features of the border serenade are replete with interest to me.

14 JULY '72. SUNDAY. Leave camp through town on Fort Sill road N at 1 o.c. P.M. hot & sultry - - - in tolerably good order leaving Chandler, Peters & Count Crenneville behind, in town to follow tomorrow. Through musquite trees & jutting rocky prominences and a tolerable road with conglomerate croppings came to halt in post oak forest at 5:15 o.c. P.M. and came (W. fork of Trinity) near a bridge over a sluggish stream of red & muddy water. Distance 8⅓ m. Temp 88 at 5:30. My tent was left behind because Peters could not get his magazines of nonsensicals out in time to start with the train. The evening was sultry with lightning. McCarty offered me the shelter of his fly under knarled, stumpy wide-spreading oaks. In the night the storm broke upon us, and the wind drove the rain in upon me, which united to an overflow of the flat fly thoroughly drenched me. I laid in my wet blankets without sleep still 3 o.c. Got an hours slumber, crawled out after daylight well soaked—but not unthankful that the storm had superceded

the persistent nips of musquitoes which were more unbearable. A sharp look out was kept during the storm as we are now dependent *entirely* on our own vigilance for safety. These are the first musquitoes to annoy us in Texas. *We are now fairly launched* on our way to the object of our journey, but without Chandler—Peters—or Roessler. The last two from sheer negligence & laziness—the former to settle up affairs in Jacksboro—get another wagon & other business—with several officers the worse for town *condiments,* the Indians might bag us.

15TH JULY '72. MOND. Near Jacksboro, Texas. I am drying myself at a large fire—internally blessing friend Peters for depriving me of my tent and a night's sleep & rest so much needed in my present weak state. Our boys got roasting ears at a neighboring field and we roasted them in the campfire. The cook boiled some and spoiled some by frying in hog grease—still with rather good bread & coffee I filled up a large vacancy of yesterday's fasting—as its dinner was only bacon, the *infernal* bacon. Verily in the midst of plenty of Texas there is famine—neither beef—chickens—game or vegetables or decent bread to be had for love or money. The little milk we get is not even a taste all around. I bought in Jacksboro 2 lbs of raisins for a dollar and they help to keep off hunger—everything in these parts equally dear. Soldiers of the fort *possessed* our cub as we came away. May they keep him! I wish I had had half the care he did, and I should have been well. But I didn't have fleas and a scabby back—and *cry*—how could I expect it? The 4 useless hounds and dogs are also behind, but I have no hopes of their staying so. *Temp 94.* A muddy disagreeable camp. Word comes in that Roessler was injured by runaway in buggy going to old camp—but will follow us tomorrow. I make my bed in ambulance—a storm in night but get a good night's rest—as we had killed and eaten a stray beef for dinner—

16TH JULY '72. TUESDAY. No signs yet of the laggers behind—and send animals out to herd. Walters was out hunting yesterday—got nothing *but saw* a large cinnamon *panther* and heard Indians whistling. ———— has just returned from a hunt of an hour or so and saw three mexican lions—*splendid* ones. I asked Col Johnson about Lions and he says they are still to be found in Texas, and gives me some notion of their habits from personal experience, as he has been a frontiersman for 40 years. He is like old Sam Houston in physique though not so large—but his fine cranium—martial bearing and cool common sense and modest deportment inspires me with great reliance on his judgment & action in case of danger. I wish he had important—or in other words *some* command among us that his courage & experience might be of some use to us. He knows how to mix & chat with our wild element of frontier boys, and yet preserve dignity and esteem. They would *forward* to any command of his—and follow also with alacrity. I have many quiet talks with him & am struck with his simplicity and intelligence and manliness. He will always be found at his post of duty. I believe he is only with us to point out certain localities rich in minerals & *without salary*—though results may induce the Company to compensate him financially. He commanded at ——— the first battle of Texas against the Mexicans[53]; a hero honored by his state & people is moving with us without ostentation or reward, prompted solely by the good he supposes this scientific expedition may prove to the future of his state. Sometimes sorely disheartened by its impractical & tardy movements, and the dangers its want of knowledge & discretion may involve us, he sticks to us still, quietly inoculating us with greater care harmony & wisdom. The air is still hot, sultry, & cloudy. Storm apparently not yet over. The camp lifeless—animals human & beastly all out of sight except McCarty, Loew, & Johnson. Some hunting—some fishing—some sleeping & some gone again to town. How I wish our vicinity were townless & no fine drinkers & poison whiskey to be dragging us from an onward sober march—Only then do I hope for the death of a demoralization which has slowly manifested itself—but *surely*. The tumblebug has taken possession of the deserted camp, and will soon clean it of the refuse of our stock—what a wonderful & useful scavenger—numerous as the locust of Egypt. I have had many a lesson from them in watching their skill & their instinctive powers. They are certainly no ornament to the camp—but they are as certainly useful and withal without the power or nature to annoy us. Some beautiful ones are to be found in color & form—reminding me of the sacred Scarabei of the Egyptians. Our camp is full of mud holes & mud and to pass through it a nuisance to all. But it is picturesque with tents and flys & wagons straggling without order amid the post oak trees, upon the ragged branches of which our wet & muddy clothes & blankets are spread to dry

---

[53] Johnson was a captain during the Anahuac disturbances in 1832 and he led a division of Texans into San Antonio at the time of the siege of Bexar in 1835.

and air. Troutman yesterday made a negative or so of the scene—a scene not fixed up for effect—where every eye is turned toward his lens as usual—Oh how naturally vain are the best of us.

Flying & brilliant clouds but weather unsettled. Photo of trees. P.M. so threatening that there is danger of overflow from the W. Branch of Trinity, the banks being already nearly full - - - that we pull up tents and move in body back across the bridge & continue towards Jacksboro about a mile—strike off to the right through musquite prairie roadless, say two miles to the base of one of the many low abrupt ranges of hills overlooking this country and go into camp with good grass & water. The night commenced with a moon which was lost in the clouds by 1 o.c. A.M., after which a steady light quiet rain set in lasting till morning. I slept in ambulance with Troutman but musquitoes annoyed me much— and got up unrefreshed

WEDS 17TH JULY '72. Temp 8 o.c. 73° - - - 2 o.c. 90½° - - - Cloudy morn. An ambulance is sent to town by order of Chandler and we are not likely to get away for a day or so. I hardly know how many men are now in town & out of camp shooting. What all this delay means is a marvel to me and I sometimes think it indicates a grand breakup of the Expedition. Webster[54] and his party of 25 left same day we did on same road—he is now ahead of us 48 hours—so much for *business*. We could have united our force to his if we were not so slow & uncertain. He has taken one of our most efficient men Crooks[55]—his own clerk in Galveston Shipping house & tells me he wishes to see *personally* the land he has already located and on his favorable report a million pounds sterling stands ready in London to exploit and work it. He is an English-

[54] Mason Webster lived in New York before moving to Galveston, where he worked for the firm of C. W. Hurley in the steamship and coal businesses. He married Julietta Knight, a niece of Mrs. Hurley. Webster was head of the grain department of the Galveston Board of Trade when he lost his life in the Galveston storm of 1900 (Samuel Chester Griffin, *History of Galveston, Texas, Narrative and Biographical*, 177). Webster, described by surveyor E. Boon of Jack County as agent for the Texas Emigration Company, persuaded Boon to lend him some state-owned guns for a period of two weeks while the Webster group explored in the areas of Haskell and Stonewall Counties. When informed of the loan Governor Davis ordered the immediate return of the guns (Boon to Governor E. J. Davis, July 28, 1872, countersigned by Adjutant General James Davidson, August 5, 1872. Davis File, Governors' Letters).

[55] The *Galveston City Directory, 1872* lists William Crooks as a clerk with C. W. Hurley and Company.

man. I saw a large snake this morn among the rocks—red sand stone & conglomerate same as at Montague. I witnessed a chase of a prairie snake by Tom Hemphill today which amused me greatly. Tom is over 6 feet high and not very active—just fitted for driving a mule team which he does well. Seeing a snake in the deep grass he made for him in full headway & jumped solidly with both feet on the snake as he supposed—but snaky turned back quickly on his trail, and before Tom could get sight of him was some 15 or 20 ft away. Tom at him again with another jump & full stop—snaky playing some trick and so the two kept it up to the shouts of the men—*"go it snake," "go it Tom"* for several minutes when Tom did actually get his big feet on his *longness* which somewhat diminished his headway & confused his brain. So Tom seized him by the tail—held him up to view in triumph and when we saw the length of Mr. Snake we considered it a triumph indeed! and cheered accordingly. The reptile was brought into camp still alive until the boys had their fun out in torturing him to death and his body cast out again. When Loew returned to camp from a slight distance, I told him of the *"magnificent specimen"* we had for him laid away down in the grass yonder. The "little Doctor" as Loew is familiarly called, is about five feet high & stout in proportion and as he made high & rapid steps into the tall grass after Snaky's carcass nothing but his head & shoulders were visible until he stooped to his prey when even these disappeared altogether. He dragged back to camp the "specimen," shrieking out "By Jove by Gimminy! by ——— who kill him? By Jove! what big fellow!" and stretched him at length in front of McCarty's tent. Mac claimed his skin for a belt, and out with knife and with the Doctor's help soon peeled off the hide and left the naked body for Dr's experiments. "Look, look, by Gimminy 'how vat he am! by Jove he all vat—vat all over!" and he picked at him with his knife from head to tail in the greatest glee. "Vot he eat? vot he eat? by jingo I dissec im & see!" and he dropped on his knees and cut away at the intestines and opened them. "Oh look here—look here by G—— grasshopper! he eat grasshopper. Oh ho, Oh ho, now I know what makes him so vat—grasshoppers by jingo!" and out tumbled one 2 inches long. "And here's another by Cot—only see another! he all grass hopper—dat ist proof bositive dat grasshopper good to eat—he make vat all over. I try im py jimminy vor my dinner! tam sight better dan de dam bacon by Cot—don't you tink so professor Kellogg"—and the professor agreed with him of course—but left the doctor to the more quiet and studious analysis of a Texas "Coach Whip" six feet long, whose hide is to grace the waist of the gay and gallant commander of the Expedition.

THURS 18TH JULY '72. After another night's steady rain the ground is covered with water and rivulets of pure water give us clean water to drink & wash out our clothes. An improvement on the muddy branches loaded with lime & magnesia thus far used in this camp. Robins starts on horse for town on some business but is turned back by the deep & overflowed ditch nearby, which was dry as we passed it on entering camp on Tuesday afternoon. No news yet from our fellows in town. Maybe they know what we don't—*who is the Baltimore nominee?*[56] The sky is still covered by wet looking clouds and we are hemmed in by deep impassable streams or Mac would get out of this *on route*—leaving "those other fellows" to find us as best they can. Yesterday I cut shorter a pair of Tom's soldier pants to fit myself, as I needed a looser pair than those I exchanged with Tom. This exercise made out another dull day in camp. I cannot go out sketching because of the bad weather. Our animals are eating grass of excellent quality and filling up extensively against the laborious days awaiting them. I notice some cacti as large as a foot across—showing that we [are] bordering close upon Mexican plants. Few flowers are now in bloom—nothing but the different shades of green cover the ground. Some fine elms & live oak give beauty to the masses of scrub oak & post oaks which form the dark lines of forests overlying the hills in all quarters about us. Temp 82°.

FRIDAY 19TH JULY '72. White comes from Chandler & Winchebach & others two miles from here at a ranch where they stopped last night because of floods. White nearly lost his horse who could not swim and came in drenched himself. Says Roessler cannot be moved for a few days. Dennis goes over to the ranch & comes back with orders to send two horses, which are sent led by two horsemen. It seems evident we cannot move ahead without Roessler. Col. Johnson & Winchebach come back on horses—the flood having somewhat subsided. Sky still lowering at 1 o.c. and I am airing the ambulance seats which have been wetted by rains. This morning I washed out some little things at a pond. No one being appointed to wash for us, we do it ourselves—at least some of us

---

[56]Horace Greeley was nominated by the Liberal Republicans.

who stick to camp & its duties. Breakfast again is the old bacon—beans & hot heavy biscuits—mine merely biscuit & coffee. I cannot get up health on this kind of food. If the beans were not soaked & rancid with bacon grease I could eat them with benefit. I am the only one who seems to have flesh on his bones, but I shall soon be reduced to their skinny look proportions. I wonder to see so many persons long & lank as these texans & imagine it must be from want of nutritious healthy food—but bacon & beans suit their taste exactly—if we believe their word. They are half savage in their habits as well as tastes—and lie down and act like half civilized animals. Cards & vulgar slang & stories of Indian adventures form the staple of their mental exercises. Whiskey they drink without regard to its pernicious & destructive qualities—adding to it various medicines to counteract Diarrhea—[illegible] chills—boils &c which I am Hebrew enough to imagine might not have troubled them much but for the filling of their stomachs with the salt pork—called bacon. Even the bread is made from dough well saturated with its grease. So that to eat at all I am forced likewise into the savage ranks unprepared by previous habits to withstand their cursed food. Even when we get fresh vegetables they are immediately cooked in the same grease—and all my begging for them in their raw state is in vain. I have sometimes seized an onion, tomato, or cucumber at the cook's before he had time to manipulate them with his universal poison. Our dinner today was less bad than usual, a stray beef was killed and afforded some nutritious juices. This complimented by a dried peach pie made a comparatively marvelous dinner and the boys even duplicated their usual number of dishes. Up to dinner time 4 o.c. we had an hours shower, and I had cleaned & arranged the ambulance contents nicely—when an order suddenly came to take them all out and let the ambulance go over to the ranch to bring a load of things. Our things were thrown pell mell into the wet grass and we were left to get them into a tent the best way we could. My pistol, bundle of clothes and sketch book being left in the seat box—and sketching chair & umbrella hung up in the rear. Thus I am deprived of both ambulance & tent or any proper accommodation either for work, study or a chance for convalescence. I was treated similarly once before—but intend not to be again. The ambulance returned before dark & I resumed my place in it, but I had taken cold, lying on the damp ground of tent after overheating myself by moving my things, and slept poorly. A cool breeze from the north struck up indicating clearing weather—a bright moon nearly full gave a lovely sight.

20TH JULY '72. A wonderfully fine sunrise, amid amber & pearl clouds. I took a stroll on the hill south of camp and sketched the extensive view South towards Jacksboro which was not visible and returned north of camp through rocky ravine—seeing several cacti of large size say 6 in diam. Rocks of sandstone project from hill amid trees—and of fine tints of lichen and moss. I should like time to study them. Troutman is out promising me a foreground for my sketch which gives a fair interpretation of the general topography of this part of the country. The day turned out cloudless and very warm but good air from S. Temp 94. Dinner today was something marvelous—good beef, green corn *without* bacon grease—cucumbers, cheese and watermelons! But these were accompanied by underdone biscuits which I did not touch. Neither did I the beef as I had no appetite. I suppose all this luxury came of my growling long continued & serious. I had made up my mind & expressed it freely that with such living and treatment I should leave the party now & here. There has been almost devilish actions in the quartermaster dept. knowing well & constantly how *bacon* was avoided—disliked—& thrown away by cooks & men—& its baneful effects on many of us—whilst there were plentiful supplies in his wagon of cheese, canned fruits, chocolate—tea, hard biscuits, codfish & other things—which properly distributed would have kept our men content & healthy. All these things were taken from his wagon this morning to air and such were the sarcastic remarks of several lookers on that probably a better dinner—for once at least—was the result. The leaders feast in town daily and seem not to regard the denizens of tents who stick properly to their duties. They are there yet or on the road, where they can get milk & fresh vegetables to repletion—but forget to bring or send us any. I suffered much from want of attention & the actual necessities of an invalid for 10 days or more unable to do anything for myself & far away from the cook & had it not been for Troutman I might have starved for all the care bestowed upon me. But when he was engaged all day out of tent I was left literally alone & helpless.—Peters & Chandler residing for the time in town—Twice Mrs. Buell was kind & thoughtful enough to send me a pot of nice tea & toast & jelly which was actually *all* the acceptable food I had for more than 2 weeks. McCarty brought me ½ bottle champagne which helped quench my thirst for a day or more. The water is good—but so far off that I was often without any whatever. Lusk - - - a teamster - - - now & then thinking of my situation and bringing me his keg full. Only small canteens are furnished & these so few that there is a constant struggle to get one—especially if it have any fresh water in it. The whole management of affairs is disgraceful in the extreme & how the men keep from mutiny is a marvel unless it be that they have no *written* agreement as to their wages & fear to break loose without them for as far as I can learn *not one* has received his monthly salary since with us. At sundown Chandler appears, and tells me he has another tent and a man to wait on us—and that in the future we will get on without trouble & annoyance. In the tent Peters finds a place with a boy to wait on him. I understand by this time what all this amounts to. I will remain in ambulance tonight, and have a talk with Chandler in the morning, whether I stay or go the question. Peters & Roessler still behind.

21ST JULY '72. Clear bright morning—entirely cloudless—with Southern breeze. We shall have another hot day. Have had a candid talk with Chandler telling him how matters had gone with me during his absence and that I had my box out ready to leave the party here but only waited to see him and know if there was to be a radical change or not, before leaving. He frankly admitted that I had good reasons for my decision—but that all these troubles would now cease as he had hired an Englishman to attend to us specially—bring water put up tents and other labor to relieve us—besides another man to cook for our mess and wait upon us. Our tent was to contain only 4 persons—and that his intention now was to take more command of matters. I told him plainly many things he ought to know as to the dissatisfaction, almost mutiny among the men at the conduct of affairs, and the chances of entire failure of the Expedition—That he had greater responsibility than any one else, and the Company would hold him as the most responsible—and that it was due to himself to act with vigor and decision in correcting the glaring and abominable faults which he had witnessed ever since we started from S. Canadian and not give way to the whims & ignorance of a vain, impracticable and assuming schoolboy like Peters, or the changeable notions of others without the necessary capacities of their position. He said these things would all be changed in the future — of that I may be assured. The present decision was to go direct from here to the *objective* point as fast as possible, that he intended to get through & return to Washington in 6 weeks time. If what he had told me was to be carried out in earnest I said I would continue with him—but that in all my travels I had never been in company with men so utterly disorganized and where so much suffering—physical & mental had been *needlessly* inflicted upon them. For myself I understood from him & others that there had never been an expedition so well fitted out in our country—everything for personal comfort & safety being liberally provided and it was from this report that I had acceded to his request to accompany it, but that I had been utterly disappointed and that it was only out of respect to his feelings & friendship that I had thus long continued to suffer indignities and privations. In fact I expressed myself frankly & decidedly —and have at last decided to move on with him under the above conditions.

Major Mizeler[57] of the Fort drove up with Count Crenneville last evening and slept with us. Today whilst sitting chatting with him in the tent we heard several distant reports of fire arms and soon our camp were called to arms—animals driven into corral and every moment we expected an Indian raid. We knew that the Count and others went to swim in the direction of the shots, and supposed they may have been surprised & attacked by Indians. All was confusion—scouts sent out—stragglers called in—rolls called of armed men—howitzer put in position—one of our guards rushed in from the woods horseless and with an arm useless by injury - - - horsemen, headed by McCarty off to the front to see what the matter was—the Count & companions galloping in, leaving shirts & stockings to the enemy, having heard voices and some 70 shots fired by two different parties close to them—couldn't tell whether by Indians or not—and what with surmises & preparations for the worst the day wore on until McCarty returned from a neighboring ranch where he learned that a company of cavalry were returning from Fort Sill to Richardson and had discharged all their arms after the wetting by recent floods and proceeded towards Jacksboro. Thus ended the *second* scare of the Expedition. If it will serve to get them into better order for real

[57]This must be John K. Mizner, major of the 4th Cavalry, who served at Fort Richardson from May 5, 1871, to October 15, 1872 (Cullum, *Biographical Register of the Officers and Graduates of the U.S. Military Academy*, II, 662–663).

trouble & fighting I shall be very glad of it. We suppose the cavalry was that commanded by Major Webb which left Richardson some two weeks since on a raid towards Sill—expecting to return about this time. All this excitement was got up with the *Therm standing at 98 in the shade.* It was a *hot* encounter to say the least of it. We now receive orders to prepare to march early tomorrow to a better camp near by—where we shall continue to wait for Peters who has gone to Weatherford for more arms—and for Roessler's recuperation. Troutman is out again, since the scare, to finish his days work. He has already some admirable negatives of the scenery & woods about here. Peters drove to Weatherford instead of taking stage & returning, using up two days and only 10$ fare. As it is, no one can guess at the time he will be gone, nor the expense—but it illustrates Peters' way of doing business. Major Mizeler an old campaigner on the border agrees with the views I have herein expressed as to the Indian policy of the present government and cites many strong instances to sustain them. The major drove back to his Post, taking Count Crenneville along. Another splendid moon for tonight which is about the hottest I have felt.

22 JULY '72. Last night was passed battling musquitoes—their number being myriad & hungry. I caught a nap now & then with a handkerchief over face—but got up at sunrise fatigued and unrefreshed. After breakfast we moved off to a new camp about north—the best I think we have yet chosen. My wishes were this time consulted as to pitching my tent which has heretofore been so arranged as to admit the least air & most sun possible. There appears no brains in the whole party for arranging camp conveniently. The tents are far from both kitchen and water; to get to either the whole corral of dung—or a circuit of the wagons is to be passed, when the whole thing should be reversed. Then the kegs for water are left *drying up* around camp empty, so that when wanted they won't hold water. The result is that there is a general hunting for water—the drones as usual getting the greater part of that brought by the industrious & liberal; and they seem to be eternally sneaking around hunting up a full canteen which must be carefully watched & kept out of sight and *air* or the owner loses both them & their contents. No *detail* is made to supply camp with water—and for the last 6 days I have had to go through grass wet or dry, in sun or rain 150 yds to get a wash of face or hands—& so has every one else—with *plenty*

of empty kegs hanging *useless & shrinking* under the wagons. The natural consequence is want of cleanliness decency & health. No inspection is made of the condition of tents or grounds—nor appropriate places chosen for the repose of men without tents or wagons to cover them from dews or rains. So that the men lie about under wagons & trees or among rocks—or on the open prairie—never twice in the same spot and positively unknown to officers in case they are suddenly needed for duty. They leave camp without permission—and when wanted are shouted for again & again before appearing. They have to be told again & again to do the simplest routine duties or they neglect them. Valuable & necessary things are lost and destroyed which cannot be now replaced and which we have carried hundreds of miles for important uses in time of business far away in the wilderness and without which the grand purposes of the Expedition are either jeopardized or brought to failure and loss. To give instances—a liberal supply of expensive tools & instruments were bought—such as axes, hatchets, hammers &c, only one axe remaining, two hatchets and two hammers! Then as to pails & buckets and wash basins & tin cups, why there only remain enough battered & broken to make comfortable 10 men (yet we have 45 on the list) and they are scattered about in the grass, or under the wagons or among rocks & holes where they must be sought when needed. For the last 5 days the tool chest has been left open rain & shine—rasps, augurs, coopers - - - knives, saws, nippers & other similar things lying on the ground all night as well as day to be broken by mules & horses or to seriously wound them, or at the least to be rusted, broken and lost. In fact we have scarce half the tools we started with and we are only now on the threshold of the journey where they will be most needed & useful. To all this waste, & negligence I have drawn the attention of officers so frequently without a change that I am disheartened - - - disgusted—& silent for fear of offence. At the beginning of the journey I was very active in saving and picking up stray things of value—but the labor became too great for half dozen men and I have now nearly ceased doing the duties of those *employed and paid* to do them. I could run on enumerating similar facts enough to fill a volume on the waste & extravagance of this party —but cease with the above which are given merely to sustain the general denunciations heretofore expressed by me. We sent back to Jacksboro 1000 lbs ammunition the second day after we left it, so as to lighten our wagons: a labor which could have been saved by leaving the ammunition when it *was* there. But such lack of thought to save trouble & expense is chronic. The day has been beautiful, clear & temp 93. Lines of ropes are now covered with slips of beef to dry.

TUES. 23 JULY '72. Last night had a good sleep free from musquitoes. The sounds heard were those of the wilderness—wild bulls measured subdued roar upon their midnight march and the Mexican cougar's cry on their track, the quick sharp yelp of the coyote—excite wonder but this is robbed of terror by the more tender and homelike notes of the mocking bird, the cricket and the quail. "Chuck Will's widow" was again among us after a silence of some weeks—I thought the mournful bird had feared to accompany us to the battlegrounds of poor Lo! The ambulance was sent to Jacksboro this morn to bring out Roessler, driven by Walters—Col. McCarty & Alexander rode in. Troutman on the hills. Engineers adjusting instruments. Myself stretching & mending cot. Loew dissecting more skunks. Chandler playing [illegible] whilst airing his clothes. As yet only a single white crane has been seen—flying slowly close above our camp—not at all times—our last camp by the fort. Grasshoppers have greatly thinned out but a large horsefly—a similar but grey—to the greenhead which tortured & bled our animals so unmercifully in the Ind. Ter. It seems harmless and walks about in the walls of the tent in friendship with the grasshopper. All four of our dogs have got back to us confound their luck the useless hounds, which a few dog courtiers insist on keeping as tent companions though obnoxious to most of their comrades who inflict many a curse and blow upon them as nuisances. They run *very* fast at the hogs which sometimes have troubled the camp, but then the hogs run *faster* at them and the men have to come to the rescue or the end of the dogs would be nigh. As to watching! they sleep like babies on the breasts of their friends until their enemies kick them out in the morning—their noses are in everything —from the sly private stores in our pallets—to the water bucket in shady nooks. But they now wisely avoid my tent *widely* as I once or twice tried the virtue of Peters' foils upon their hides—the only virtue I believe they possess. Little Bruin is still confined at the fort by his old playmates the soldiers—may he "stick." A single stubborn selfish man can give unceasing annoyance to a whole company and yet not get knocked in the head. Chandler does now begin to set his foot down—and forbid the driver of the ambulance from bringing back any whiskey for anybody and denied the request of another person to send for 5 gallons to carry with him privately. Every device will be no doubt had to get this drug to accompany us. Musquito hawks (Devil's darning needle species) are today upon us in great numbers—if they do actually make way with musquitoes they will be welcome. They are a singularly beautiful fly with four long wings & rapidly fly. Notwithstanding the effort of Chandler to keep whiskey out of camp, one man who went to town today left it on horseback drunk as a madman—carrying several bottles of whiskey behind him—his comrade could not persuade him to continue on to camp. He ran his horse furiously—threw his gun away—bundle of whiskey fell off—sat his horse sideways—and altogether could not be controlled—all at once he sent off his horse full speed and disappeared on the wrong road—his comrade Humphreys coming in to camp alone. The ambulance & McCarty came out part of the way & returned to Jacksboro. *Temp* 93°.

WED. 24 JULY '72. Brown and Newman start in search of Alexander. The scouts kill a beef and are now jerking his beef in the woods. McCarty sends word to Chandler to come to town to have an important talk as to another movement—also to send 6 men & 3 days rations to go to Fort Griffin[58] and get some Tonqua Indians to scout for us as this can be done by the time the creeks are low enough to allow us to proceed. Chandler after a talk with White (wagon master who says he can already take our train through the creeks) sends word to McCarty to come *out here* and have the talk and send Roessler in the ambulance—as we are anxious to move on fast as possible. Go down to pond where our cook does a little washing for me and return rather knocked over by the heat. Cover a canteen which occupies rest of day. Alexander is found and brought into camp well bruised up and keeps his tent to convalesce. Roessler comes in ambulance and put into tent. He is not fit for work & I doubt whether he ever will be for us. Troutman's gallon of alcohol has been drained - - - gone no doubt where so many bottles of Jamaica gin-

[58] Fort Griffin, established in 1867 and named for Major General Charles Griffin, then commanding the Department of Texas, was located in Shackelford County on the Clear Fork of the Brazos about twenty-five miles north of present Albany. Troops from the post escorted government mail, surveying parties, and cattle drivers in addition to searching for depredating Indians. The fort was not abandoned until 1881 (Carl Coke Rister, *Fort Griffin on the Texas Frontier*).

ger - - - Bay Rum & Cologne have preceded them—down some human throats. This mania for liquor plays the devil with the Expedition—it has had no greater foe—and that too among the minds that should be most steady, calm & active, *especially* in the Scientific Corps. It is only from the uniform sobriety and work & watchfulness of *a few* determined, conscientious & capable men that we are not now ruined and separated and a laughing stock to all who have expected from the noise we have made of wonderful things from us. After smoking tents the musquitoes annoy us but little—cool breeze for the night. Very little dew has fallen for several nights. Our living has been better lately—the beef supercedes the *bacon* & now & then a good potato or cucumber or melon makes a good dessert. We are rapidly diminishing rations in *idleness*, & before leaving here may have to replenish. *So we move!* Temp. 90.

THURS. 25 JULY '72. Peters returned to Jacksboro from Weatherford night before last. The count and he are together at the Hotel. This morning an ambulance has gone to town to be mended—it however was fully occupied by passengers who always find something *necessary* to be had in town whenever they wish to go. Some did not go as they were *denied permission* to bring back whiskey with them. Troutman went for alcohol—Plummer to have a tooth pulled. The ground we now occupy is historical in Indian annals. It is the Comanche country proper. The Waco & Caddos still south of this. A Waco chief married a Comanche squaw or rather wished to, and was taking his sweetheart home when they were attacked & both killed in the pass just north of us called —————. The Comanches refuse the right of their tribe to intermarry out of it. The number of our party now, since late additions is 49, mostly Texans, young hardy and used to roughing it. Many are over 6 ft high. Robins the Engineer 6 ft 4½—and Loew say 5 ft, the two extremes. Few are natives—generally from the cotton states; several daredevils with their pistols ever ready for a melee—then there are English, Irish & Germans to give variety—a few discharged soldiers are among us and very useful and accommodating, knowing this kind of wild life well, having been in contact & fights with the Indians. Altogether the company is formed of excellent material—but so dreadfully mismanaged that as yet it has done no *work*. All the negroes are now out of the party. Temp 93°. A large, vicious cowfly is bleeding the horses terribly—a

small, thin kind of housefly is doing the same by us all day—& quick as lightning.

FRIDAY 26 JULY 1872. Ambulance with Troutman, Robins & Winchebaugh returned at 8 P.M. I woke up in the night & found Peters & the Count lying in my tent. So Peters has *at last* got to camp. *Maybe* we will go forward now—if nothing happens. Wagons are packed and the decision now is to haul out at 10 A.M. Very clear cloudless morning. During breakfast a very unpleasant altercation & threats of shooting between Peters & McCarty owing to ———— on going to medicine chest without leave. Peters & Crenneville go back to town in his new wagon. An ambulance with Newman goes also, to return here today after we have left, & take in Roessler sick who awaits it here under a tree—

Start off *en route* West at 9:30 A.M. - - - at 10 o.c. turn to N.W. 60° after crossing a rough pass over point of hill into "sand valley" a few days since overflown—and a few years ago was covered with cattle. At 10:45 cross "Spring Creek" & water mules—the valley opens without trees or bushes to a mile in diameter each way, bounded on N by ridge of low hills—covered by wood—"Spring Creek" nearly dry. Passing through mesquite trees in plenty—and increasing groups of cacti - - - the fruit red but unripe. Arrive at & cross W. Fork Trinity 1:30 P.M. Water muddy but sweet and 7 feet across in steep sandy banks. Move on 2:10 N 30′ W. Mesquite plains—Sugarloaf hill bearing N.E. one mile dist. Hills on W. receding from River. Encamp under trees at 2:25 P.M. - - - tolerable grass. Evidence all today of the great freshet of W. fork. Temp 94.

SAT 27 JULY '72. Built fires before tents with Buffalo chips and suffered none from musquitoes. No news of Peters—Roessler & those still behind. If they attempted to come after dark they could not get through —road so bad & blind and in some places so stony—As to the W. Fork its passage might destroy the ambulance at least. McCarty has sent two men back to see what the matter is with them. My head and eyes pain me—too much walking in hot sun yesterday. Slight sun stroke. At 6:45 A.M. off *en route* - - - course N. - - - clear & still—through musquite thick. Snake through my tent yesterday. 8:15 A.M. - - - come to two isolated rocky broken hills 50 to 60 feet high and 2 to 3 hundred ft long in the open prairie. Examine them, find *rich* specimens of Iron (magnetic) and indications of copper—this is on our location. Webster has left his marks before us in wagon track and camp ground. Fine breeze now—and we water mules from a good hole full between the two knolls. Leafless musquite trees scattered over prairie—a few *cacti* and many flowers of a lovely blue. Sunflowers show themselves occasionally. We go into camp at 8:45 P.M. near grove of post oaks on border of prairie. Dist 4¼ miles. Water very good. Must be near the E. border of *Archer* Co. Temp. 95°.

SUND. 28TH JULY '72. Very ill today with sunstroke. Peters & Co get up today and we pull out at 5 o.c. P.M. Nearly N—cross open prairie ascending, making our own road through tufty tall grass, with no rest for my head which is knocked about in a painful manner until 7 o.c. P.M., when we camp near a little pondy water. Distance 3 m. Temp 95.

MON. 29 JULY '72. I suppose this may be termed our *first* day's journey towards its object. All men together and cut loose from settlements —cast upon our own resources—Only think of our having laid about Jacksboro a *whole month*—the *very* month too when we should have been on the scene of our labors. Leave camp at 6 A.M. - - - cross road to Phantom Hill at 6:50—Stop water mules at a hole of pretty good water - - - 7:30 A.M. - - - still ascending our course N.W. by W. I hear that Augur has ordered Buell to take all available force & join McKenzie at Pope's Wells,[59] to drive back the Indians *for certain* to their reservation. At 10:10 come to dry Wichita—Dist 7 m. - - - not able to pass its deep banks, go into camp and begin preparations for bridging it. Good breeze. Saw 3 fawns run the gauntlet of our lines safely though two shots were fired at them—this was yesterday. Today our advance guard saw 4 fine bucks—maybe will have some of them today—our mules are pegged out with the difficult road which they have to make over hard lumps of grass. In this region no animal subsists. I hear now & then a quail—grasshoppers live on in spite of Indian inroads—locusts are few—snakes plenty—we got one for Loew yesterday—shot half his head off—a noble rattler of 11 years. One, a whip snake passed through my tent on Friday - - - 5 ft long—I was on a chair writing as I saw him come in the front of the tent and pass, straight as a serpent can, between my legs whilst I called for the Doctor to come and get a "splendid speci-

---

[59]Named for John Pope of the Topographical Engineers, who commanded an expedition to search for water in the Texas High Plains area. The well was near the Pecos River at the Texas-New Mexico line.

men" as his snakeship passed out of the tent behind me to be looked for in the tall grass by the learned chemist. My head is still in a bad state—when on my feet I am too faint to stand—twice fainted away & carried to my tent. Dr. Brown gave me yesterday two doses of quinine, & 2 of seltzer—declaring the disease chills & fever, as sunstroke is unknown in Texas—which I don't now believe, and don't today take his proposed extra dose of quinine—those of yesterday rang loud & long enough in my ears. He says tomorrow will tell whether it is chills or no. I tell him that in Texas every disease is treated as chills & fever—"well" he says "quinine is a good remedy for everything." I think that decent food & rest and nursing is a great deal better one. Count Crenneville has a fine box of Homoe [?] medicines which I shall in future call on if needed. Buffalo tracks were seen today by our scouts—so that a few may be in this region though the wrong season. McKenzie is beyond *Double Mts* and says if he had a few hundred men to guard his train—that he has the Indians where he can force them back to the Reservation from which *all* have gone on the war path, so that several forts on the border are denuding themselves for his support. Buell starts from Richardson with all he can spare - - - say 200 - - - in a few days—as soon as he can get his horses shod &c - - - This being the case we *may* get to Double Mts without trouble—yet the Indians *may* flank him & then look out for the *Red devils all along these borders.* So we go on the *Peace* principle of the government—so fine on paper! Our camp is in the base of the bowl formed by ridges nearly straight & horizontal with scarce a tree upon their whole waving outline—and on the southern bank of the School creek which is slightly marked—here & there by low trees & bushes covering its bed. Though there would scarcely [be] a suspicion of a stream now—when fed by rains from the surrounding amphitheater of hills it must become wide & deep, rapid & impassable. Buffalo chips are plentiful near camp on the trail across the stream—indeed our scouts saw three buffalo bulls, who saw us afar & made rapid strides away. The night was cool & with fire, musquitoes not troublesome.

TUES. 30 JULY '72. Left camp at 6 o.c. A.M. - - - crossing dry bed of School creek at our new bridging successfully, and with a perfectly cloudless sky & good cool breeze make on our course N.W. by W. - - - ascending gently—to the watershed dividing the two branches of School creek, the line made prominent on the north by a fine *fortress like* work commanding extended views—a prominent landmark for many miles. Descending into the valley of the fork of School creek which we reach at 8:20 A.M. and halt to make a crossing. The stream is outlined by low timber & bushes running in a semicircular sweep from S to W & N. Cross at 8:40 & at 9:15 cross Griffin & Fort Sill trail. At 9:50 get to a creek of good water lined with nearly ripe plums, cotton wood & elm—mulberry. Stop and build bridge and pass it at 11:40 A.M. & continue *en route* W. Passing slowly over rough rolling bare prairie without interest. Many sunflowers in groups—old Buffalo chips—neither game nor birds nor even grasshoppers—various species of cactus—here & there others seeing Webster's tracks pretty fresh—some fine mesquite grass—shaley sandstone cropping out—until we come in view of several broken ranges of mts south of us—our general course being S.W. We go into camp at 2:50 P.M. under the W. face of an acropolis of rocky & broken form running N & S 40 to 80 ft high—& 500 ft long. From our camp we have an interesting lookout to the W. upon lines of bright green timber in picturesque forms above which are seen high & level plateaux which cut the horizon. Temp 96°.

WED. 31 JULY '72. Yesterday eve. sketch of headwaters of S. Fork of Little Wichita looking south. This morn continue same looking West until we start off on back track to strike the Belknap road. So that we shall see no more of the Wichita region—and I have made the only sketch or picture ever taken of it—so far as I know. We leave at 6:25 A.M. - - - a cool fresh wind. Bad night's rest on hard ground under tent & feel weak & feverish. We take a course S.E. to strike our yesterdays, and jog along over an open, denuded prairie, and rough hillocks of common "sedge" grass, on a slow walk. An antelope was killed en route by McCarty and added to our stores. Long rolling knolls with large sandstone cropping from their sides form the distinguishing features of the landscape. At 9 A.M. we stop on the edge of a thin line of trees in the valley of the fork of School creek which we bridged yesterday morn. Here we make another bridge. Halted to lunch from 10 till 2:20. At 4 o.c. P.M. strike the road from Buffalo Springs[60] & Fort Belknap thence

---

[60]Old Buffalo Springs Fort in Clay County was the extreme Texas border post in 1861. The nearest settlement was Queen's Peak and the nearest post office was at Weatherford, seventy miles distant. In 1867 the soldiers at Fort Richardson were removed to Buffalo Springs and to Fort Belknap, but drought caused their return to

to Fort Griffin which we follow S.W. after having come S. since we lunched across an open boundless prairie making our walking way over detestable tufty grass—impossible to write upon—no animal life visible today.[61] Temp. 98. At 4:40 P.M. come to fine grove of postoak and park-like intervals and cross W. Fork of Trinity in their midst passing out into a fine open valley with fine view close on the S.E. of a rocky bluff running back & merging into the rising ground of the prairie. There we camp at 5:10 P.M. having made 11 miles—and are now within 20 miles again of Jacksboro. Thus far Roessler has been too ill to examine or note the character of many interesting points in this quite unexplored or unsurveyed territory. I have stood the tiresome journey very well indeed, and am cheered with the fact that we are *now* pursuing the object of our contemplated tour - - - *Double Mtns*. Chandler is now getting pluck enough to be stubborn & assume responsibility in this movement and to avoid Fort Griffin and its temptations. Our company are now all sober and doing their duty well. Last night we passed in one of the most dangerous positions regarding Indians. Had any appeared they would have had a warm reception—I think. I learn that we are the first party known to have passed over the region we have today. McCarty chased a stray pony this evening and caught him and added him to our stock—much needed as some men *foot* it—and 2 horses are on the lame list.

Secor shoots & brings in two splendid Turkeys—this looks like having a supply of fresh meat—wild at that—I have heard the thing *promised* now for 2 months. The brave hunter was heartily cheered. Dist 11 m.

THURS. 1ST AUG. '72. In the night threat of rain. Troubles in not being able to fix my tent—the new man *Graham* having no experience in tent pitching. To make the night sleepless, the consumptive cook was bitten by something and kept Dr. Brown and 2 or 3 assistants at work

---

Fort Richardson in 1868 (Theronne Thompson, "Fort Buffalo Springs, Texas Frontier Post," *West Texas Historical Association Year Book*, XXXVI [1960], 156).

[61]Fort Belknap, established by General William Goldsmith Belknap and named for him, was located in 1851 in present Young County at a site selected by Randolph B. Marcy. The post had a beautiful location and a number of permanent structures, but an inadequate water supply finally caused its abandonment (Carrie J. Crouch, *Young County History and Biography*, 5-8).

for hours. How dangerous he lies now I know not—but he called piteously on his Maker for mercy and writhed in agony. He is very profane in character—his fright may make him penitent until he either dies, or revives. This is the usual measure of such men's deserts to enter Heaven. A slight shower this morning is all the result of the gathering of the elements—though it may yet "give us Jessie." All clear in the South—and Turkey feathers wave on many a man's hat. Leaving camp 6 A.M. - - - course general S.W. Tolerable road—day clears up with scattering white cumuli—Landscape reminds one of Indian Ter. - - - long rolling prairies & post oak reaches—At 11 A.M. road becomes so lost that we lose *it*, and after hunting & turning here & there—our scouts in all directions on the lookout for it—we gave up & went into camp at 12 m. the mules going ravenously into the fine mesquite grass. Water is good and we are supposed to be near "Salt creek." The hills & timber bordering the Brazos lie close ahead, and I suppose tomorrow will find us at Belknap. I pick up a few specimens of iron & possibly a *pink marble* in camp—Also the conglomerate similar to that of Montague. Our greyhound performed his first feat of usefulness today in catching a young jack rabbit. No other wild animal seen. No birds—no flowers but sunflowers—straggling by the roadside. I doubt whether *Whiteman* ever camped here before. This district *ought* to be explored—it never has. I must speak of a lovely little flower seen during the last few days growing in clusters of a delicate purple—feathery thistlehead—also one of clear charming blue—a rarity always. Grasses exhibit a *great* variety to make wild our New England lassies—if they set eyes on them. This evening was bathing feet in a pond near camp when Tim, who was near me was startled by the rattle of a snake about 6 feet from me. He called on Hall the herder near by, who got a big stick & broke the serpent's back and hung him across the stick & carried him to camp where Loew soon had his head off as trophy. The reptile had 10 rattles and was 1½ in diam. Having only slippers to walk in I made my way *very* cautiously back—fearing Mrs. serpent might take vengeance on me for the loss of her Lord. I had been searching a long way on the banks of the muddy, steep ditch for a chance to get my feet in some pool, when the thought struck me that my slippered feet might invite a nibble from a "snake in the grass," and I made for Tim's wash hole & found a seat at its muddy edge —and a snake on its bank. Roessler says he has been over this region—

it contains coal & iron of not good quality—I doubt his having *explored* it or ever looked at *much* of the land about here.[62] Temp. 86.

FRI. 2ND AUG 1872. Last night was cool—no musquitoes—and I really enjoyed a full night's sleep—the first for 6 weeks—& I am refreshed & cheerful as the effect. The sun rises lovely amid a few flaming clouds to accompany his chariot, and the shadows of its wheels diverge in grand lines across them—while Phoebus, just above the scene, awaits in her declining days to salute the coming of her glorious Sovereign to be absorbed in his lifegiving bosom. Our animals have had a good fill of the nutritious mesquite and are being harnessed for a long & hard day's work to arrive at the banks of the Brazos. I hear a quail, and see groups of sociable prairie black birds sailing about us almost within reach—"without fear & without reproach" certainly. In the evening a kind of heron—small as a dove, & with a long tail, sails rapidly around seeking some food or other among the ponds or pools scattered over the dreary prairie. The dense forest on the border of the approaching river spreads its dark line just across our line of march within a quarter of a mile and we shall soon penetrate its unknown bosom. We start now at 6:37. Course W.S.W. 7:30 - - - In the woods & *in a mess.*—lost! Division in council has led us here. Found again 8:50 by returning to open prairie and taking a course Easterly until we struck our yesterday's road going S. All right now for Belknap—through mesquite timber and grass on excellent soil. At 10:30 cross a running stream with deep steep banks. "Whiskey." The wagon sticks badly on coming out. Our ambulance twists its axle tree & is disabled. At 11 we proceed—deserted & ruined ranch—soon a cattle pen solidly wormfenced with post oak timber—on left of road; facing it is a stockade ranch & farm lately deserted. Here we await the construction of a bridge on the bank of a creek called "Salt" which is completed by 12 M. by using the rails of the ranch fence carried down by all hands. The water runs visibly and the direction of the creek is N. & S. Its width is 25 ft at the ford between banks 15 to 20 ft

---

[62]In 1854 Captain John Pope reported that at Fort Belknap an outcropping of coal along the river valley was used as fuel by the post blacksmiths (Martin L. Crimmins, "Captain John Pope's Route to the Pacific," *The Military Engineer* [March–April, 1931]; reprint with unnumbered pages). The town of Newcastle was founded in 1908 because of a coal mine in operation a few miles north of Fort Belknap. The Wichita and Southern Railroad promoted the industry, which reached its peak of production between 1910 and 1917 (Crouch, *Young County*, 206).

high - - - Ambulances cross safely but the first team sticks in the corduroy rising of the Western bank. The day is so breezy, with clouds obscuring the sun that this delay is not *very* objectionable to any of us—anxious as we are to reach Belknap this evening. We have yet to cross Salt creek - - - We have two fine turkeys and the hindquarters of a yearling beef hanging to our wagons—the trophies of a morning raid by our hunters—the essentials of a proposed feast this evening. We cross a grand valley of mesquite trees and encamp at 6:30 in its fine plain. This morning at sunrise the *Temp* was only 69°, the coolest since Gainesville (63) and at 2 P.M. 89°. Peters & Secor still behind—somewhere. They have returned having failed all day to find us. The Count Crenneville had been with them hunting but lost them & after hunting for them, or us, an hour or so got *himself lost*, as he really was—and had it not been for his horse's sagacity might have died in these solitudes. Even Peters & Secor had a hard time in getting to camp again. This kind of thoughtlessness in getting out of sight of camp has lost many a man his scalp. These gentlemen have not so much confidence in themselves as they had, and the lesson will not be lost upon them.

SAT 3 AUG. '72. The morning opens finely after a heavy dew—so scarce of late. The men all got a dram issued last night. I am very happy to see that they are limited in their libations—and can keep a keener eye to business with less noise in camp. We are *right in the line* of some of the most horrible massacres ever perpetrated upon the white man by Indians. 6:30 Haul out on the old road. S.W. course in good order. Arrive at Belknap 8:20 A.M. Ruins of the Fort.[63] A postoffice in one of the old buildings. Get nice fresh milk & watermelons. Arrived at the *Brazos* at 9 A.M. A reddish line of banks enclosing water of similar

---

[63]Fort Belknap was abandoned as an infantry post when the United States property in Texas was turned over to the Confederacy in 1861. In April, 1867, four companies were ordered from Fort Richardson to Belknap with a view to the possible rebuilding of that post. H. H. McConnell, in charge of one of the companies, said that they found it dilapidated and in ruins. His description ran: "Sand, sand everywhere; dead buffalo lying on the parade ground; a few ancient rats and bats looked on us with an evil eye for disturbing their repose, and my first night's rest in the old commissary was broken by visions of old infantry sentinels stalking ghost-like on their beats, and the wind howling through the broken roof." After five months' occupancy the fort was evacuated, and Fort Griffin, forty miles to the west, became the new post (McConnell, *Five Years a Cavalryman*, 62–67).

color, runs along the base of hills from 50 to 200 ft high on the South—the old Fort lying on a level plain on the northern shore. Islands of sand dot the stream which is here 300 ft wide—but as much within its banks. Our horsemen pass & repass the river to ascertain its depth and the solidity of its quicksands—for the safe passage of the wagon train—Men wade over with trousers above their knees—& many lie down & have a good play spell—imagining they are swimming—All the teams pass over with 8 mules—I crossed on horse and at 1:10 we march on our course *beyond the Brazos*: N.W. on the regular mail route to El Paso, a deep sand & broad road. About 3 miles from the river we go into camp in a mesquite bottom surrounded by Postoak timber at ——— A.M. After repose & dinner we were enlightened and amused by a lecture of Dr. Loew on metals—with pretty experiments.

SUN 4TH AUG '72. A nice cool morning. Here Brown the commissary & Atchison leave us to return to "the States," (as if they were a foreign country to this—such is the habit of speech of Texans, who seem to deeply regret their annexation.) Yesterday before we reached Belknap, our men were excited in picking up bits of coal & iron & speculating on their qualities. The Iron was very rich—almost solid—coal inferior because on the surface perhaps. A government mule train from Griffin to Jacksboro passed this camp at 6 A.M. and Brown & Atchison will join them at the Brazos ferry. By this train we learn that Gen. Mackenzie's Headquarters are now about 100 m N.E. of Double Mts.—had seen only 5 Indians as yet! At 1:30 Webster came forward & met us—from his camp just ahead—He was on his return from the Double Mts Fork—having left Jacksboro when we did. Thus much *for business*. He accompanied us back to his camp and we camped near his at 1:40 P.M. We then enchanged notes—he gave us his route & all the information he could as to our proposed location of land—and showed us the *richest kind* of specimens of copper ore taken from the D.M. Fork on his location. We bought one of his horses and hired three of his best men to return with us. Cowan will also go with us—We have now secured some men who have *actually been to the region* we are marching for & can point us to the richest of it this side of Double Mts itself—where we expect to go. A whirlwind took away our tents as soon as they were pitched—and our camp fire was started into the prairie grass—which was for a time very dangerous on its rapid flight but our men got after it with blankets and after a hard & vigorous beating whipped it out after it had licked up a couple of acres. Whiffs of wind continue to give us business in holding down our tents. The count did not come to dinner and we sent out men to find him—asleep under a tree alone just beyond camp. He is determined to get lost or scalped. Webster & party at 4:30 proceeded on route to Jacksboro. He tells me that a letter awaits me at Griffin—the most cheerful news he could bring. I shall hear from Somers. I am getting on my feet again—without the aid of the cursed quinine —or anything else but quiet—good sleep—and better food. Webster's party saw hundreds of Buffalo & had their fill of their meat—killing more than they needed—as every fellow must have his shot. Wolves— Rattle snakes & Prairie dogs in frightful numbers. Indians were about in small thieving parties—we have to fear the loss of our stock from them, nothing else. Dist 12½ m Tem 98.

MON 5TH AUG. '72. A cool quiet morning, with thin filmy clouds. Our camp is just at the base of a low spur or knoll running S.E. & N.W. 30 feet high covered with low scattered oaks and exposing loose red sandstone rocks on its face. Red sandstone is the rock of this district. Depart from camp on same road to Griffin at 6 o.c. sharp, going over the northern limb of the spur and on to a high plateau affording a very extensive view of level land on all points & still rising over high ridges of very rich soil sparsely covered with mesquite trees: the road lined with wild sunflowers. Range after range of swelling ridges of like character of soil & herbage until 10:30 A.M. when we begin the descent to the bed of the *Clear Fork* of the Brazos," which we cross at 12 m. - - - a fine running stream of clear water rumbling over a rough rocky bottom & about 50 ft wide, most cheering to behold. Ahead of us rises the range of bare hills with gentle inclination with a direct road leading up to the Fort—its houses & flag crowning the crest of the hill. Part of our horsemen ascend directly to the Fort—but the wagon train keeps on around the eastern base of the hill—passing the tents of the *Tonkhua* Indians & their dark inhabitants—men—women & naked babies & children standing around silently gazing at the retinue of pale faced strangers. The painted chief in a dirty calico gown drawn closely around him stands by the roadside and says "How" with a flourish of his hand in oriental style—which I return in the same style. We pitch our tents on the declivity of a hill—a mile from the Fort & beneath it, out of view in a hot & arid place—a nice creek of fresh water near by—but wood & grass scarce and the *Temp* 97° with a cool breeze. Chandler goes to town & I hope he will bring back letters for me before night. I cannot yet bear the sun—and now come the Indians to prevent my rest—seating themselves like orientals in front of my tent. An old Tonkhua* chief and his squaw—He hands me a dirty paper to read. It purported to be from some one who knew the old Indians history—he was 117 years old & had served the whites faithfully—in 1812—in the Texas war &c &c. The old man evidently wanted money "heaps." I gave none of course to the beggar as it would bring the whole tribe down upon me. Had I been well I would have sketched him. Very soon several women & papooses & girls came & silently took their stand to see what I had for them—but I stuck close to me cot "heap sick" & failing to get anything or even notice they went about to other tents "Heap hungry" as they saw dinner was getting ready—& so they prowled about until the Commissary ordered them all away. Ah Lo!

Towards eve Chandler brings me 4 letters from Post—*Sheldon* 2—*Evans—Suydam*.[64] All giving me the same good news of Somers—but no letter from her which I so set my heart upon. After dark the Post officers came to camp & the Band followed & gave several pieces of music in "Circus style" - - - took a drink, & after I had fallen asleep departed—I declined being introduced to officers as I needed rest & did not feel like talking two or three hours after bed time. I expect to visit the Post tomorrow.

TUES 6 AUG. '72. Go up to the Post & see several officers—write letters to Sheldon & Suydam & Somers, and intend to make some sketches about the Post before the day is over, and conclude to send these sketches by tomorrow's mail. So close them here.

Col. W. H. Wood[65]—command of Post. 11th Infantry.

*Ton-ka-wa [Kellogg's note].
[64]Probably P. M. Suydam.
[65]William H. Wood, of Massachusetts, was a cadet at the United States Military Academy from 1841 to 1845. He served in the 7th Infantry during the Mexican War and was on frontier service in Texas until 1851. During the Civil War he attained the rank of colonel. In 1870 he was assigned to the 11th Infantry, commanding the regiment at Fort Griffin from February, 1871, to December, 1872, and at Fort Richardson from 1872 to 1876. He retired in 1882 and died on January 1, 1887, aged sixty-six (Cullum, *Biographical Register of the Officers and Graduates of the U.S. Military Academy*, II, 245-246).

Don't rub the pages much as the writing is not much yet fixed. K.
Please post the letters to Suydam & Evans.
[In different handwriting at frontispiece of notebook]
Tonkawa

Chief "Campo"[66]—

Campo the old chief of the Tonkawas served in the war of 1812 under Old Chief (Jackson)—big fight. White man [illegible] fought under Sam Houston in his war of Independence of Texas in the years 1834 & 35—also in the Mexican War 46/48 which can be proved - - - signed by Col Hayman [?][67] of the U.S.A. The Tonkawas have been a peaceful tribe and have always been friendly towards the whites. Campo is (117) one hundred & seventeen years old and is still in good health. When I came to this post in 1870 he was 115 years old

Yours truly
D. B. Taylor[68]
Lt. 11th In U.S.A.

[66]In 1864, during the Civil War, Campo was at Waco with a group of Tonkawa. The Indians were ordered back to Fort Belknap, where they acted as scouts for rangers and later for U.S. troops (James Buckner Barry, *A Texas Ranger and Frontiersman: The Days of Buck Barry in Texas, 1845–1906*, 164). Edgar Rye describes Campo as the "ancient medicine man of the tribe" (Edgar Rye, *The Quirt and the Spur: Vanishing Shadows of the Texas Frontier*, 54).

[67]Perhaps this is Samuel B. Hayman, lieutenant in the 7th Infantry during the Mexican War. He was breveted brigadier general in 1865 and retired as lieutenant colonel in 1872 (Cullum, *Biographical Register*, II, 148–149).

[68]David Brown Taylor, born in Scotland, served in an engineering battalion in the United States Army from 1860 to 1867, when he became second lieutenant in the 24th Infantry. He was transferred to the 11th Infantry in 1869, and made first lieutenant in 1873; he retired in August, 1886, and died December 12, 1886 (Heitman, *Historical Register and Dictionary of the United States Army*, I, 946).

"Texas Land and Copper Company" 3
Texas Expedition
1872
Miner K. Kellogg—
New York.

[On end sheet] Dist. 5280—14th Aug - - - 2810 back from River to - - - camp - - - 6⅓ m - - - 25 Aug.
1st Sergeant J. W. Foley, Co. H 4th Cavalry, Fort Griffin, Texas
Sheldon - - - 102 Montague Place, Brooklyn
Edwards [?] - - - 456 Washington Ave. Brooklyn

FORT GRIFFIN—TEXAS.

WED. 7TH AUG. 1872. Yesterday Temp 98°. Sent by today's mail letters to Sheldon, Somers, Evans & Suydam—written at the sutler's store—where I dined—played a game of billiards - - - made some sketches—paid respects to Lt. Wood commanding Post. Bought drawers & thick jacket. Peters & the count amusing themselves shooting arrows on the parade ground & buying Indian costumes, securing all that these lazy people had to sell. I had no show for getting any. How agreeable to have money & time to seize the rarest of things before other people get their eyes on them. Came to camp & had a good night's rest and found this morning only 59 and myself cold under blankets. Camp ground covered with goods being re-arranged to be packed in less space—leave

THE JOURNAL 127

Howitzer & 1500 lbs ammunition in store at the Fort till our return. Another evidence of ignorance—bringing the troublesome gun all the way from St. Louis, and then part with it just as we get to the country where it was intended to be serviceable. Sent to Sheldon also my *notebook to date*.

The Ton-ka-was are filling our camp and McCarty is presenting them with beads & jewels. Squaws & papoose abound & annoy us much. The treatment of these *always* friendly Indians is a disgrace to our government, which allows them no support whatever except a little for their scouts—whilst feeding & clothing the bloody & savage enemies to the North of us, which have by constant warfare against our allies reduced their warriors to 47 from 2500. *Temp 97*. Coyotes wake me with their cries near tent—our hounds responding.

[Insert on opposite leaf] I am wrong here. Sergt Foley says they draw rations enough for their support—but a late law of Congress or order of War Dept will deprive them of this scant allowance.

THURS 8TH AUG '72. Go up to Sutler's, and accept Hicks[69] offer of a tub of cool water & sponge & have a fine bath. I dined with him yesterday—made sketches about Post—one for Sergeant Foley. Cavy. of his cabin & gave [it to] his wife—they showed me attention & I lunched & supped with them. He promised to get some little things made by the Indians in my absence—for Somers—and gave me specimens of silver ore he got at some of the ancient abandoned mines near the Rio Blanco from one of his military party. Came to camp & took to the ground again as Clune needs the cot—a bilious fever to cure. A fine roseate aurora & during the night a high wind from S. & clouds threatening a change in the fine weather. *Whiskey* very noisy tonight as he always is near towns & plays the Devil with order & progress. Chandler in the Post. Temp 97.

FRID. 9TH AUG. '72. Yesty sent tintypes of self & others to Sheldon. Chandler comes to camp this morn—said he tried to find his way last night, but lost his way & after several miles wandering got back to the Post & slept. He tells me now that things will go better as he has actually

---

[69]W. H. Hicks, who with J. E. Adams entered into a contract to carry on a trading business at Fort Griffin in June, 1872 (Margaret K. Donoghue, "An Abstract of Biographical Data in the Texas Supreme Court Reports, 1874–1881" [M.A. Thesis, The University of Texas, 1938], 4).

assumed entire command. At last he finds he *must* do so or the whole thing explodes. But he will have a large unruly Elephant to conquer. I hope he can do it! We have quite a gale from S. & are preparing to move on. The train started at 11 A.M. but we passed to the Fort Sutlers & after laying in hats & shirts for the 6 Ton-ka-was—alike in kind and color that we may know them from *wild* Indians & not shoot them. Then came a wind & dust storm and then further delay & then at 4 P.M. we start the ambulance for the train which we find camped in a narrow valley among the bare ridges on a creek where men were fishing. We left the other & *wounded* ambulance & must do without it now as best we can. Peters & Count & McCarty still behind at dusk. Plummer on the sick list. Loew taking quinine for sun stroke. Edwards nursing a huge boil on right hand. Chandler used up already, but all are ready to stand by & follow him. But I know he has not the decision to keep them to the mark. No experience & too fond of talk when action is essential. Cat fish are caught in the creek. See Indian rubber tree for first time. Moccasins abundant—many killed. Cloudy night—coyotes—sultry. Musquitoes—bad odors.

SAT. 10 AUG. '72. Leave camp at 7 A.M. - - - course W. to turn ridges on North. Mesquite covering valleys. Beautiful specimens of cactus of which there are 40 different kinds in Texas. 8 o.c. steep ridge passed—all on foot—rare specimens of fossils everywhere on these limestone hills. Wagon wheel broken & gives out in ascending rough pass. Extended view back to East. Ambulance taken & broken wheel put on it & I took charge of the mending—with Hall as driver—brought it back to Post, went to Quinby[70]—QM delivered Chandlers note—& he conferred with Lieut Wood, and they ordered the carpenter & Blacksmith to do the job if possible—the wagon maker being absent at Ft Richardson. I accepted the hospitality of Sergt Foley to dine & sup & to sleep in his quarters—to give stabling to mules for the night. A heavy storm came on & continued all day—clearing off at sundown with beautiful rainbow.

SUND 11TH AUG. '72. Breakfast with Foley & go to Blacksmith. The

---

[70]Ira Quinby, of New York, was first sergeant of Company D, 2nd Colorado Infantry, in 1861. He transferred to the 11th Infantry in 1869 and served as regimental quartermaster from April, 1869, to September, 1878. He advanced to rank of captain in December, 1880, and became a major in the 1st Infantry in June, 1898, retiring March 13, 1899 (Hamersly, *Complete Army Register*, 706).

storm had put out his fire yesty eve & couldn't put on the tire of wheel but was obliging enough to go at it early this morning—*altho Sunday* —and it was finished by 7:30 A.M. when I took the wheel on rear of ambulance & left for camp Leaving a note of thanks for Quimby. Peters & Count behind in bed—& we were without escort or rifles—only a shotgun & revolver. Morning cool & cloudy—road heavy. Storm wheeling around us to the East & S. Troutman left Post yest. PM in storm— for camp alone. We notice his horses tracks this morning & suppose he found his way all safe. Arrive in camp 11:30 A.M. Several men on sick list. Baird,[71] Hemphill & Roessler. Troutman in camp all right. Leave camp at 12:10—pass in rain through splendid agricultural valleys and lovely scenery surrounding mesquite trees dead & scattered like a *"played out* orchard" as one of our boys termed it. At 2 o.c. arrive at a stream with very steep banks which detains us. I ask Roessler if this is Clear Fork—he says no but deigns not to tell what stream it is—*if he knows.* There is no information to be got out of him—& he is as brusque & mad looking & silent as a tiger. I am sadly disappointed in the companionship of this scientific man. He is reticent with all of us—yet he says he knows all this country well.[72] Cross the stream at 2:40 and encamp on its left bank on a fine high plateau with good mesquite grass. The East or right bank is precipitous & 60 feet high with horizontal ledges of limestone here & there upon its face. Here the fellow hind wheel of same wagon gives way and we must send it to the fort to be mended—and await it. There is dry rot in the spokes which no doubt is the case with other wagons bought in St. Louis as *new*. How we are to get to the Double Mts with this outfit is a question. Chandler confers with me and it is decided to send the wheel in on a pole by Charlie

---

[71]William Miller Baird was born at Knowlton, Warren County, New Jersey, in 1849. He attended Knighton's Academy, at Belvidere, and Pennington Seminary before taking up the study of medicine at Bellevue Hospital in New York. He located in Washington, D.C. in March, 1877 (New Jersey Legislature, *Legislative Manual of the State of New Jersey, 1887,* 212; information supplied by New Jersey State Library, Division of Archives and History, Trenton).

[72]William Fletcher Cummins (1840-1931), geologist and Methodist minister, accompanied a geological expedition in Texas in 1859 and 1860 and saw copper deposits in Archer County. According to his reminiscences, it was he who sent the copper to DeRyee for the manufacture of Confederate percussion caps. Also according to those reminiscences, Roessler was sent by the United States Geological Survey to Texas in 1871, and Cummins went with him, with a military escort from Fort Rich-

Miller - - - Edward to go. I write notes to Quimby on the subject—and to Dr. Koerper[73] for Quinine—for at least six are down with chills & fever. Our cook John is down with whiskey—the special cause of most of the diseases in camp.

12TH AUG '72. MONDAY. Sketched "Clear Fork" valley to the S. from the E. bank of a creek emptying into the Fork from the N. The scenery is fine & soil excellent—with mesquite grass & a bull thistle covering the ground. In large masses this thistle makes a good adjunct to foreground—like candelabra of many lights of brilliant purple on light pea green branches. The precipitous banks of these streams present strata horizontal of limestone blocks of good building material—and the ground pebbles of hard stones & flint. The swift running waters are musically brought to my ears by the southern breeze, & grateful it is too—for it is the first sound of running waters which has greeted me on this long journey. But no cries of coyote or song of birds are heard. Our hunters find no game—fishers get some catfish of 6 pounds in the creeks and they furnish a much grabbed-for addition to the bacon to which we are again subjected. McCarty gets & cooks a turtle & makes a tolerable soup for a few. The "Tonks" get all the fish they need—for they are *fishermen*. They have rigged up wigwams under the slight mesquite trees with their rags of blankets. The squaw with axe & strong grass for strings has made a picturesque lodge for herself, wherein she sits on the ground, showing some of her gay calico wrapped in its shade to much advantage. How silent they all are—scarce a word above the breath. A chief accompanied me & shades my paper as I work—looking on delighted & appreciative—knowing all the points & trees as they are transcribed. They ask me often for colors to paint themselves—but as

---

ardson, to examine copper deposits on the Little Wichita. They were deterred from further exploration by an Indian intrusion (Elizabeth Stiles, "Life and Reminiscences of W. F. Cummins," typescript, 34, 145). In 1880 Cummins explored Archer and Baylor Counties for the Texas Copper Mining and Manufacturing Company and reported limited quantities of copper in different forms (Texas Copper Mining and Manufacturing Company, *Charter and By-Laws of the Texas Copper and Manufacturing Company . . .*, 9).

[73]Egon Anthony Koerper, born in Prussia, served as assistant surgeon in the Pennsylvania Infantry in 1861 and 1862. He became a U.S. Army assistant surgeon in May, 1867, a major in the Surgeon General's Department in 1885, and lieutenant colonel in 1898. He retired in February 1900 (Heitman, *Historical Register and Dictionary of the United States Army*, I, 608).

they use powdered dry ones I regret my inability to supply them. They are now in full colors for the war path.

13 AUG. '72—TUESDAY. The wheel came in last evening all mended and we are off again en route at 7:30 A.M. on N.W. course ascending a long rise gradually—denuded of trees & reach a summit in an hour overlooking a vast reach of rolling smooth hills, good road but rocky at times as this scrawl proves. At 9 A.M. arrive at a magnificent level plateau of mesquite trees & scattered about among them is the first Prairie dog town yet met with. A dog is bold enough to sit upon his house & chirp until our shots fired upon him—dead. Walters the shot. The town extended quarter of a mile & a few dogs seen. At 11 A.M. we are detained by a broken tongue of wagon. Still continue on similar open prairie—getting hot & sultry—the clouds & breeze fast going. 11:45 A.M. arrive at "Paint Creek."[74] Water 12 ft across, good current, very steep banks, requiring extra mules to wagons—color of water reddish & turbid. 12:35 start on S.W. Span extensive plain, with sunflowers & other yellow weeds—excellent mesquite grass & dead trees of same. 12:20 another Prairie dog town. Dist. today 12 m. Killed a rabbit. Now comes a great crack in the prairie—a kind of wash—showing red soil nearly denuded of verdure—2000 acres of it below the general surface opening gently upon the vast prairie to the N.W. our course now being W. & S. to turn it. Descending into it fine specimens of copper are abundant on the surface. Went into corral at 3:20 P.M. - - - a very hot sultry day somewhere near 100° I judge. Good grass & mules tired & hungry. Distance 15½ m.

WEDNESDAY 14 AUG 1872. Because of disturbance by Peters & friends until late at night adjoining my ambulance I last night took refuge under a wagon. Midnight came up a heavy rain with thunder & lightning—continuing two hours; this morning is cooler and clear—fair prospect of nice travel and good distance. I picked up a few pebbles & copper specimens in the red banks of the creek near camp which empties into Otis creek.[75] Where the copper comes from I know not—Roessler says it is washed here—but I have no confidence in his candor

[74]Roessler's 1874 map shows this creek flowing from southwestern Haskell County into the Clear Fork of the Brazos in western Throckmorton County.
[75]The Roessler map shows Oteys Creek rising in Jones County and flowing across southern Haskell County to join the Clear Fork of the Brazos in Throckmorton County.

on such matters—& observe for myself as usual. Chandler is pleased with the apparent progress he has made in bringing some kind of order out of chaos. Buffalo are said to be seen & we expect to meet them tomorrow. He is confused & irritated by little matters to the neglect of weighty duties of his new position; but experience will correct this error —perhaps!

At 7 o.c. A.M. start *en route*, turning the washes & then crossing creek full of water & steep banks called "Otis Creek." Course N. & N.W. on Webster's trail through mesquite trees & tall rank grass & weeds. 9 o.c. A.M. dogtown & level prairie of magnificent mesquite grass, also flowering milkweed in grand masses as far as eye can see. Ascending ground. 10 o.c. descending. McMillan killed an antelope—last dog town was a mile & half long. We have made 6⅓ m. 10:30 McCarty killed a Bull Buffalo, a mile from our route. We sent 4 men to help skin him & bring in meat. Yesterday & today "Flat Top Mtn"[76] in view in distance today bearing S of W. A long level ridge with precipitous sides N. & S. Mesquite trees today numerous but dead, making a dreary sight. Milkweed entirely disappeared & Sunflowers superseded them & this may be termed *Sunflower Prairie* since they cover the land. Our ambulance mules give out—I whip them up for a mile or so when a horse was put to and we caught up at the camp at 1:15 P.M. in a basin of the plain, with holes of water of last night's rain. Two more buffalo were killed by this time by McMillan & Troutman & Dennis. Peters still behind somewhere hunting. The day has been pleasantly breezy. The time has apparently *at last* come when we shall have fresh meat—and my health improve. Pruet has shot another Buffalo. "It never rains but it pours." I saw four at a distance today. Peters got back—after we had prepared to send 2 men after him—lost his way of course.

THURS 15TH AUG '72. A splendid & comfortable morning after a night of roseate Borealis, and falling stars, and a slight dew—a thing scarce now a mornings. I watched & mediated much on the bright constellations above my bed upon the ground. This morning at breakfast time White, Cunber, Edwards & two others returned—We were anxious about them; they left 3 days ago for pack saddles at a ranch some distance back but got none. Saw tracks of Indians. So did another man yesterday—some 16—so now we are certainly watched by them and in

[76]On the Haskell-Stonewall County line.

danger. Chandler called up the men & read some good rules for their guidance in future. Coyotes had a grand howling feast last night on the remains of our buffaloes left in the neighborhood. Pull out of camp en route at 7:30 A.M. in good order & *all* present except a horse lost day before yesterday—course N.W. 8 o.c. Extensive dog town—and the skeleton mesquite wood disappears entirely, and a grand prospect before —on gently rising ground strikes us as a real desert—not a tree or bush or weed is seen—but it is not a desert really—the excellent soil bearing a thick carpet of mesquite grass—in seed—and of a withered green color. Delicious food for animals. As we ascend we view Flat top Mtn in the blue distance bearing S.W. and on the summit opens a most extensive level plateau of same character of barrenness. At the N.E. is the first mirage I have seen in this country—as complete a one as seen in Arabia —a long blue belt of forest suspended in air close to horizon—on observing it a wolf or other large wild animal passes before the belt in the nearer land—and from him to our path the hillocks of Prairie dogs form the foreground, with here & there a sentinel upon them guarding his domicile. We are now two miles from camp, "Flat top" bearing S.W. nearly invisible. We are evidently slightly descending. 9:45 A.M. halt to water in shallow holes filled with rank grass. Dog town still continuing & the dead mesquite trees reappearing. 10:15 the level plateau ceasing—and undulations commence. The grass now green again. Soil rich yellow sandy. Buffalo trails very many crossing our path—& Dog town ends. Mesquite trees assuming life at roots. Buffalo wallows in all directions, clearing off the grass exposing the ground in circular patches 10 ft diam. 10:30 ascending gradually to the watershed - - - at 10:40 descry Kiowa Peak[77] in the distant - - - fine range of high hills bearing N.W. 55° and the Double Mtn. also bearing S. 60 W. All descending from wagons & horses and group themselves together on the highest portion of our watershed and view the beautiful & long sought region with delight. The two mountains are connected by a long range of mountains of nearly equal heights, very picturesque, which are called the *Mtns of the Brazos,* Double Mtn. rising above them beyond, distinctly defined as the atmosphere intervenes. Descending watershed on our course for a miles—pass a basin dividing this from another watershed a mile in advance which hides the mountains from view, we temporarily

[77]In the northeast corner of present Stonewall County.

make our camp for dinner—& rest & feed animals in the heat of the day. Large ponds—one 500 ft long receive the washings of this amphitheater, and create a joyous homelike sensation—so long have we been without the sight of any bodies of water. The ponds are partially fringed with hackberry of small size, but the water is of as muddy a color & consistence as the Mississippi at flood. It is however drinkable & our cooks use it for want of better. All my suggestions of providing kegs & filling them with good water when we can, amount to nothing—only six small kegs are now found & they are dry inside the wagons! Nothing but great suffering in these arid countries will beat into their heads the propriety of my old fogy notions on this point. We have been singularly favored by rains or suffering from thirst by men & animals would already commence.[78] The Temperature has varied little from my last notes of it —somewhere in the 90's. I always regret not having brought my own instruments—and not be depended [dependent] upon absent or ill-natured owners. Chandler & Troutman being with me in ambulance have given me the time & a little 50¢ pocket compass I thoughtfully purchased in St. Louis. With these helps—but without an opera glass for distances, I manage to make these observations. Distance 6½ m.

16TH AUG—FRIDAY. Yesterday while making the above sketch of Double Mtn [pencilled in notebook] the sun prostrated me so that I had to keep myself on the ground or in the ambulance—quite torpid on the brain. This morn we made start *en route* at 4:40 A.M. - - - the "Kiowa Peak" our point to guide us—but division of opinion in Webster's men who were to conduct us, led us too far W—and we wandered about with the whole train to the left and back again to right, losing probably 2 m in time without progress until we started again for *Kiowa Peak* & kept that line until we made sight of the bright river beneath us ahead. For this we skirted the deep ravines and finally got down to its banks over deep washings & gullies of red sand and buffalo trails—very rough —with blocks of white gypsum scattered about & other minerals & carnelians, we went into camp at 7:30 A.M. having made only 5 m. progress in 3 hours. We passed another dog town just out of camp & buffalo

---

[78]The Nolan, or "Lost Nigger," Expedition of 1877 experienced tragedy from lack of water in Lynn County, west of Stonewall County. See W. C. Nunn, "Eighty-six Hours without Water on the Texas Plains," *Southwestern Historical Quarterly*, XLIII (1939/1940), 356-364.

tracks fresh in all directions—but no buffalo. Our hunters yesterday frightened them all away. A splendid "lofer" [lobo?] wolf loped finely by our train—Safely! And now we are down in the flat among the cottonwood and plum trees. Shots are heard profusely among the turkeys— a skunk passed my ambulance and Count shot it after Peters failed, and ran up to dispatch it with a stick, accompanied by Loew, and both were perfumed *intensely* thereby—to the amusement of witnesses but to my disgust as Count is in my mess, and his perfumed jacket will drive me or him out of it. The camp odor is now unbearable—but as we are to move today this can be borne—the jackets of Count & Doctor Loew are however to be with us—for our constant disgust. Chandler thinks *now* that it is time to stop this skunk amusement. Loew is insane on the matter of *assaying* the delicious substance of the polecat, and has been giving 2$ a head for him—& has already many skins to take with him & a bottle of the *essence*. Plums are ripe & fine—covering acres, and we are feasting our fill. We are only 200 yds from the Eastern bank of the stream but it is not seen between its high red banks. Fearing chills & fever in this river flat—sometimes overflowed, and after picking up some of the minerals & hard stones plentiful here—we again started to higher ground to fix our abode for a few days, & go out of this flat at 2½ o.c. P.M. in our coming track and encamped on the plain above the eastern banks of the stream about 2 m distant, overlooking the vast plains of the river ("Double Mtn Fork") to the S.W. with the whole range of Mtns bounding them on the W & N. Our camp is fixed near a pond of rainwater - - - shallow & 100 ft long with but a single clump of hackberry trees on its border to shade us when out of tents. The whole plain, rising gradually from the N. clear around Eastwards to the South, is only about ⅓ of a mile in diameter, with the pond in its centre— showing it to be a large flat basin only, which in dry seasons is entirely dry. Buffalo trails lead through it from all sides passing down the steep washy banks to the river. We protect this precious pond as well as a general *request* can do such a thing—but horses & mules will naturally get into & cross it—& stir up its deposits—against all the shrieks & curses which our men are so well schooled in towards these poor animals as well as towards their own Christian race. The view of this basin is melancholy & wild—No pastures of flowers—no large spaces covered with young green grass to cheer the spirit against the sadness produced by the knarled trunks & branches of the short & scraggy mesquite trees —without a leaf upon their dead carcasses, yet still standing & clinging to the hope of resurrection from the life yet remaining in their roots. For these are the skeletons by day & the bogies by night which spread themselves thinly over the ground in all directions. All is death, but the now parched mesquite grass which imparts health & strength to our jaded animals. Temp about 95.

SAT 17TH AUG. '72. Slept very little last night. Musquitoes—Tonkawa war dance & sickening odor from the 20 mules corralled within 10 feet of my bed upon the ground to leeward of them.

SUNDAY 18TH AUG. '72. Yesterday was a trying day to me. Fainting —vomiting—& chills & fever & bilious—altogether wrong. Nothing else to be expected and *no one to blame.* Is there not the same kind of food for all? Buffalo meat just killed in the greatest plenty—isn't that good enough for anybody? And haven't we got hot bread every day? & good water, if it *is* muddy, to wash them down—besides tea & coffee? What more can a reasonable man need? I admit I am unreasonable & need a vegetable of some kind—*extra*—or rather my stomach is unreasonable. It would like a potato, or a little rice—or maccaroni or beans—or more unreasonable still—prunes or dates, or raisins—& even canned fruits! But all such luxuries were eaten up long ago. To be sure some of them such as potatoes, & rice might have been replenished at Jacksboro & Griffin—but this was too expensive for the Company's exchequer! So that when we are entering the deserted regions where it was intended such things were to be our only healthy food, we go upon our hot & weary journey and live upon the medicine chest—or die. A glorious record to read of the "most completely and comfortably fitted out expedition which ever went to Texas." But what will the *men* of it say? I have had, since leaving Griffin, only two healthy & palatable dishes—a turkey soup and one of Buffalo. The venison I have eaten, but it is hard & disagreeable—and the Buffalo bulls' worse yet. I took some pills and lay in a torpid state all day until the musquitoes drove me out of the ambulance under a tent about which fires had been smoking. The wind sprung up and let me back in a hour or so to my ambulance scarcely able to climb into it. A tolerable nights rest and the pills—have cleared me of stupor & fever—but instead of doing an important day's sketching I am confined in the ambulance without a fly stretched at its side in which I can bathe or change position, because the man whose duty it is to do such service, says it's too hot to work, and would rather stay in the shade himself! *Altho he has nothing whatever to do.* This laziness & insolence is owing to the absence of Chandler who has the right of command. Where is he? I forgot to record in its place, but was led away by the story of *the Feast.*

On Saturday Chandler took 17 of our best men on horses & a pack mule across river to the range of mountains to look into the value of the land located by the Compy. If it is valuable enough to survey & Possess, he will on returning take the remaining members of the Engineer Corps to effect it. When I will "assist." My ill health prevented my going with Chandler yesterday. After he went, arrangements were made for a more secure & comfortable place for our corral about the pond—and towards evening it was so placed. Thirty of us guard the wagons & mules, and the few horses that remain. Col. Johnson, with Winchebach in command—Chandler & party expect to get back today or tomorrow—but I have learned to give them leeway as to time. It is the general opinion of our men & officers that Kiowa peak is only 6 or 8 m from here. I think it double that distance and if the exploring party explore it as is intended, they will not reach camp until Tuesday or Wednesday at least. In the meantime I hope to be well enough to make careful drawings of the important views from this point. 97°.

MON 19TH AUG. '72. Yesterday I had another spell of vomiting—heavy chill & fever which laid me up under blankets & medicine till this morning—I am now pretty smart. I suspect that a bath all over was the cause of yesterday's attack. Wind coming up while I was naked & chilled the skin. But I got a good sponge wash at any rate & I would have paid a heavy penalty for it. I felt so filthy. No means are at hand to get a wash readily, water being either too far off to carry or too inaccessible when near to profit by its presence. What is a muddy pond full of weeds—and not a tub or other vehicle large enough to hold a quart of water which may be used for ablutions?

20 AUG '72. TUES. Yesterday after the above notes, came a repetition of the fainting, vomiting, chills & fever only more painful & dangerous. Dr. Brown gave me quinine in afternoon which gave me horrible nightmares all night—this with a high wind upon me through the ragged covers of the ambulance, chilling me whilst perspiring—and shaking

the ambulance like a small boat among the breakers. The Chandler party got back yest. eve. and tolerably well satisfied with their hasty view. They ascended *Kiowa Peak.* It is apparently 400 ft above the river, and 2700 above sea. Principally of gypsum and shale. 12 m. distant they say.

21 AUG. WED. Passed bad night. Quinine devils. Today fixed in ambulance—too weak to descend. Here is a party without a proper wagon for a sick man—a *rich* party sending out 50 men into an arid wilderness without any proper means of preventive or of cure of such diseases as are known to endanger every strangers health & life. "Put not your faith in princes." I cannot return neither proceed & must endure this accursed region of 99° and no water fit to drink until such time as the Company of rich men choose—*for their own interest,* to make a way for my getting back to a civilized land. As to the *Double Mts.* I can see it far off 60 m or more—that is all I wish to see of it—at present—and the Co. may yet send some of our number to explore it to save their credit—and make a "good report"[79] to sell their bonds &c—That now is all they will or can do—and could always have been done for an outlay of less than a fourth of the present. Chandler has today sent a party of Engineers to survey the Co's locations examined yesterday. He follows today with a small party to look at some spots McCarty says he missed yesterday—*very* rich—which he wishes to locate if the Co. wont. *Whereat* Chandler wishes to see them for himself or to hold them for the Co. And thus two parties are now working near each other for somebody. The skein is getting tangled—and *I know what does it.* 20 men are thus separated beyond assistance from us & *vice versa.* Peters in camp is preparing rations to move in two or three days to *Dbl Mtn* with 20 men or more—leaving wagons here till they explore & see whether any copper or ores are rich enough to call us all down there to stay & survey locations already or to be made by Co. Some such devilish wild movement is decided upon apparently without a thought for the mens' safety from Indians or their health & comfort. A Report *must be made, and of the Double Mtns,* the important point from the beginning of the Association's labors. With

---

[79]In his report to the stockholders Roessler wrote: *"The copper is the main thing,* but besides this, our investigations developed results of still greater interest, from which the fact is established, that in Haskell county, near Kioway Peak, occur in combination with numerous copper veins, varying in thickness from a few inches to

the outfit of 6 weeks ago it could have been done *honestly* & *faithfully* —with the present *leavings* of an outfit it cannot. Indeed we cannot properly explore the space lying before our camp where our location is —it could not be done under 2 months hard, honest labor—and yet this Co is to report upon it after *two* days hasty glancing at the surface of a small locality near their *supposed* rich veins—for they don't know even that there are any veins of the specimens of ore they find upon the ground about which their locations may cover. It is to this hasty makeshift labor that this party has come at last, and I am not so *old* a fogy as I feared I might have been in predicting a grand & mean fiasco to the whole affair as at present conducted. I may speak now more bitterly than if hearty & moving towards some possible object of attainment. Still there is *no* language too strong to use on this occasion with my life still in the terrible hands of this unfeeling Co. and should I die here it will be because it gave me no means of preventing disease nor after it was incurred afford the *most ordinary* means of personal comfort or nursing or bed or food suitable for an invalid—not because they could not do any of these things—but that there was *no effort* made to do them by anyone having command, responsibility or means. Temp 99°

22 AUGUST '72—THURSDAY. The anniversary of my birth has been very near that of my death—for yesterday I was confined to ambulance all day & night—too weak to descend. Peters found some prunes & canned tomatoes in his private stores & these made some life for me, with the aid of tea & hard tack—the first food I had taken for 4 days! Is not this time to give up the Ghost? Quinine may have broken the fever & chill, but it also played the devil with my brain—I cannot even get into a doze that horrid nightmares do not seize me & torture me till I can arouse myself again & so day comes & brings no additional strength to begin to convalesce.

I managed to hear Roessler converse a little today about the resources —mineral, agricultural & otherwise of Texas. He told me there was an *Iron Mtn* 60 m from Austin *unlocated*—yielding 1st quality Hematite & magnetic Iron like the Swedish, excellent for maleable Iron & hence steel—It could be had for small sum & railroads already projected to or

---

several feet, extensive deposits of *bituminous coal*, which will exercise a most important influence in connection with the Southern Pacific R.R." (A. R. Roessler, *Geological Report of the Property of the Texas Land and Copper Association*, 1–2).

near it.[80] Accompanying this metal are others, and rocks of primary formation—granite—prophyry. From his opinions weighed, & my own observations I should say that there are many better ways of spending money than among these wild inaccessible mountains of the Brazos in other parts of this great state. Temp noon 95°. Move camp to higher ground 1 m. North—near or in a grove of yellow plums—unripe in which men make their little tents of blankets with greater comfort. Better water from pond—at all events we are clear of the obnoxious deleterious effluvia of buffalo carcass, & other foul odors & miasmas. We take apartments in the center of a dogtown—& the count, with consistent pluck goes at the innocent inhabitants gun in hand, and shoots one from his housetop—as brave a soldier as a boy shooting a caged squirrel enjoying his little exercise at a wheel! Oh Count Crenneville! how brave an act you can relate in your book on a "Tour in Texas." After all that has been written about them these animals appear & act just like grey squirrels turned into burrowing ground squirrels.

FRIDAY 23 AUG '72. Night's rest very troubled by dreams but after bitter tea and a bit of buffalo I feel on the mend. I had a *waking up* talk with Chandler regarding my dangerous condition, and he saw at last that no more neglect of me would do—the camp was moved and he got a bottle of claret & some sugar for my use, this has strengthened me much, and I am in less pain & sketched "Double Mountains" after sunrise when its outlines were very clear. It is said to be 60 m dist.

SAT 24 AUG. There is a great, though subdued excitement among the men and leaders, as to the projected branch expedition to double mts. It shakes the whole camp. A row happened just now between the scout Windus & commissary Baird and I saw them draw pistols on each other within 30 ft of me. Peters & McCarty have been at swords points for a month—but I don't in these notes intend to be personal in unpleasant matters: but foresee great trouble to the Expedition on account of personal quarrels, and repugnances & misunderstandings of the leaders. I hope, through everything—for honorable ending to our work. Chandler sent couriers to Engineer's camp at Kiowa Peak where they

---

[80]When the Expedition broke up in September, Roessler, according to his report, was accompanied by Peters to the General Land Office in Austin. They then went to Llano County, where they examined deposits of iron and located three sections "in this silver–lead region" (*Ibid.*, 8–10).

have worked since last Sat. They sent letter & map of labor to Chandler, but Graham the carrier arriving near camp showed them to a Tonky and on coming to Chandler to deliver them found them non est and off he went for Indians & papers in a high wind. Of course they were lost & Chandler awaits some other communications today to *know* what to do regarding starting the Dbl Mtn expedition under Peters tomorrow. I really enjoyed a plate of Turtle Soup today—canned. Peters' stores—& with *almost* drinkable water—& claret & sugar to make it so I am cheered & stronger. Wolves & coyotes make wild howlings near camp, to which our hound responds. Buzzards in flocks whirl about over the remains of buffaloes heedlessly killed around camp.

SUND 25 AUG. '72. McCarty & Engineers came in last eve. This morn McC gave me a specimen of ore he has found among the hills between Kiowa Peak & Double Mtn where he says many veins of it are. Shields & McMillan were with him. Wishes Co. to locate them before going to Dbl Mtn—or let him. Better specimens than those he showed in Washn. which were from head of Miller's creek[81] in the neighborhood, but which is suspected by leaders here may be a *mythical* place—One thing certain, Mac has given me a number of specimens of the *very richest* copper, also fine pebbles—jasper, carnelian &c—and a piece of gypsum he took from Kiowa Peak in this excursion. They speak for themselves. The copper he brought from some 20 m. beyond the present workings of Engineers, "Carters Creek"[82] & near. Indeed this whole Mtn chain is full of rich copper—the only thing is to strike a lead or vein—which must be near by. His representations have put an end to the present *immediate* movement to Dbl Mtn and Chandler, Peters, & Roessler have just taken my ambulance & gone on a lookout for the *new treasure* & put extra force on the Engineer Corps where it now is—leaving the Mtn. Expedition to the future.[83] Col. Johnson & I agree that this work should be

---

[81]The Roessler map of 1872 locates Miller's Creek in southwest Haskell County, flowing into the Double Mountain Fork of the Brazos.

[82]Roessler's map of 1872 shows Carter's Valley between Croton Creek and the South Fork of the Brazos, just west of the Haskell County line.

[83]In his report to the company, Roessler stated that when they reached the Double Mountains they found the formations changing entirely from the Permian to the Cretaceous. They found little timber, and the precipitous bluffs and broken character of the country created barriers to common wagon roads. "In consequence of these disadvantages," he said, "the southern route of the Pacific Railroad could not well

prosecuted rapidly & finished *then all the train to go to the Mtn together*. This will be the safe, rapid and economical plan—and quiet the incipient rebellion among the men who are determined not to be left in this camp with half the force, and not armed at all well—with all the sick and mules & wagons and property to defend—*which could not be done*—if 50 Indians *choose to take men & all*. The sick & incompetent now rate high—bad water & overwork in a hot sun at 95° keeps many on their backs—even Dr. Brown has succumbed—& McCarty is overcome—& so is Shields. Newman is down & I cannot tell who else. A nice party to gobble up—at pleasure—But I am satisfied we will not be left alone—because we can take horses & mules & get back to Griffin if we were. We won't thus risk life & starvation in this dangerous wilderness—*that's certain.* We are 45 m. from Griffin & 100 from Jacksboro —the limit of civilization.

MOND. 26 AUG. '72. Slept again—under a "fly" with fresh air—and looking out into the beautiful heavens between periods of sleep less disturbed by fever demons. Meteors are many from the Zenith to the S.E. Wolves are less tumultuous and altogether I am better: but still too feeble to walk 100 yds without vertigo. So I keep under fly—making these notes & arranging little things in my valise—so as to be ready to move at any moment. My eyes are too weak & smarting to risk their use in any careful work. McCarty, Troutman & others have again crossed the river to the surveyors camp, and the camp, with men reposing is silent as the grave. At 8:30 P.M. a rocket was fired to light party to camp from *Kiowa Peak*: Chandler, Peters—Plummer—Roessler.

TUESD. 27 AUG. 72. Arrangements are again being made to start the D. Mtn expedition under Peters. I made a sketch of the mountain by sunrise when it was very distinctly seen by glass. Capt. Shields came in from Engineer's camp, saying three horses and a mule were lost by them —McCarty's mare—Robbins' horse—Troutman's mule & Dennis' pony. McMillan was sent to hunt them. Carelessness in not hobbling & picketing them. This *inevitable* accident comes at a wrong time when it is with greatest difficulty & delay that Peters can make up his desired quota of animals for *Dble Mtn*. Capt. Shields gave me pieces of copper ore

---

penetrate this region, and as, with the exception of some salt springs, no minerals exist, the certificates which were intended for that section were raised by my advice" (Roessler, *Geological Report*, 6–7).

he has just found in a *new* & unknown locality today during his horse hunt. I wrap them in separate parcel—marked as from him. At 5 o.c. P.M. Peters at length departs for Dble Mtn with 18 men—himself deputed by Chandler as commander in his place: & Smith (Indian) - - - Shields advised Plummer today to locate more sections near Croton Creek for the association—believing the locality of exceeding richness though he never examined it. But if the Co. do not, he says a man he knows will take the whole as soon as it is known it is to be had. Shields seems the only one among us who is thoroughly acquainted with the mineral resources of this region from very many years exploration of it personally. He is not able to spend any more money than he has on this speculation, having largely invested for his means, years ago.

WED 28 AUG. '72. Peters & party left in an uproar full of liquor & deviltry. I opposed my opinion to his & Chandlers to giving the men a parting drink—because it would not stop with one drink—but would extend to a *general drunk* & demoralization before it was done with. The kegs of Brandy & Whiskey were taken from the Commissary wagon and placed under my fly for protection—and they were by my head safely. The men had got a large taste & had this precaution not been taken there is no knowing what evil would have befallen the camp—with pistols in insane hands pointed at innocent heads on slightest occasions. It was with most surprising exertion that enough men could be had for this new Expedition. Some because they disliked the commander (who is very unpopular) others that it was too dangerous to separate the Expedition—others that they were doubtful of their pay on getting back to Griffin—and it was an exciting day in arranging private pecuniary affairs among the men in separating—which had to be done by transfers of notes &c through Chandler. This morning there is ill feeling towards Peters for having nearly denuded us of arms—and Humphreys & White have gone to his camp 2 m. distant to get some back again. I am happy to know that he did not succeed in getting most of the good & experienced of our men and we are not left in a miserable & helpless condition. We have Johnson & Humphreys & White & McMillan & Robbins & McConnell & other men to be depended on and had we *arms* would feel more secure. There may be no danger whatever from Indians —yet there *may* be. Buffalo yesterday were rushing by within 2 miles of us by the thousands, making a humming or rumbling noise like Niagara at a distance—and where they are in such numbers the Indians are likely to follow. McKenzie & his army 60 m dis to the contrary notwithstanding.[84] This whole frontier is exposed to inroads from Red men—and a Tonky tells me that this place where we are encamped is their regular running & hunting ground. And here come buffalo into our camp. Having no gun at hand I got no shot at them—there were more than 100 of them—McCarty and others popped away at them—Mc killed a fine fat young bull, as they passed previously by our camp within 100 yds. *Peters* came back to us just now in answer to our request for arms & says he has none to spare & so returns to his men who are on their route. I copy at Chandler's request letters said to be from Plummer to Robbins—in C's account book. It is decided that we return by next Saturday to Griffin as we are not secure here without proper arms. Men are dissatisfied & officers too. I may venture to Kiowa Peak today to get a sketch of country & see the copperland. I feel convalescent—but as to strength to go 8 m on a mule am uncertain. Thus is true all my surmises & counsels regarding the disorder & non organization & headlessness of this Expedition. May we yet get out safely & profitably. That *loads* of wealth are within sight of us is certain—but I suppose the D.M. Expedition is made from positive instructions from Washn & to satisfy conscience of leaders—not hoping for anything as rich as what is now being surveyed.

At 10:40 A.M. left camp - - - all hands, and made another at 12:15 P.M. 2 miles N.E. by a pond of better water than we have lately had. Weather very hot—say 95°.

THURS 29 AUG '72. Determined to cross the Brazos before going back home I took a mule & accompanied by Col Johnson & Col McCarty started for Kiowa Peak at 6:00 A.M. - - - cloudy rather - - - and crossed the Brazos at 9 A.M. stopping to pick up precious stones on the shores—passed over in a hurry for fear of quick sand—safely—two miles below Kiowa Peak on Brazos. Now in the promised land—unlike Moses, who only *looked* across Jordan, and died—ascending breaks in the 50 [foot] high banks of the River on North side—the Southern be-

---

[84]Mackenzie marched from a supply camp at the site of old Camp Cooper, near Fort Griffin, to the Staked Plains, where several villages of the Quahada Comanches were scattered along McClellan Creek and the North Fork of Red River. He destroyed the largest of the villages on September 29, 1872 (Nye, *Carbine and Lance*, 207).

ing a low overflowing plain—of great richness—go over high plateau of mesquite trees, see 2 of our lost horses wild as mustangs who fly from us—we pursue to drive them to Engineers' camp, but my mule gets into a *"vine needle cactus"* and being covered by its dreadful points on belly & all four legs commenced most furious kicking and lunging until my friends came to my assistance & held the animal till I could dismount, and with knife, stick & ramrod and a half hours dangerous labor got off the principal part of the needles & I got on & we pursued our journey to the Peak—losing all sight of the lost horses. Ascending the Peak nearly to its summit we saw the fly of the Engineers just below us & hailed the inmates. Sitting on the side of Peak in sun took a Birdseye view of a whole range of Mts to S.E. & to the W &c including the whole location of the mines of the Company in the "Copper Valley" as I have named it. Getting specimens of gypsum from the Peak, descended to "fly" unsaddled & rested ½ hour, then Johnson & I with Winchebach on McCarty's mare (he being overcome by heat & exercise) we descended to base of valley, crawling among gulches—ravines & creeks of the dreaded gypsum—sulphur & copper waters. Stopping to examine the various surface & other deposits of copper getting specimens returned to "fly" rested ½ hour—then with McCarty & Johnson started on return through other deposits in gulches—richer & richer than before to base of picturesque creek with high—richly colored bluff, which my friends named "Kellogg's Creek" in honor of their artist friend—the first artist who had delineated & entered the country beyond the Brazos. Passed down this to Brazos when a shower passed & wetted us as we hastily crossed the River opposite "Kellogg's Creek"—2 miles above where we had crossed it this morning. Striking East for camp, McCarty killed a fine young doe —and putting it on his mare went onward till dark came cloudy & showery—without a star to guide us—wandered on and struck a pond of our late camp of china trees. Col Johnson went back in dark to find our old camp for certain—finding it, we then went Eastward stumbling through dogtown holes & against dead mesquite trees, until seeing a rocket at 8:00 from our camp were certain of our course & went on by occasional light of two other rockets got us safely into camp.

30TH AUG. FRIDAY '72. Engineers came in & we are now ready to go to Griffin on the *backtrack*—there to wait for Peters & the D.M. party. Start off at 1:40 P.M. Course S. to hit our coming trail and at last get into it and keep it for an hour when by some misunderstanding of signals of leaders from distant elevated ground get out of it and camped at 4:30 P.M. by a small pond of water which was dirty & thick from wallowing buffalo.

31 AUG. In our course large herds of Buffalo—by hundreds were seen on all sides. Shields & McCarty shot two nice fat ones & brought meat to camp—enough to supply us until reach Griffin. McCarty tied up his mare at the spot he intended we should make our camp and went on foot for Buffalo nearby—after skinning it dark was upon him & on coming to camp it was too dark to go back & find his mare—so he awaited the morn to hunt her. Wolves made such terrible howling in all quarters that we would not have been surprized to hear they had devoured her. In the morning he & others started to get her & an Indian succeeded in getting her just where Mac had tied her—all safe & brought her to camp, saddle & all. Mac still being out on the hunt. Slept cold on ground, a lovely starlight. Tem of day say 88. *No therm now with us.* Since Loew went to D. Mts. I am now in Peter's wagon, & Chandler—a rickety concern with thin white cover—hot enough to bake our heads—but it will probably last to Griffin which I don't expect my old ambulance will—it was so overloaded by Peters for D. Mtns.

A sweet clear morning; & start *en route* at 6:07 A.M. Buffalo in herds & some shooting at them. Stop to water at our old camping ground at 8 o.c. On the way Humphrey killed a grand rattle snake large as wrist and 4½ ft long 17 rattles—traveling fast in the cool of the morning. This has been a "game day" - - - Buffalo on all sides in large herds. Swift antelopes. Troutman killed fine young bull buffalo just near my horse (as I was riding McCarty's) - - - Got off & saw him die & men's knives soon had him mutilated & the beautiful dark & scarlet blood oozing from the many wounds. Troutman got his tuft & Tom his tail as trophies of their shooting—I got a tooth as reminder of the incident & Troutman. Then of course everybody wanted a tooth—a thing they never thought of before. Camped at Otis Creek, our former camping ground at 12 m. Collected a few more pebbles & made a sketch of dead mesquite trees during shower & slept in large tent as well as could for talking & snoring.

1ST SEPT. '72. SUNDAY. Left camp *en route* 5:20 A.M. Cross Paint

Creek at 9 o.c. with some trouble—and resumed position in our former camp on *"Clear Fork"* at 11:27 A.M. seeing the debris as we left it—old bottles, boxes, envelopes & ashes. After dinner took a good bath & swim in creek & slept on open ground pretty well. Muscle soup for supper with McCarty—excellent.

MON. 2ND SEPT. '72. Up at 3 in morning bright & cool—start off at sunrise 5 o.c. The color of landscape quite changed since here—autumnal tints of green and flowers & weeds going to seed—thistles all bright purple & in places entirely covering ground. Saved some fine muscle shells. A distant shower yesterday evening raised creek considerably & it rumbled a delicious melody over its rocky bed. What a blessing to get once more to clear sweet healthy water. Our road yesterday was dusty but this morning worse because of deeper sand. Arrive at *Fort Griffin* at 10:20 A.M. & camp ½ m. west of it. With Chandler go to Fort. No letters for me. Send some provisions & letter to camp. Hicks offers me room & hospitality whilst I stay and wishes his portrait. Not knowing when Peters will return can make no promises. Lieut. Ira Quinby Q.M. gives me quarters with him & there I slept—taken with diarrhea & suffered much pain all night.

3 SEPT. '72. Next day Dr. Alexander administered Squibs preparation & lying torpid all day became better at night of 3 Sept. 72 & slept again at Quinby's, taking meals in his mess with Hicks & Hodges of S. Pacific R.R. Surveying Party. Peters & party returned.

4 SEPT. WED. Much better this morning. Some of our men in guard house & others ought to be—for drunkenness & disorder. Roessler says he climbed several peaks of Double Mtns—no copper—but gypsum plenty—Mtns 4000 ft above sea. Says that my drawing was of the Mtn though McCarty has always told me that it was Baylor Peak, the Mtn lying behind it. Peters party saw no Indians or impediments of any kind. I cannot venture down to camp yet & risk my bundles & sketch books in charge of our Cook John, who is very likely to get drunk & let them take care of themselves. Chandler says we will stop only a day or so. Of course I cannot get ready to paint anything here. This morning McCarty, White & Shields left for Jacksboro. Later this afternoon Peters & some ten men left for same—a kind of gradual breaking up which I think I comprehend. Diverse interests & suspicions & dodges as to claims to

what has been accomplished & putting in new locations to what has not yet been explored or known. Such is the *fever* regarding the copper manifestations.

5TH SEPT. 72. THURSDAY. Took a bath in Quinby's quarters after a good nights rest therein & change underclothes by a suit bought at Sutlers—no chance of getting washing done. All my things yet in camp 1¼ m. distant where I cannot go & they are at the mercy of a mob of drunken & ½ drunken men who may at any moments fancy march away with what they can grab. One who came from D. Mtns. with Peters—*Edwards,* received certain intelligence which hurried him away on horse. He had been State Constable, and the Govt. has offered $1000 reward for him. He left his overcoat with me when he went to D. Mts—possibly it is still with my things in camp. Yesterday I requested McConnell who is sober to bring my pistol from camp—if to be had. Says our cook John is sober & likely has taken care of it. Chandler says we are to go to Jacksboro today. I am well enough to try it. Call on Sergt. Foley who is unwell—tell him I will possibly send him result of investigation of the stones from Brazos that he may know their value—he can then furnish any number of best. 4 P.M. our train left camp en route to Jacksboro passing around Post—leaving my old ambulance here with my luggage transferred—and Plummer sick within—both stopping for the night to take Chandler & me tomorrow morn to camp.

6TH SEPT. FRID. '72. After another comfortable night at Lieut. Quinby's am tolerably well & able to start for Jacksboro. 1st Sergeant J. W. Foley will send me the moccasins (promised by Tonky's) by mail when he can get them. He is very kind & amiable & worthy as a man & I hear a first rate officer. Plummer is better & goes in my ambulance today. Feeling very grateful for attentions from officers at this post—I take leave of them and leave Griffin in ambulance with Chandler, Roessler & Plummer at 10 A.M. for Jacksboro, via Belknap and catch up to our train in camp 16 [?] m. at 4:30 P.M. Suffering somewhat for lack of water—none fit to drink on road—pools dried up. Mesquite trees now in pod which I gather fine specimens. Cactus magnt & abundant.

7TH SEPT. SAT. 6:30 A.M. Start in shower which lasts but ½ hour. Cloudy until we cross Brazos at 12:30 through fine mesquite trees in pod. River half size of when we passed before—got through with little trouble from quick sand. Altho threatening storms from every quarter no tents were pitched. Watered ourselves & animals at good well of the old Fort - - - got milk & lunched at a woman's dwelling in one of the abandoned stone quarters. Sketched the remains of Fort Belknap[85]—plenty of goats of all colors looking at me. Curse of the place is the sandburs which covered everybody & his blankets—stinging like needles heavy rain comes on at dusk. Chandler & others take refuge in the woman's house amid vermin—I in rickety, leaky ambulance. Roessler plunges in on me in night and we have some sharp words—and he at last leaves me—pass tiresome wet & windy night Dist 13 m.

8TH SEPT. '72—SUNDAY. Fort Belknap. Cloudy. N.W. wind—probably more rain today. Leave for Jacksboro. 9 o.c. A.M. Course East. Deep sandy road. Lost king bolt of a wagon at 9:30. Detained ½ hour. Cactus *none this side river.* Death of negro cook Jim by shooting at Jacksboro. Death of White cook Jim dropped dead at Griffin—both consumptives & never ought to have been engaged. 12 M. Clearing off n. wind. Heavy roads & stony. Descend slowly to deserted ranch of Peverel[86] near "Salt Creek" and passed over later at 2 P.M. Steep muddy banks and camp above on left of road. Have passed through oaks & mesquite nearly all the way. Turkey tracks abundant. Distance today 7 m. & half.

9TH SEPT. MOND. Leave camp 6:10 A.M. E. open treeless prairie—noted for Indian massacres—the most dangerous place in this region—At 7:10 stop to view graves of the four men who were killed two years since—negroes—one Brit Johnson[87] a famous Indian fighter—driving one supply wagon from Weatherford to Griffin—day fight—15 or 20 Indians. Hat full cartridge shells found around their wagon where they

---

[85]One wonders if the sketch was of the military establishment or of the Belknap village, which before the Civil War was an important western town on the Overland, or Butterfield, Mail Route. In 1859 Belknap had five general stores, three hotels, a blacksmith shop, two wagon yards, and a number of homes (Crouch, *Young County,* 29).

[86]David Peveler (Kellogg's *Peverel*) and his family settled in Palo Pinto County in 1856 and moved to Young County in 1858. Will R. Peveler was a meat contractor at Fort Belknap. Lewis Peveler was attacked by Indians at the Peveler ranch in 1870 or 1871 (Joseph Carroll McConnell, *The West Texas Frontier; or, A Descriptive History of Early Times in Western Texas,* I, 159; II, 115–116).

[87]The wife and two children of Brit Johnson, a slave on Allen Johnson's ranch and a respected member of his community, were captured by Indians in the Elm Creek raid of 1864. Brit made four trips to the Kiowas in the Texas Panhandle before he secured their release. On those trips he was able to secure the release of other captives. In the spring of 1871 Brit and two other Negroes were en route to Weather-

fought—Scalped & mutilated—bowels taken out and body stuffed with meal from the wagon. Antelopes seen this morn—Mts. of Brazos disappearing in rear—a conspicuous isolated hill ahead in our path. Yesterday at Salt Creek found plenty of iron & red chalk, got specimens. 10:25 A.M. came to Monument to 7 men massacred—50 yds left of road 18 May 1871 - - - Inscribed as follows: Sacred to the memory of seven brave men killed by Indians at this place on Thurs. May 18 '71 while in discharge of their duty defending their train against 150 Comanche Indians. N. S. Song—Wagon master. Teamsters: J. S. Elliott, Sam Elliott, N. J. Baxter, Jas Williams, John Mullins, Jesse Bowman.[88]

Temporarily encamp just beyond monument near pool of water from 11 to 1 P.M. & lunch. Sketch some sunflowers & thistles on a low hill near monument [where] the Comanche Chieftain Satanta[89] said on trial he was there looking on at the massacre but had no part in it—only wanted to see if his young men could fight! *Big Tree* is in penitentiary.[90] *Satanta* also. See records in co. court *Jacksboro* where they were tried & convicted. 2:45 P.M. come to Crosstimbers the hills on S. entirely & thickly covered with oak. Conglomerate & red sandstone—a part of country evidently same characteristics as that at Montague and "Head of Elm." We have now passed the most dangerous prairie in all Texas

---

ford for supplies for the ranch when they were surprised by Indians near Turtle Hole. More than one hundred shells were said to have been found around Brit's body (Crouch, *Young County*, 47–50).

[88]The Salt Creek, or Wagon Train, Massacre took place near the present town of Graham in southeastern Young County. A wounded teamster walked to Fort Richardson and reported the raid to General William T. Sherman, who had just been over the same route. For a detailed story of the massacre and its aftermath see Nye, *Carbine and Lance*, 159–190. In the winter of 1872 (January or February) Troop F of the 4th Cavalry, under Captain Wirt Davis, built a monument at the site of the massacre. The monument of oak, pyramidial in shape and painted olive color, with the inscription in black, was made by the quartermaster at Fort Richardson. The State of Texas erected a monument at the site in 1936 (Huckabay, *Ninety-four Years in Jack County*, 169–170).

[89]At first, Satanta, the "Orator of the Plains," boasted that the honor of leading the attack on the wagon train belonged to him. When told that he would be sent to Texas to be tried for murder, he revised his version, saying that he had been present but had not killed anyone and that he had only been prevailed on to accompany his young men to show them how to make war (Nye, *Carbine and Lance*, 178).

[90]Big Tree was released from prison in 1873 but was returned to the penitentiary in 1875. He was again released, became leader of his people after Satanta's suicide, and lived until 1929.

—if rumors be true—& not an Indian! Encamp at Butterfield Ranch near good water hole in rocks. 4:30 P.M. ———— Dis. 14¾ m. Sketch abandoned Ranch of Butterfield from ledge of sandstone rocks over water hole. It lies in a bowl surrounded by rugged oaks, the road running through centre.

10TH SEPT. '72 TUESDAY. Slept alone in ambulance. Cool night. Soils very rich all way from Belknap—immense milkweed 6 ft high in flower. The ranch an old stage tavern—10:30 A.M. after rolling beautiful land come to Ham's Ranch—once important—now abandoned. Roads sandy with heavy rocky declivities where we walk—all red sandstone. Precipitous rocky bluffs of hills jut into valley and conical sandy hills naked—called "Potato hills." At 10:45 come to temporary camp to rest & feed jaded mules, on a beautiful plateau of 50 acres—surrounded by wood—the sun sometimes obscured by clouds which with a nice breeze makes travelling comfortable. Altogether the scenery this morning has been picturesque from the varied vistas of hills beyond hills—as much as any I have seen in Texas

At 1 o.c. P.M. continued *en route* N.E. and ascending bad roads we reached the high land on the North of Jacksboro viewing with delight the town a mile off in the plain below—a long straggling village ended by the Fort Richardson on the South with its flag flying amid the comparatively large buildings of the Post. The little town really looked large to me after being so long straying in the uninhabited wilderness of the Brazos. We descended the hill and camped a mile W. of the town on the headwaters of Cleveland creek upon which we had formerly camped a month & which I shall ever remember as a place of suffering and idleness & ennui on our journey towards the Double Mountain Fork of the Brazos. We arrive at 4 o.c. In the evening it commenced thundering & lightning & rain which continued nearly all night. Chandler immediately went to town & slept there, I in tent on damp blankets & damper ground.

11TH SEPT. WED. Peters & his outfit are camped within hailing distance on the N.E. and further side of the creek. It is the general opinion that the Expedition will go to the "Big Wichita" in a week or ten days.[91] Chandler says he must see Peters before deciding. I am repacking my

---

[91]Roessler stated that he was not required to examine the locations made in Wichita, Jack, and Wilbarger Counties, which were not visited in 1872, but he added:

effects to go to N. York as I will continue no longer with this party, and it is time that I was looking after my daughter and establishing a studio somewhere now that I am free to do so.[92] Chandler has returned & tells Troutman that he himself intends returning in a few days to Washington. I hope so & I shall have company. He slept in tent with me. Heavy fog.

12TH SEPT. '72. THURSDAY. Chandler & I go to town in Ambulance he to settle with men & I to get box for packing minerals, & help him in accounts should he need me. Meet D. W. Patten a man 55 years old who accompanied Webster's Expedition to Kiowa Peak. Described Double Mtns minutely, and it appears that my drawing of it was of a range this side on Salt Creek. He has been to D.M. 3 times. First in 1856 with J. R. Baylor.[93] Says D.M. consists of 2 peaks similar to Kiowa Peak connected at the base on the elevated plain. That it would take at least 10 days to reach them and return to Griffin from Kiowa Peak. They are *entirely* separated from any other mtn—and there is no other mountain or high hill within 30 miles of them. The D.M. Fork takes its rise from a lovely small lake of *fresh water* 25 or 30 m. beyond on W. course from them. Patten is now going to another excursion to Kiowa Peak to locate & survey lands farther West or above those that we have just located. He is with Hill's party as guide, getting his own certificates located & surveyed. He is also engaged for other parties, R.R. and private for future work. Thus it seems that our party has awakened an interest unknown before in regard to the mineral riches of Texas. For this the State is deeply indebted.

After a long talk with Patten I presume that Peters' party did not in fact get to the Double Mtn but only to what I drew as such which hides D.B. which lies 30 m. beyond. A *dreadful* mistake if it be one. Dined at Thompson's Hotel, a good meal most acceptable indeed to my needy feeble stomach. Chandler *privately* informs me that *we alone* will likely

---

"I am able to say that there are good copper lands at the mouth of Beaver Creek, Wichita County, where about six sections were secured for the Association" (Roessler, *Geological Report*, 8).

[92] Apparently an oblique reference to Kellogg's divorce or to his wife's remarriage.

[93] John R. Baylor became Indian agent for the Comanche Reservation on the upper Brazos at old Camp Cooper in 1856. Baylor Peak, mentioned by Kellogg, is not shown under that name on the Roessler map. For a biography of Baylor see J. Evetts Haley, "John R. Baylor, Irrepressible Rebel," in *Men of Fiber*, 6–12.

start for Sherman tomorrow with two mule wagons, getting there ahead of the train which still follows us—most of the men receiving their discharge today, leaving Peters to send it on—then leaving it & go to Austin himself. This may be said to be the *End of the Expedition* of the "Texas Land & Copper Co." So mote it be.

13TH SEPT. '72. FRIDAY. Go to town to breakfast at Thompson's Hotel with several of the scientific corps—our cuisine & cooks being in such a dilapidated state. Go to pay my respects to Gen & Mrs. Buell at the Post. Then back to camp to pack for a start—then back to town to assist Chandler in making out accounts which employed us till evening. Day before & yesterday, & today the sky has been obscured by myriads of grasshoppers. Dews are heavy here.

14TH SEPT. '72 SAT. I am now apprized that Chandler will go immediately to Washington & I to accompany him in wagon to terminus of M.K.T. R.R. I regret not knowing this sooner. So as to get some clothes from my boxes left in the baggage wagon of train which will follow us too late for me to get any change of linen or decent suit for civilization. - - - But *en avant*. Another talk with Patten confirmed him in the opinion that Peters & party never went to Double Mtns. He says there *are* minerals—silver lead & copper in abundance & salt likewise—that he has filed upon the land and been there & *seen* what he speaks of that he can take any party there & prove it. He is awaiting Hill of another party of Explorers—expected this evening & he is to guide them to *Dble Mtn*. Hill[94] is locating mineral land for some R.R. Co.—possibly "Southern Pacific."

Left Jacksboro at 2:30 for Decatur in Peters' ambulance, without cover—with Chandler & Humphreys; course E. when we got 10½ m. took wrong road & after keeping it 10 m. until after sundown—though with bright moon—we came to a ranch & enquired our way—found where we were & got lodging in King's an empty ranch, where we

---

[94]Hill seems to be identified in a note in the Dallas *Herald* of September 7, 1872. Entitled "Off for the Frontier," the item reads: "Our friend from Austin, familiarly known as Capt. Wash. Hill has been in our city the past week with a party destined for the frontier. This party in charge of Capt. Hill, is sent out by the Central Railroad to survey and locate lands for the Company in the counties of Hardeman, Knox, Wilbarger & Baylor, etc." The *Mercantile and General City Directory of Austin, Texas* located the residence of Captain Wash Hill on Live Oak Street between Guadalupe and San Antonio.

cooked coffee, took crackers & potted meats - - - spread blankets on floor & had a good night's rest. Wolves, cocks & geese music with bull-fights accompanied by moonlight—one having a bell to toll as to its progress.

SUNDAY 15TH SEPT. '72. This morning made coffee in Ranch & with crackers & potted ham & turkey a tolerable breakfast. This is a stage Station from Jacksboro to Beal's station[95]—the landlady had no eggs or milk or bread, it was lucky we had some food with us or we should have suffered hunger. We left on the back track at 6:30 A.M. & reached the proper road at 9 o.c. then turned to N.E. from a S.E. course and crossed West Fork Trinity at 12:20 - - - got excellent water & stopped to lunch & feed mules near a ranch on banks which could give us no eggs or milk - - - So we fed as before—making coffee at camp fire—a couple of teams from Jacksboro, lunched their drivers & animals same time & we had a friendly chat. At ——— we start *en route* for Decatur refreshed. The district passed through from Jack's is rich & picturesque with many fine hills & views—generally rolling prairie & timber—with good mesquite trees—in the creeks Pecan, large cotton wood - - - Burr oak, Hackberry, Hickory &c. Going slowly over sandy roads & stumpy ones—knocking my spine to pieces, we finally gradually ascend long hills till reach Decatur on the most elevated spot in the region—overlooking an immense region—surpassing all yet seen in Texas. The blue distance extends like an ocean on all sides—the horizontal line almost perfect—only one point in the prairie equal or exceeding the height of Decatur—on the East a green smooth regular slope or mound. A few isolated houses & ranches are scattered about the declining slopes of the Decatur hill, but the general aspect was that of a desert with this lovely green oasis in its midst. The hill is limestone—water hard as flint. We stopped at *"Decatur House"* 6 o.c. kept by Shoemaker an old borderer—from Virginia.[96] The little town has a frame *Court House* in a square sur-

---

[95]Kellogg spells this *Beal's*, but he may have meant Veal Station, a Parker County village established in 1857 thirteen miles northeast of Weatherford (Smythe, *Historical Sketch of Parker County*, 373).

[96]In October, 1872, Tom Bomar wrote in the first number of the *Advance Guard*, Wise County's first newspaper: "Upon my arrival at Decatur I was directed to the Decatur Hotel, a single story, double building, which, if my memory serves me right, was a part frame and part log structure, conducted by Captain A. H. Shoemaker, where I was entertained in the most hospitable old-time Texas manner" (Cliff D.

rounded by wooden stores & shanties of recent building, which form nearly the whole of this frontier county town—where the people of the county are is more than I can guess as no habitation is visible in the great distance of the prairie surrounding. After putting our mules in the stable we got a supper at 7 o.c. without either eggs, milk or butter—things our mouths had watered for all day. Get lodgings—I on floor on my own blanket. Chandler in bed with *companions* I avoided. He found it better however to take a blanket & pillow out on the porch before morning to get a little sleep. The cats & rats had nice sport about my head but I got a tolerable rest—though the landlord got up & attended often to calls in the night from wayfarers who he could not accommodate. His bed was in the same room with me & his noisy boots & voice proved that he didn't mind my presence at all.

MOND 16TH SEP. '72. After breakfast of similar deprivations—not even milk for coffee we got away at 7 o.c. A.M. on the Road E. to *Denton* our next point for night's lodging. Passing over excellent hard black roads & rolling denuded prairies—sometimes without seeing a single tree anywhere—but covered with the green & prolific broom weed with yellow starlike flowers. We crossed *Denton Creek* at 14 m - - - 10½ o.c. where we watered—keeping on with a jaded or lazy mule which took all the strength out of Humphrey's arm in flogging him we arrived at a woody shady place to lunch & feed near a ranch on "South Hickory Creek" at 12 & left at 3 o.c. P.M. The woman at Ranch was sick but gave us buttermilk & eggs—In return we give can of Lemonade, much to her comfort. Distance 21 m from Decatur—Cross N. Hickory at 3:40 - - - arrive at *Denton,* co—town of same name - - - 5:30 P.M. put up at *Denton Hotel.* Walk round square with old forest trees—post & rail fence. New houses are going up about it and there is evidence of life in the town. Even a weekly paper is printed here—and its sign *"Monitor"* shows itself on a modest frame shanty on the square. Clean hotel but no milk or eggs—landlord says they are not to be had as camp meeting has starved them all out for 3 weeks. Slept well on my own blanket & after a tolerable breakfast—*with fried* eggs & butter!!

On 17TH SEPT. '72 started for "Pilot point" at 7 A.M. Weather always clear—hot & with breeze enough to be comfortable in shade.

Cates, *Pioneer History of Wise County from Red Men to Railroads—Twenty Years of Intrepid History,* 467).

Crossed "Clear Creek" at 9 A.M., a clear little stream of cool water—filled canteen - - - crossed "Foot of Elm" creek at 11 o.c. ———— hurried lunch & *fixed* harness a little and passed on over most fertile soil & woody belt which comes from "Head of Elm" through very shady roads—and by many fine farms of cotton & corn & ranches grow numerous until we made "Pilot Point" at 1:30 P.M. Hotel & supper—sleep fighting coon & fleas on feather bed.

18TH SEPT. WED. Town larger than *Denton* - - - the county town of this county—built around central sq. Situated on a slightly elevated point above the great flat prairie which it overlooks—and thus makes a point of pilotage to Indians & travellers.

Leave "Pilot Point" at 7 A.M. in co with Alexander on his way to Sherman as we are. The prairie is well marked in all parts by extensive fenced fields of corn and well built farm houses—no longer rough ranches. Prosperity & civilization are come again & we have turned our backs on the wilderness & its savages.

8 miles distant we stop to water mules at a spring near farm house its well affording too little to be used for such purpose—and we do not expect to find water for some hours march—nor inhabitants nor cultivation. Road hard & excellent—but mules not yet active & hearty. 16 m. is the "divide" or watershed between Pilot Point & Sherman & called "White Ridge" from a cropping of white limestone—seen afar—& on the road which has uncovered it by abrasion of travel. From here is seen Pilot Point indistinctly. 18 m—is a new shop & Restaurant for travellers—much needed in this waterless desert—not a ranch for 10 m. nor water. Here we feed ourselves & mules—several travellers stopping to refresh from different points—roads cross from Kentuckytown to Gainesville and from Sherman to Pilot Point. The proprietor has dug 30 ft for water unsuccessfully & bring it a mile from a spring. We shall find it as we go about 1½ m. on road. Hay stacks are here very large in store for the projected R.R. across Texas—"Texas Pacific." Day very hot—but fine breeze. Proceeded at 4 P.M. and watered mules in pools in a creek 6 m from Sherman—thus making 18 m. without water. Arrived at our old camping ground at Duggen's[97] near Sherman at sundown

[97]In 1836 the David Dugan family helped establish the first Grayson County settlement near present Pilot Grove. Descendants of the original family still live in Sherman and at Bells, located at the intersection of the Katy and the Texas and

where we found corn & fodder for mules & hospitality of supper & lodging on the open porch till 12 midnight when we hitched up & started by moonlight at 12:45 for Red River, making it by 6 o.c.

19TH SEPT. THURS. Getting some groceries at the "First & Last Chance" store at the Colbert Ferry.[98] Seeing many shanties on the road erected for accommodation of R.R. traffic since our visit—also many teams & camps of travellers & porterage to & from the terminus of M.K. & T.R.R. now within 50 miles. This exhibition of traffic already proves that when the R.R. reaches Red River there will be plenty for it to do, and a consequent benefit to all this part of Texas which looks earnestly & impatiently for this means of reaching the Eastern market and of facilitating immigration to its most fertile & healthy region. I find my sketch book has been left at Duggens in our night's hurried departure. How fearful I am that this sole evidence & labor of my long Texas trip will be lost—though Chandler promises to telegraph for it to be sent by Express to Washington.[99]

Delayed at Ferry by placing another rope across it until 8:30 A.M. - - - the river is much lower than when we passed it 3 mo since and much more business for ferrymen because of the nearer approach of M.K.T.R.R. We counted 16 teams awaiting ferriage on this side after 8 had crossed & they were continuously arriving and the road was encumbered by them for a mile. What a business will spring up when the R.R. bridge is completed & the road reaches it! Then good bye to the enormous profits of Colbert's ferry. We paid one dollar in coin for our wag-

---

Pacific. Mr. Dan D. Dugan, of Bells, has not heard of the Expedition or of any unidentified water-color pictures possibly still in Grayson County, but he does say of the family: "I am sure that the Dugans mentioned were our folks. They came to Texas in 1835 and have been around here since. There were always folks stopping with them as there were not many people here at that time" (Dan D. Dugan to L. Friend, February 28, 1965).

[98]Kellogg mentioned the First and Last Chance but not the name of the ferry when he made his notes on crossing into Texas. Named for its builder and operator, Benjamin F. Colbert, the ferry was the crossing used by the Butterfield Overland Mail. Colbert was influential and wealthy when he established the ferry in 1853, and a warm welcome and a good meal were reported by travellers who stopped at the Colbert home-station (Roscoe P. and Margaret B. Conkling, *The Butterfield Overland Mail, 1857–1869* . . . , I, 278–283).

[99]It is sadly ironic that Kellogg was so critical of other members of the Expedition who failed to perform adequately their assigned chores, and then lost the fruits of his own labor.

ons & selves to cross it. One mile from ferry in Indian Territory we made fire - - - coffee & breakfast. Weather threatening rain - - - at 12m. proceed *en route* through deep sand, (as have for 5 miles on the other side of river) with forest & fine timber of much variety & large—to a great blank prairie, rolling & high, outlines of timber at great distances & a lively fire spreading rapidly over the dry grass. Day hot with little breeze made time & distance pass slowly & uncomfortably until we reached *"Carriage Point"* in the midst of this blank uninhabited region. At this Point roads cross to Colberts Ferry—to Rock Bluff ferry 7 m above to Gainesville. Stages stop here and have several horses in stable. There is a store and a nice farm house of Mrs. Colbert where we had accommodations.

20TH SEPT. FRID. After a good dinner yesty, clean bed, & excellent breakfast this morning, we were satisfied & pleased enough to forget how many hounds slept in our rooms, or barked outside—how many cocks crowed, or geese cackled, or ducks quacked during the night. I am refreshed—Chandler indisposed. Alexander[100] joined us this morning— and we start *en route* at 8 o.c. A.M. over the naked prairie—then through the same forest of deep sand where we had formerly such a fearful tornado outward bound—and came to *"Blue River"* a fine clear running stream at 12:15 A.M. [noon]—passed the long high bridge and took bread & milk at Folsom's nice farm house. He is toll taker—1200 head of cattle are in pens on way to R Way Station where we are going. Our mules are fagged & we give them a lunch of corn whilst we rest in the shade. The limestone formation here is peculiar & filled with shells. Day hot, road dusty, but good breeze at times—Many emigrants on way to Texas—one returning & with family—says it costs too much there for a poor man to get a start. Very likely true. Broom weed still fills the prairies—very large in rich blossoms. Sunflowers have almost disappeared since we left Sherman—as also the milkweed. Osage orange or Bodoch [bois d'arc] trees are plentiful and filled with fruit—very provoking. Since we can get no eatable fruit of any kind in these parts. Indeed we have scarcely had any kind of either fruit or vegetables since we left St. Louis more than three months ago. But we are fortunately on the road towards such rare enjoyments. I bought a few apples yesterday

[100]Presumably J. M. Alexander, of Sherman, whose name Kellogg notes at the end of his journal.

at 4 cts each—they were all the way from Nebraska. Crossed "Rockyford" at same place as on our coming down—it looks picturesque as before. Road "really fearful" as Chandler says for dust—we can hardly drag through it on a slow walk, at 4 P.M. and arrive at "New Boggy" at 6 o.c. P.M. - - - put up at *Nichol's Hotel,* a nice roomy frame house with spacious porch in front. This village has been nearly all built up since we were here in June—consisting of several frame houses in expectation that the M.K.T. R Road would pass by it. How disappointed they are—of course.

21 SEP. SAT. Good supper & bed last night & breakft today—we leave at 7:35 A.M. through woods, sand & dust for R.R. Terminus. Alexander with us on horse. 8:25 Toll bridge—arrive at "Middle Boggy," or now *"Atoka"* the present terminus of M.K.T.R.R. at 11 o.c. A.M. This is a RW station and quite a village has sprung up since June last—out of the silent wilderness. There are tents & shanties and some frame houses lining the R.Way track—much business already done in merchandize & shipments of cattle & cotton—and there is actually a "Newspaper" published here called the "Vindicator"—supporting the policy of sectionalizing the Indian Territory, and finally bringing it into the Union as a state. Chandler disposes of his wagon & mules for $150. So that we now end our tedious & tiresome journey into the uncivilized regions, and take an easy seat in the cars upon a road only just commenced as we passed its track three months ago. Such is Yankee enterprize contrasted with the lethargy of the semisavage character of this western border. Soon all will be made bright & comfortable by the progress of the Iron Horse, which will leap the Red River into Texas before next New Year's day. At 12:30 A.M. we take our seats in the comfortable cars of the M.K.T. R way for St Louis, and start for home—home!!

22D SEPT. SUND. We are now steaming through the Indian Territory on a new & remarkably smooth & solidly laid track, passing the Limestone Gap over a fine bridge at 1:30 A.M. on which our car rested 15 minutes above the fine rapid stream, to water its Fiery Steed. Here is a difficult & deep cutting through a Limestone Ridge & over a sudden turn of the river. It strikes me as a fine piece of engineering skill. Another & excellent bridge lower on the stream has been constructed by the RW Company for wagons. When we crossed here in June it was over a very old & rickety structure. After a few hours fitful slumber the daylight displays the great prairies, without a tree or bush, with great black spots & patches marking the extent of prairie fires now gone out—(but one of which cast its lurid & fitful light over the vast expanse during the night) the grass now turned into the "sear and yellow" stage of the declining year. Here & there refreshing lines of dark rich green forest project a welcome presence into the denuded landscape, or allows us to run through its dark & picturesque shades—which often shelter a clear delicious stream beneath. The road generally passes through the centre of great vacant plains, bounded on one side—at times on both—by hills of singular geological forms, generally divested of any kind of verdure. Conical hills rise abruptly from the plains, solitary and without apparent reason as beacons to the lost wanderer; some truncated, others entirely flat adjoining. Then will come into the scene in the middle distance long ridges—even mountains with gently undulating summits, entirely covered with the densest forests of heavy timber—suddenly ending or losing themselves in the absolute level of the naked prairie—and as suddenly rising from it in their course shorn of all evidence of fertility—mere blank, smooth surface of buff colored sand, strongly defined against the agreeable misty lines of the blue mountains in the far away distance. Though entirely destitute of human life, the scene is not altogether lifeless. Prairie chicken—quail and other birds often spring from the grass —frightened by our rattling train—and skim away over the land in numbers enchanting to the heart of a sportsman. Such is the usual aspect of the Indian Territory on the line of the great Railway which is in time to cause it to blossom as the rose and to receive and support millions of civilized human beings—instead of the very meagre number of semi-civilized aborigines living unseen amid the luxurious forests of this unexplored region which divides one section from another of the great continent of American states.

Passing across the territorial line into Kansas there is no noticeable change in the natural features of the country but a very decided and marked one in its artificial. From utter absence of all human habitations or human labor, the land at once is changed as by magic to the most cheering evidences of both. Well built farm houses and capacious barns —fields teeming with ripe corn, hay stacks dotting the level surface of the prairie with pyramided stacks, glistening far & near upon the enraptured vision—the enormous spaces of earth closely shaven of its grassy covering in sharp straight lines by the mowing machine—stake & rider fences marking the limits of fields running in chequered lines across the verdant landscape and dotted by little mounds of the gathered grass—these are some of the silent witnesses of man's intelligence & toil & ambition in subduing the earth to his gain & comfort. Then become prominent the positive proofs that he has not labored in vain—that his labor is blest with abundant reward. A natural love of his race & the social instincts prompt him to come nearer to his kind and he creates villages in the midst of his well cultivated fields—that he may more readily communicate with his neighbors; exchange thoughts & aspirations and receive the news of what is passing in distant places—Educate his children in Christian paths, and live & act among his fellow men with greater usefulness and honor. So here in distant Kansas do the villages spring up & their neat, modest, white church spires sparkle upon the travellers sight, conferring the most agreeable emotions as to the future greatness and prosperity of his country. In these points we notice immediately the passage into civilization from the aboriginal inertness & ignorance of the poor denizens of this great Indian Territory.

23 SEPT. '72 MOND. Arrive at St. Louis at 6:30 this morning, breakfasted at a Restaurant, crossed the Mississippi to the R.R. Depot and started for Vandalia, Ill. at 8 A.M. Weather continued clear & hot. Since leaving Indian Territory the breeze has grown warmer & warmer as we get North. There and in Texas it was invariably cool & delightful—here similar to Sirocco blast.

Knowing Chandler to be very short of money I have not asked him for money due me—and shall have to get to Washington in my filthy uncouth prairie attire, as I am shorter of money than Chandler himself. Miss dinner & supper except sandwich & coffee for latter. Arrived at Indianapolis about dusk—Greeley is here speaking - - - nothing but his followers is heard along the line.

24 SEPT. '72. TUES. A *tiresome* rest all night on car seat. Gen. S. F. Cary[101] aboard—has stumped N. Carolina and now doing same in Ohio —he leaves at Cadiz station to speak. Opinion is that Greeley will carry Penn. - - - Ohio & Indiana. *"May be so"* as Indian says. Ohio & Indiana

---

[101]Samuel Fenton Cary (1814–1900) was born in Cincinnati, Ohio. He was a national leader in the Sons of Temperance, was commissioned general during the Civil War, and was often in demand as a public speaker during presidential elections.

present fertile fields & lovely scenes—frost has touched some trees. Ohio near Steubenville is especially beautiful in the narrow valleys through which R.R. runs—Steubenville is seated in one of the loveliest reaches of the Ohio imaginable—Its furnaces furnish smoke & steam in rich clouds against the green forest hills in Virginia—opposite—a fine *character* painting could be made of it. The bridge is a magnificent & bold structure—though fragile & graceful not offensive as bridges generally are spanning great streams—Cattle on the sandy edges of streams in the bright sun and the richly wooded hills rising boldly from the river flashing around their bases, softened by the smoke & mist of the city's factories in the plains of the foreground, form a striking & lovely scene which only a Claude[102] could adequately render—as seen from the bridge miraculously held in the air over the *"Beautiful River."* We passed into ——— at noon and soon lost sight of it in the narrow picturesque valleys, cultivated where possible & enlivened by the huts & hamlets and cattle of the modest laborious farmers. The trees & foliage of all this section are remarkably fine & varied, the verdure fresh & rich —just the favorable time for the landscape student.

25 SEPT. '72. WEDNESDAY. 5 o.c. A.M. arrived in Washington, via Harrisburg, Balt. &c—lodge at Mrs. Williams 620 P. Av. Remain in Washington some days & leave for N. York—and go to my old friend P. M. Suydams in 51st St. accepting his hospitality.

OCT. Go to Flushing & take Somers to Brooklyn—because of ill treatment and other causes by Sisters of Academy.

[In the back of the notebook]

[Sketch of] Mesquite trees—near Belknap, Texas. Sep 72.

[Sketch of] Wild sunflower - - - Texas 9th Sep. 72. From 1 to 7–10 ft high. Covers prairies for miles in places. Gone to seed - - - brown bolls spherical.

[Sketch of] Bull thistle - - - Texas. 9 Sep. 72. Purple like bowl and green—green stalk & leaves. Sometimes 4 ft high—covers great spaces making bright purple masses across prairies—interspersed with sunflowers.

AUGUST 8. Buy & charge to Chandler at Sutler's Fort Griffin—

He served in the Fortieth U.S. Congress (*National Cyclopaedia of American Biography*..., XI, 480).

[102]The French painter Claude Lorrain (Claude Gelée).

Socks—1.20
Shirt—1.25
Jacket—2
Drawers—4
drawers 4

Clothes at Griffin 2 times Sep.

Dr. Wisewell—Prof Roessler to send him a brief of the trip of Expedition for use in his writings.

D. W. Patten—Jacksboro, Texas—guide to Fork

F. W. Johnson, Austin

J. M. Alexander—Sherman, Texas

BIBLIOGRAPHY

HISTORICAL BACKGROUND

Manuscripts

Barton, Henry W. Letter to Llerena Friend, January 20, 1965.
Davis, E. J., File. Governors' Letters, Texas State Archives, Austin.
Donoghue, Margaret K. "An Abstract of Biographical Data in the Texas Supreme Court Reports, 1874–1881" (M.A. thesis, The University of Texas, 1938).
Dugan, Dan D. Letter to Llerena Friend, February 28, 1965.
Election Register, 1872. Texas State Archives, Austin.
Graham, E. S. Graham Papers, Archives Collection, The University of Texas Library, Austin.
Land, Robert H. Letter to Llerena Friend, February 23, 1965.
Pease, E. M., Papers. Austin-Travis County Collection, Austin Public Library.
Stiles, Elizabeth. "Life and Reminiscences of W. F. Cummins." Typescript, Archives Collection, The University of Texas Library, Austin.

Books

Barry, James Buckner. *A Texas Ranger and Frontiersman: The Days of Buck Barry in Texas, 1845–1906.* Edited by James K. Greer. Dallas, Southwest Press, 1932.
Bentley, H. L., and Thomas Pilgrim. *The Texas Legal Directory for 1876–77.* Austin, Democratic Statesman Office, 1877.
Carter, R. G. *On the Border with Mackenzie.* ... Washington, D.C., Eynon Printing Company, 1935.
Cates, Cliff D. *Pioneer History of Wise County from Red Men to Railroads —Twenty Years of Intrepid History.* ... Decatur, Texas, 1907.
[Charlton, John B.]. *The Old Sergeant's Story: Winning the West from the Indians and Bad Men in 1870 to 1876.* By Captain Robert G. Carter. New York, Frederick H. Hitchcock, 1926.
Conkling, Roscoe P., and Margaret B. Conkling. *The Butterfield Overland Mail, 1857–1869* ... 3 vols. Glendale, Arthur H. Clark Company, 1947.
Crouch, Carrie J. *Young County History and Biography.* Dallas, Dealey and Lowe, 1937.

Cullum, George W. *Biographical Register of the Officers and Graduates of the U.S. Military Academy at West Point, N.Y. from Its Establishment in 1802, to 1890* ... Boston, Houghton Mifflin, 1891. Vols. II and III.

[Edmund J. Davis]. *Message of Governor Edmund J. Davis to Twelfth Legislature. April 28, 1870.* Austin: Tracy, Siemering & co., printers, 1870.

———. *Message of Gov. Edmund J. Davis, of the State of Texas.* Austin: J. G. Tracy, state printer, 1871.

Dictionary of American Biography. Edited by Dumas Malone. Published under the Auspices of American Council of Learned Societies. New York, Charles Scribner's Sons, 1943.

Foreman, Grant. *Down the Texas Road: Historic Places Along Highway 69 Through Oklahoma* (Historic Oklahoma Series, No. 2). Norman, University of Oklahoma Press, 1936.

Foreman, Grant (ed.). *Adventure on Red River: Report on the Exploration of the Headwaters of the Red River by Captain Randolph B. Marcy and Captain G. B. McClellan.* Norman, University of Oklahoma Press, 1937.

Forney, John W. *What I Saw in Texas.* Philadelphia, Ringwalt and Brown, Printers [1872].

Galveston City Directory, 1872. Compiled and Published by John H. Heller. Galveston, Texas: Printed at the "News" Steam Job Printing Office, 1872.

Gammel, H. P. N. *The Laws of Texas, 1822–1897* ... 10 vols. Austin, Gammell Book Co., 1898.

Glass, E. L. N. (ed.). *The History of the Tenth Cavalry, 1866–1921.* Tucson, Arizona, Acme Printing Company, 1921.

Griffin, Samuel Chester. *History of Galveston, Texas, Narrative and Biographical.* Galveston, A. H. Cawston, 1931.

Haley, J. Evetts. *Men of Fiber.* El Paso, Texas, Carl Hertzog, 1963.

Hamersly, Thomas Holdup Stevens (comp.). *Complete Regular Army Register of the United States: For One Hundred Years (1779 to 1879)* ... Washington, D. C., T. H. S. Hamersly, 1880.

Heitman, Francis B. *Historical Register and Dictionary of the United States Army, from Its Organization, September 29, 1789, to March 2, 1903.* 2 vols. Washington, D.C., Government Printing Office, 1903.

Henderson, Jeff S. (ed.). *100 Years in Montague County, Texas.* St. Jo, Texas, IPTA Printers [1958?].

Hill, Robert Thomas. *The Present Condition of Knowledge of the Geology of Texas.* (Department of Interior, *Bulletin* of the United States Geological Survey, No. 45 ...). Washington, D.C., Government Printing Office, 1887.

Huckabay, Ida Lasater. *Ninety-Four Years in Jack County, 1854–1948*. Austin, Steck Company, 1949.

King, Edward. *The Southern States of North America: A Record of Journeys in Louisiana, Texas, the Indian Territory, Missouri, Arkansas, Mississippi, Alabama, Georgia, Florida, South Carolina, North Carolina, Kentucky, Tennessee, Virginia, West Virginia and Maryland*. 4 vols. London, Blackie & Son..., 1875.

McCarty, W. C. *A Few Practical Remarks about Texas, Her Resources, Climate and Soil, with Many Important Facts and Extracts from Reliable Sources*. By Col. W. C. McCarty of Texas. New York, Great American Engraving and Printing Company, 1871.

McConnell, H. H. *Five Years a Cavalryman; or, Sketches of Regular Army Life on the Texas Frontier Twenty Odd Years Ago*. Jacksboro, Texas, J. N. Rogers & Co., printers, 1889.

McConnell, Joseph Carroll. *The West Texas Frontier; or, A Descriptive History of Early Times in Western Texas; Containing an Accurate Account of Much Hitherto Unpublished History...* Vol. I, Jacksboro, Texas, Gazette Print, 1933; Vol. II, Palo Pinto, Texas, 1939.

Marcy, Randolph B. *Thirty Years of Army Life on the Border*. The 1866 Edition unabridged. Introduction by Edward S. Wallace. Philadelphia, J. B. Lippincott, 1963.

Masterson, V. V. *The Katy Railroad and the Last Frontier*. Norman, University of Oklahoma Press, 1952.

Mercantile and General City Directory of Austin, Texas—1872–73... By Gray & Moore. Austin: S. A. Gray, Book and Job Printers, 1872.

National Cyclopaedia of American Biography. New York, J. T. White & Company, 1892–19——.

New Jersey Legislature. *Legislative Manual of the State of New Jersey, 1887*. Trenton, 1887.

Nye, Wilbur Sturtevant. *Carbine and Lance: The Story of Old Fort Sill*. By Captain W. S. Nye. Norman, University of Oklahoma Press, 1938.

O'Beirne, H. F. *Leaders and Leading Men of the Indian Territory. With Interesting Biographical Sketches* . . . Chicago, American Publishers' Association, 1891.

Österreichisches Biographisches Lexikon, 1815–1950. 3 vols. Graz-Köln, Wein, Verlag Hermann Böhlaus Nachf, 1857.

Richardson, Rupert Norval. *The Frontier of Northwest Texas, 1846 to 1876: Advance and Defense by the Pioneer Settlers of the Cross Timbers and Plains*. Glendale, California, Arthur H. Clark, 1963.

Rister, Carl Coke. *Fort Griffin on the Texas Frontier.* Norman, University of Oklahoma Press, 1956.

———. *The Southwestern Frontier, 1865–1881.* Cleveland, Arthur H. Clark Company, 1928.

Roessler, A. R. *Geological Report of the Property of the Texas Land and Copper Association.* N.p. [New York, 1872].

———. *Reply to the Charges Made by S. B. Buckley, State Geologist of Texas, in His Official Report of 1874 against Dr. B. F. Shumard and A. R. Roessler.* N.p. [New York? 1875?].

Rye, Edgar. *The Quirt and the Spur: Vanishing Shadows of the Texas Frontier.* Chicago, W. B. Conkey Company, 1909.

Smythe, H. *Historical Sketch of Parker County.* St. Louis, Louis C. Lavat, 1877.

Texas Bureau of Immigration. *Texas: The Home for the Immigrant from Everywhere.* Published by Authority of the Legislature and under the Auspices of the Bureau of Immigration of the State of Texas. Austin, John Cardwell, State Printer, 1873.

Texas Copper Mining and Manufacturing Company. *Charter and By-Laws of the Texas Copper Mining and Manufacturing Company, A History of the Company.* Letter from the Department of the Interior, by Joseph S. Wilson, Commissioner. Prof. Wm. DeRyee's Geological Report. Dallas, Herald and Commercial Steam Printing House, 1880.

Texas Geological and Agricultural Survey. *First Annual Report of the Geological and Agricultural Survey of Texas.* By S. B. Buckley, A.M., Ph.D., state geologist. Houston, A. C. Gray, state printer, 1874.

———. *First Report of Progress of the Geological and Agricultural Survey of Texas.* By B. F. Shumard, State Geologist. Printed by order of the Eighth Legislature. Austin, John Marshall & Co., state printers, 1859.

———. *A Preliminary Report of the Geological and Agricultural Survey of Texas.* By S. B. Buckley. Austin, State Gazette Office, 1866.

Udden, J. A., C. L. Baker, and Emil Böse. *Review of the Geology of Texas* (*Bulletin* of The University of Texas, 1916, No. 4). Austin, 1916.

The War of the Rebellion: A Compilation of the Official Records of the Union and Confederate Armies ... Series I, Vol. 48. Washington, D. C., Government Printing Office, 1896.

Articles

Crimmins, Martin L., "Captain John Pope's Route to the Pacific," *The Military Engineer* (March–April, 1931), reprint.

Ewing, Floyd E., Jr., "Copper Mining in West Texas: Early Interest and Development," *West Texas Historical Association Year Book*, XXX (1954), 17–29.

Geiser, Samuel Wood, "Men of Science in Texas, 1820–1880," *Field and Laboratory*, XXVII (1959), 127–128, 187–188.

Kimbrough, W. C., "The Frontier Background of Clay County," *West Texas Historical Association Year Book*, XVIII (1942), 116–131.

Loew, Oskar, and A. R. Roessler, "Erforschung des Nordwesttheiles von Texas im Jahre 1872," *Petermanns mitteilungen aus Justus Perthes' geographischeranstalt*, XIX (1873), 453–457.

Mabry, W. S., Early West Texas and Panhandle Surveys," *Panhandle-Plains Historical Association Review*, II (1929), 22–42.

"Minerals of Texas," *Texas Almanac for 1872*, 160–162.

Nunn, W. C., "Eighty-six Hours without Water on the Texas Plains," *Southwestern Historical Quarterly*, XLIII (1939/1940), 356–364.

Roessler, A. R., "Mineral Resources of Texas," *Texas Almanac for 1872* (Galveston, 1871), 126–138.

―――, "Texas Minerals," *Texas Almanac for 1873* (Galveston, 1872), 111–114.

Sellards, E. H., and Glen L. Haynes, "An Index to Texas' Mineral Resources: Descriptive List of Texas Minerals," *Texas Looks Ahead* (Austin, The University of Texas, 1944), 91–117.

Simonds, Frederic W., "A Record of the Geology of Texas for the Decade Ending December 31, 1896," *Transactions of the Texas Academy of Science*, III (1900), 19–285.

Thoborn, Joseph B., "The Tropical and Subtropical Origin of Mound-Builder Cultures," *Chronicles of Oklahoma*, XVI (1918), 97–117.

Thompson, Theronne, "Fort Buffalo Springs, Texas Frontier Post," *West Texas Historical Association Year Book*, XXXVI (1960), 156–175.

Young, Keith, "The Roessler Maps," *Texas Journal of Science*, XVII (1965), 28–45.

Newspapers

Austin (Texas) *Daily Republican*, March 21, 1870.
Austin (Texas) *Tri-Weekly State Gazette*, May 27, 1872.
Dallas (Texas) *Herald*, May 4, June 1, June 8, July 6, August 3, 1872.
Galveston (Texas) *Daily Civilian*, June 12, 1872.
Norfolk (Virginia) *Landmark*, April 18, 1876.
Sherman (Texas) *Democrat* (Centennial Edition), September 19, 1948.

LIFE OF KELLOGG

Manuscripts

Callery, Joseph S. "A Short Biography of Miner Kilbourne Kellogg" (194—?). Photostatic copy of typescript from Frick Art Reference Library, New York City.

Jackson, Andrew. Papers of Andrew Jackson, 1st Series, Vol. 104 (1840). Microfilm (Reel 53) of originals in the Library of Congress.

Kellogg, Miner K. Miner K. Kellogg Papers. Chiefly letters addressed to Kellogg. Xerox copy of the originals in the Archives of American Art, Detroit, Michigan.

———. Notes and Memoranda. Approximately 159 pages, of which 67 are numbered consecutively and others are unnumbered; labelled "Notes for an Autobiography" (1886), "Notes for Autobiography" (1887), "Mems," "Powers," "Fish and Fox," etc. Xerox copy of the originals in the Indiana Historical Society Library, Indianapolis.

Kellogg, Sheldon Ingalls. "A Narrative of the Life of Sheldon Ingalls Kellogg." Typescript furnished by Mrs. John Whitney Blemer, Diablo, California.

Layard, Austen Henry. Layard Papers. Manuscript Division, British Museum.

Poinsett, Joel R. Joel R. Poinsett Papers. Henry D. Gilpin Collection, The Historical Society of Pennsylvania, Philadelphia.

Books

Appleton's Cyclopaedia of American Biography, VI (New York, D. Appleton and Company, 1889).

Bassett, John Spencer (ed.). *Correspondence of Andrew Jackson.* Washington, Carnegie Institution of Washington, VI (1933).

Benjamin, S. G. W. *Persia and the Persians.* Boston, Ticknor and Company, 1887.

Brown, T. Allston. *History of the American Stage.* New York, Dick and Fitzgerald, 1870.

Cist, Charles. *Cincinnati in 1841: Its Early Annals and Future Prospects.* Cincinnati, printed and published for the author, 1841.

Cist, Charles (comp.). *The Cincinnati Miscellany; or, Antiquities of the West and Pioneer History and General and Local Statistics.* Compiled from the *Western General Advertiser* from October 1st, 1844, to April 1st... [1846]. By Charles Cist. 2 vols. Cincinnati, C. Clark Printer, 1845–1846.

Dictionary of American Biography. Edited by Dumas Malone. Published under the Auspices of American Council of Learned Societies. New York, Charles Scribner's Sons, 1943.

Dictionary of National Biography. London, Smith, Elder & Co., 1900. Vol. 61.

Enciclopedia Universal Ilustrada. Barcelona, Espasa-Calpe, S. A., 1923. Vols. 50 and 51.

Encyclopedia Americana. New York, Encyclopedia Americana Corporation, 1940. Vols. 27 and 28.

Ford, Henry A., and Mrs. Kate B. Ford (comps.). *History of Cincinnati, with Illustrations and Biographical Sketches.* Cleveland, L. A. Williams & Co., publishers (from Printing House of W. W. Williams), 1881.

Graves, Algernon. *The Royal Academy of Arts. A Complete Dictionary of Contributors and Their Work from Its Foundation in 1769 to 1904* ... London, Henry Graves & Co. Ltd. 1906. Vol. IV.

Groce, George C., and David H. Wallace (eds.). *The New-York Historical Society's Dictionary of Artists in America, 1564–1860.* New Haven, Yale University Press, 1957.

Hawthorne, Nathaniel. *Passages from the French and Italian Notebooks (The Complete Works of Nathaniel Hawthorne, X).* Boston, Houghton Mifflin and Company, 1883.

History of Cincinnati and Hamilton County, Ohio; Their Past and Present, Including ... Statistics; Biographies and Portraits of Pioneers and Representative Citizens, etc.... 2 vols. Cincinnati, S. B. Nelson & co., 1894.

Hopkins, Timothy. *The Kelloggs in the Old World and the New.* 3 vols. San Francisco, Sunset Press and Photo Engraving Co., 1903.

Kellogg, Miner Kilbourne. *Documents relating to A Picture by Leonardo da Vinci, entitled "Herodias," (from the Mariahalden Gallery).* London, W. Allen and Co., Printers, 4 Brydges Street, Covent Garden, 1864.

———. *Fine Arts in the United States: A Paper Read before the American Union Academy of Literature, Science, and Art, at Washington, D.C., December 27th, 1869.* Washington, J. L. Pearson, Printer, 1870.

———. *Justice to Hiram Powers. Addressed to the Citizens of New Orleans.* Cincinnati, 1848.

———. *Mr. Miner K. Kellogg to His Friends.* Paris, Simon Racon and Co., 1858.

———. *Observations on the History and Qualities of a Painting Entitled "Herodias," by Leonardo da Vinci* ... New York, C. H. Clayton & Co., Printers, 1879.

———. *Researches into the History of a Painting by Raphael of Urbino, Entitled "La Belle Jardinière," ("Première Idée du Peintre")*. London W. Phillips, Printer, 1860.

Kitto, John. *Scripture Lands; Described in a Series of Historical, Geographical, and Topographical Sketches.* ... London, Henry G. Bohn, 1850.

Minnigerode, Meade. *The Fabulous Forties, 1840–1850. A Presentation of Private Life*. Garden City, Garden City Publishing Co., 1924.

New York National Academy of Design Exhibition Record, 1826–1860. 2 vols. New York, Printed for the New York Historical Society, 1943.

Polk, James K. *The Diary of James K. Polk during His Presidency, 1845 to 1849*. Now first printed from the original manuscript in the Collections of the Chicago Historical Society. Edited and annotated by Milo Milton Quaife. With an introduction by Andrew Cunningham McLaughlin. 5 vols. Chicago, A. C. McClurg & Co., 1910.

Rutledge, Anna Wells (comp. and ed.). *Cumulative Record of Exhibition Catalogues. The Pennsylvania Academy of Fine Arts, 1807–1870. The Society of Artists, 1800–1814. The Artist's Fund Society, 1835–1845*. Philadelphia, The American Philosophical Society, 1955.

Scudder, Horace E., and Marie Hansen-Taylor (eds.). *Life and Letters of Bayard Taylor*. 2 v. Boston, Houghton Mifflin and Company, 1885.

Taylor, Bayard. *Views A-Foot; or Europe Seen with Knapsack and Staff*. 24th rev. ed. New York, G. P. Putnam, 1860.

Thorp, Margaret Farrand. *The Literary Sculptors*. Durham, North Carolina, Duke University Press, 1965.

Tuckerman, Henry. *American Artist Life*. New York, Putnam's, 1867.

Waterfield, Gordon. *Layard of Nineveh*. London, John Murray, 1963.

Willard, Frances E., and Mary A. Livermore (eds.). *A Woman of the Century. Fourteen Hundred-Seventy Biographical Sketches Accompanied by Portraits of Leading American Women in All Walks of Life* ... Buffalo, Chicago, New York, Charles Wells Moulton, 1893.

Wilson, William E. *The Angel and the Serpent*. Bloomington, Indiana University Press, 1964.

Wolff, Joseph. *Narrative of a Mission to Bokhara, in the Years 1843–1845, to Ascertain the Fate of Colonel Stoddart and Captain Conolly*. New York, Harper & Brothers, 1845.

Articles

Boyle, Richard J., "Miner Kilbourne Kellogg," *The Cincinnati Art Museum Bulletin*, VIII (1966), 17–23.

Dwight, Edward H., "Art in Early Cincinnati," *The Cincinnati Art Museum Bulletin* (August, 1953), 4–10.

Kellogg, Miner Kilbourne, "The Geography of Mount Sinai," *Annual Report of the American Geographical Society of New York for the Years 1870–71*. Albany, The Argus Company, 1872.

———, "The Position of Mount Sinai Examined," *The Literary World*, II (February 19, 1848), 44–46.

[Macdonald, Donald], "The Diaries of Donald Macdonald, 1824–1826," *Indiana Historical Society Publication*, XIV, No. 2 (1942).

"Miner K. Kellogg," *Magazine of Western History*, IV (June, 1886), 165–166.

Powers, Hiram, "Letters of Hiram Powers to Nicholas Longworth, Esq., 1856–1858," *The Quarterly Publication of the Historical and Philosophical Society of Ohio*, I (April–June, 1906), 33–59.

Richardson, E. P., "Miner K. Kellogg," *Art Quarterly* (Spring, 1960), 271–274.

Newspapers

Toledo (Ohio) *Daily Blade*, February 19, 1889; May 25, 1937.

INDEX

Abdul Madjid (Sultan of Turkey): 37
Academy of Natural Sciences: 13
Ackworth, A. B.: 36
Alden, Lieutenant: 32
Alexander, ———: 111, 112, 156
Alexander, Dr.: 147
Alexander, J. M.: 158 and n.; 163
Alexander, William: 17 n., 18 n.
American Geographical Society: 52
Archer County: copper in, 10, 13; description of, 12; mentioned, 4, 11, 115
Archives of American Art: 21
Armstrong, Major Robert: 33
Arusmont, William Piquepal d': 25
Ashburton, Lord (William Bingham Baring, 1799-1864): 47, 49
Atchison, ———: 122
Atoka, Indian Territory: 159
Augur, General Christopher Columbus: and request for military escort, 89 and n., 94; mentioned, 92, 96, 115

Baer, Baron de: Belgian minister, 38
Baird, William Miller: commissary, 6; mentioned 129 and n., 140 /
Baker, Miss Octavia: marriage of, 9
Baldwin, Judge: U.S. attorney, 92
Ball, Thomas: attorney, 95
Baltimore and Cuba Smelting and Mining Company: 11
Barnum, ———: 91
Baxter, J. N.: 150
Bayley, J.: 49
Baylor, John R.: 152

Baylor Peak: 147
Beal's Station (Veal Station?): 154 and n.
bear (pet): 93, 100, 111
Beard, W. M. SEE Baird, William Miller
Belknap road: 117
Belzoni, Giovanni: 36
Bevan, C. N.: 50
Big Tree (Indian chief): 150 and n.
Bliss, Dr.: 32
Boon, E.: surveyor, 18, 102 n.
Bowman, Jesse: 150
Boyle, Richard J.: article of, on Kellogg, 22
Brazos ferry: 122
bridges: building of, 117, 120
Brown, ——— (commissary): injured, 97; leaves Expedition, 122; mentioned, 112
Brown, Dr.: 86, 116, 118, 137, 142
Brown, George L.: artist, 40
Brown, Henry Kirke: artist, 40
Brushy Mountain: 84, 89
Bryant, William Cullen: 45
Buckley, S. B.: geologist, 10; report of, on minerals, 11; and quarrel with Roessler, 12
Buell, General George P.: 89 and n., 90-97 *passim*, 115, 153
Buell, Mrs. George P.: 89; gifts from, 90-97 *passim*, 106
buffalo: 116, 123, 132, 135, 144, 146
Buffalo Head plateau: 73
Buffalo Springs: 117 and n.

Bullion, M. D.: on copper ore, 11, 12; surveyor and scout, 92 and n. mentioned, 95, 97
Butterfield Ranch: 151

cactus: 115, 128, 145, 148
Caddo Mounds: 70
Callery, Joseph S.: 21
camels: 36, 53
Camp "Departure": 65
camp meeting: 155
Campo (Tonkawa chief): 124, 125, and n.
Canning, Sir Stratford: British ambassador, 37; on Andrew Jackson, 38; gift of, to Kellogg, 40
Canning, Lady Stratford: 39, 48
Carr, Dabney Smith: U.S. minister to Turkey, 36, 37, 39
Carriage Point: 74, 158
Carter, R. G.: 91 n.
Cartwright, ———: British consul general, 37
Cary, Samuel Fenton: 161 and n.
Catlin, McCarty & Co.: 15
cattle herds: 79
Cazenovia, New York: 22
Central Railroad: 153 n.
Chandler, L. H.: business manager of Expedition, 6; Kellogg's evaluation of, 128; differences with McCarty, 138; mentioned, 53–161 *passim*
Charleston, Indiana: 26
Charley (Negro teamster): 81
Chetopa, Kansas: 59
chiggers: 64, 76, 87
Choctaw Indians: 66
Cincinnati, Ohio: Kellogg home in, 23–24, 27–29, 32, 33, 45
Cincinnati Art Museum: display of Kellogg works in, 22
Cincinnati Female Academy: 28
Cincinnati Western Museum: 35
"Circassian" (Kellogg painting): 41, 46
Clarke, Conrad B.: 48
Claude (artist): 50, 162 and n.
Clay County: 17
Cleveland, Ohio: Kellogg residence in, 54–56
Cleveland Art Museum: Kellogg-owned paintings in, 54
climate of Texas: 96, 161

Clune, ———: 127
coal: 120 and n.
Colbert, Benjamin F.: 157 n.
Colbert, Mrs. B. F.: 158
Colbert Ferry: 157 and n.
Collyer, Dr.: 44
Colt, Christopher: 45
Colt, Samuel: 45
Comanche Indians: 150
Connelly, James H.: 53
Cooke County: 17
Cooley, Pleasant: 84, 86, 87
Cooper, James Fenimore: 45
Coote, Sir Charles: 41
copper: 3–5, 9, 18, 122, 131, 138 n., 147; samples of missing, 11
Copper Valley: 145
Cowan, ———: 75; guide, 92, 122
Cox, J. D.: 60 n.
Cross Timbers: description of, 81; mentioned, 82, 88, 150
Crenneville, Victor de: joins Expedition, 91 and n.; supposed to write of tour, 140; mentioned, 99–135 *passim*
Crooks, William: 102 and n.
Croton Creek area: recommended for mineral location, 143
Culberson, D. B.: legislator and company director, 10
Cummins, William Fletcher: 129 n.
Cunber, ———: 132

Davis, ———: left as invalid, 78
Davis, Edmund J.: governor of Texas, 16, 17
Decatur, Texas: 154
Decatur House: 154
Delafield, Dr. Edward: 53
Delafield, Richard: 30, 53
Dennis, ———: 104, 132
Denton, Texas: 155
Denton Hotel: 155
Denton Monitor: 155
DeRyee, William: state chemist, 10; geological report of, 11; mentioned, 12, 129 n.
divorce case: 76 and n.
Donelson, Andrew Jackson: 32, 33
Double Mountains: objective of Expedition, 94, 118; description of, 152; mentioned, 18, 116, 133
Double Mountain Expedition: 144

INDEX

Dugan, David: 156 n.
Dugan's: 156, 157
Duggen's. SEE Dugan's
Durand, Ashur Brown: 34

Eckstein, Frederick: 28
Edwards, ———: state constable, 148: mentioned, 128, 130, 132
Elliott, J. S.: 150
Elliott, Sam: 150
Elopement: novel by Celia Logan Kellogg: 49, 50
Evans, ———: Kellogg writes to, 124, 125, 126
Evans, Lemuel D.: judge, 17
Expedition of Texas Land and Copper Association: accounts of, 7: disbandment of, 7, 147, 153; publicity on, 60, 61 n., 76 n., 78; diversions on, 90; intemperance on, 112-113, 126, 143; personnel of, 113

Fairfax, L.: pseudonym for Celia Logan Kellogg, 49
Ferûkh Khan: 46
fine arts in the U.S.: 35, 52, 55
First and Last Chance Store: 74, 157
Fish and Fox: female mediums, 45
Flat Top Mountain: 132, 133
flowers: Kellogg's enumeration of, 20, 64, 72, 79, 80, 88, 104, 115, 119, 123, 130, 132, 147, 155, 158
Foley, J. W.: member of 4th Cavalry, 126; hospitality of, 127, 128; mentioned, 148
Folsom, ———: toll-taker, 158
food: on Expedition, 66-155 *passim;* prices of, 78
Forney, J. W.: publicity man, 13
Fort Belknap: 6, 10, 11, 118 n., 121 and n., 122
Fort Griffin: camp near, 123; Expedition returns to, 147; mentioned, 6, 17, 112 and n., 121 n.
Fort Griffin and Fort Sill Trail: 116
Fort Leavenworth: 62
Fort Richardson: 5, 17, 65, 86, 88 and n., 97-98, 151
Fort Scott: 59
Fort Sill: 61, 62, 85 and n.

fossils: 128
Fourth of July celebration: 93
Franks, Frederick: 29
Freeman, James Edward: 31

Gant, A. B.: 18, 61 n.
General Land Office of Texas: 16, 19
Geological Bureau of Texas: 16
geology: 15, 83, 88
Gifford, Sanford R.: 50
Glenn, John W.: state geologist, 16
Gould, ———: 43
Graham, E. S.: 18 and n., 60 n.
Graham, G. A.: 14 n., 18 n., 60 n.
Graham Salt Works: 18
Graham, ———: servant, 118; courier, 141
Grand Belt Copper Company of Texas: 4
Grant, Captain John: 41
Grant, U.S.: 18, 75
Grayson County: 17
"Greek Girl" (picture by Kellogg): 46
"Greek Slave": statue by Powers, 40; Kellogg display of, 41-42; popularity of, 44
Greeley, Horace: 104 n., 161
"Green fly" Prairie: 67
Greenough, Horace (artist): 40
Griswold, Rufus Wilmot: 45

Hall, ———: herder, 119; driver, 128
Harper, ———: editor, 60
Harris, Dr.: 71
Harrison, ———: teacher, 24
Harrison, William Henry: 33
Haskell County: 138 n.
Hawthorne, Nathaniel: opinion of, of Powers, 43-44
Hayman, Colonel (Samuel Brown?): 125 and n.
Head of Elm, Texas: 81 and n., 150
Hemphill, Tom: teamster, 103, 129, 146
"Herodias" (painting): owned by Kellogg, 50, 54; pamphlet on, 51, 54
Hicks, W. H.: sutler at Fort Griffin, 127, 147
Hill, Captain Wash: 152, 153 and n.
Hill, Lena: 63
Hitchcock, Edward: 8
Hodges, ———: of Southern Pacific survey party, 147

Holden, L. E.: and contract with Kellogg, 54, 55
Holy Land: Kellogg's experiences in, 36
hotels: 59, 60, 74, 95, 97, 153, 154, 155, 159
Houston, Sam: 75
howitzer: 7, 63, 76, 93, 127
Hoxie, Vinnie Ream: friendship of, with Kellogg, 52; mentioned, 61 and n.
Hull, Isaac: commodore, U.S. Navy, 34 and n.
Humphrey, Ballard S.: captain, 75 and n.; mentioned, 112, 143, 146, 153, 155
Hunt, Anderson, and Company: 15
Hurdus, Adam: Swedenborgian, 27; painted by Kellogg, 29

Indian legend: 113
Indian mounds: 72, 73
Indian policy of government: opinions on, 86, 97, 109, 116, 127
Indian problem: settlement of, necessary, 17
Indian rubber tree: 128
Indian Territory: description of, 67; inhabitants of, 71; future of, 160
Indians: fears about, 17, 142, 144; reports about, 80, 82, 85, 132
iron: 119, 122, 150
Ives, Chauncey B.: 40
Ives Hotel: 59

Jack County: 17
Jacksboro: surveying district, 17; description of, 88, 151; mentioned, 6
Jackson, Andrew: painted by Kellogg, 32, 33
Jackson, Captain: 89
Jay Cook & Co.: 14
Jennings, ———: 24
Jewett, William: 30
Jim: Negro cook, shot at Jacksboro, 149
Jim: white cook, dead at Fort Griffin, 149
John: cook, 130, 147, 148
Johnson, Brit: 149, 150 n.
Johnson, Francis White: recommends Loew and Roessler, 17; Kellogg's opinion of, 100, 101; commander in Chandler's absence, 137; mentioned, 18 n., 75, 76, 90, 94, 104, 141, 144, 145, 163

Kansas: 161
Keen, General: 27
Kellogg, Almira Kilbourne Harris, (mother of Miner Kilbourne Kellogg): marriage of, 22; death of, 23; mentioned, 27
Kellogg, Almira Sophia (sister of M. K. Kellogg): 22, 27
Kellogg, Celia Logan (wife of M. K. Kellogg): family of, 47–48; early career of, 48; marriage of, to Clarke, 48; journalist, 49; novel by, 49–50; separation of, from Kellogg, 51; marriage of, to James Connelly, 53
Kellogg, Charles Fraser (father of M. K. Kellogg): early life of, 22–23; marriages of, 22, 23, 27; joins Robert Owen, 24; and family at New Harmony, 24–27; death, 51
Kellogg, Charles Henry (brother of M. K. Kellogg): birth of, 22
Kellogg, Eliza Smith Downes, (stepmother of M. K. Kellogg): 27
Kellogg, Elizabeth Gazley (stepmother of M. K. Kellogg): 23, 27
Kellogg, Leonard (uncle of M. K. Kellogg): publisher, 22
Kellogg, Lovell Horace (half-brother of M. K. Kellogg): 53
Kellogg, Miner Kilbourne, autobiographical materials of, 21; birth, 21; biographical articles on 21, 22; family and early years of, 22–23; interest in music of, 25, 28, 29, 30; experiences of, at New Harmony, 27; memories of, of father, 27–28; at Vevay, Ohio, 27, 28; early artistic efforts of, 28–29; as artist on the Eastern seaboard, 29–30; at West Point, 31–32; as courier for State Department, 34; in Italy, 34–36, 39, 42, 46–49; in Egypt, 36; in the Holy Land, 36; in Constantinople, 36–37; and Layard, 38; in North Africa, 39; displays "Greek Slave" in America, 40, 44, 45; and quarrel with Hiram Powers, 40–41, 42–43, 46; transfer of, to Paris, 46; as art collector, 47, 49; marriage and move of, to London, 47–48; with family in Italy, 50; and return to America and domestic tragedy, 51; lecture of, on fine arts in America,

INDEX

52; paper of, for American Geographical Society, 52; life of, in Cleveland, Ohio, 54–55, 56; agreement of, with L. E. Holden, 54; death of, 56; as official artist for Texas Land and Copper Association, 59–163; mentioned, 5, 6, 8
—pamphlets by: *Justice to Hiram Powers. Addressed to the Citizens of New Orleans,* 41; *Mr. Miner K. Kellogg to His Friends,* 41, 43; *Researches into the History of a Painting by Raphael of Urbino, Entitled "La Belle Jardinière,"* *("Première Idée du Peintre")*, 48; *Documents relating to A Picture by Leonardo da Vinci, entitled "Herodias," (From the Mariahalden Gallery),* 51; *Fine Arts in the United States,* 52; *Observations on the History and Qualities of a Painting Entitled "Herodias",* 54
—portraits by: Robert Owen, 25; Robert Dale Owen, 26 n.; Adam Hurdus, 29; Phineas Kellogg, 29; George Washington, 30; Robert Swartwout, 30; Robert W. Weir, 31; Andrew Jackson, 33; James K. Polk and Mrs. Polk, 33, 45; Martin Van Buren, 33; Joel R. Poinsett, 33; Riza Pasha, 37; Canning daughters, 37; Roger B. Taney, 45; William Jenkins Worth, 45; Winfield Scott, 45; Ferûkh Khan, 46; Sheldon Kellogg, Jr., 49; John Surratt, 52
—as member of the Texas Land and Copper Company Expedition: as revealed in diary, 20; descriptive powers of, 20; comments on being ill, 50, 62, 66, 76, 85, 87, 94, 97, 105, 115, 136, 139, 147; as photographer, 62, 63, 74; criticizes management of Expedition, 63, 64, 66, 77, 78, 84, 90, 91, 94, 95, 105, 106, 108, 109–111, 136; on breakup of the expedition, 101, 102; loses sketchbook, 105, 157. SEE ALSO Indian policy, opinions
—on sketches by, on Expedition: at South Canadian camp ground, 63; Log cabin of stage stand, 64; Head of Elm, 81; panorama from Brushy Mountain, 89; view south toward Jacksboro, 106; headwaters of Little Wichita, 117; Fort Griffin, 126; Foley's cabin, 127; valley of the Clear Fork, 130; Double Mountain, 134; Double Mountain by sunrise, 142; remains of Fort Belknap; 149; sunflowers and thistles, 150; Butterfield Ranch, 151

Kellogg, Phineas (grandfather of M. K. Kellogg): 23

Kellogg, Phineas, Jr. (uncle of M. K. Kellogg): 23, 29

Kellogg, Sheldon Ingalls (brother of M. K. Kellogg): birth of, 22; description of, of New Harmony, 25–26; tours Europe, 49; as custodian of the journals, 92, 127; mentioned, 27, 53, 64, 78, 90, 95, 98, 124, 126

Kellogg, Sheldon Ingalls, Jr. (nephew of M. K. Kellogg): 49

Kellogg, Virginia Somers (daughter of M. K. Kellogg): birth and christening of, 48, 49; marriages of, 56 and n.; mentioned, 50, 51, 52, 53; death of, 21, 56 n; Kellogg's concern for, expressed during Expedition, 64, 78, 97, 123, 124, 126, 127, 152

Kellogg, Warren Converse (infant brother of M. K. Kellogg): 23

Kellogg's Creek: 145

Kentuckytown, Texas: 156

King, Edward: 4

King, Edwin: 46

King's Ranch: stage station of, 153

Kiowa Peak: 5, 6, 18, 133–140 *passim*

Kirkland, Mrs. Caroline Matilda: 44

Kirkup, Seymour (artist): 33

Kitto, John: quotes Kellogg, 36 n.

Koerper, Dr. Egon Anthony: at Fort Griffin, 130

"La Belle Jardinière" (painting): owned by Kellogg, 47

Lane, Elder: 29, 30

Lane Theological Seminary: 30

Lawrence, ———: 24

Layard, Austen Henry: friendship of, with Kellogg, 38; on Persian women, 39; and search for Nineveh, 39; illness of, 39; sketches history of Nineveh, 45; elected to New York Ethnological Society, 44; mentioned, 48

Leavenworth, General Henry (?): 31

Lee, Philip Ludwell: 61 and n.

Le Flore, Charles: 73 and n.

Lesueur, Charles-Alexander: 25
Limestone Gap: 67, 68, 159
Limestone Ridge: 159
Lincoln, Abraham: 52
Locke, David Ross (Petroleum V. Nasby): 56
Locke, Edmund: 21, 56
Loew, Oscar: application of, for post as state chemist, 16; chemist, 62 and n.; and snakes, 103, 115; and skunks, 111, 135; mentioned, 6, 7, 8, 17, 64, 70–90 *passim,* 101, 113, 122, 128, 146
Logan, Celia. SEE Kellogg, Celia Logan
Logan, Cornelius A.: 47, 48
Logan, Cornelius Ambrose, Jr.: 47
Logan, Eliza Ackley (Mrs. Cornelius A.): 48
Logan, Olive: 47, 48
Longworth, Nicholas: patron of Hiram Powers, 35, 43
Louvre: Kellogg's research in, 46
Lusk, ———: 96, 107
Lyon, H. C.: 10

Macdonald, Donald: of New Harmony, 24
Mackenzie, Ranald S.: scouting for Indians, 17, 65, 89, 97, 115, 116, 122, 144 and n.
Maddox, ———: 84
Mahan, Dennis Hart: 31
"Maltese" (Kellogg painting): 46
Manlius Square, New York: 22
Marcy, Randolph B.: explorer of North Texas, 8, 17
Marlett, Charley: 85 and n.
Mason, John Young: 46
McAlester Station, Indian Territory: 66
McCarty, W. C.: commander of Expedition, 14; McConnell's opinion of, 6; pamphlet of, quoted, 15; on Expedition, 61–147 *passim*
McClure, William: 25
McConnell, H. H.: account of, of exploring expedition, 5–7; on Expedition, 121 n., 144, 148; mentioned, 8
McConnell, Mrs. H. H.: 97 n.
McMillan, ———: 132, 141, 143
Metropolitan Museum of Art: Kellogg paintings on loan to, 54
Mexican lions: 100

military bands: 98 and n., 99, 124
Miller, Charlie: 130
minerals: 15, 82, 120, 153
mirage: 133
Missouri, Kansas, and Texas Railroad: 59, 61, 65, 69, 153, 157, 159
"Missouri Bill": 83
Missouri Pacific Railroad: 59
Mizeler, Major (John K. Mizner?): 108, 109
Montague, Texas: 82, 150
Montague County: 17
mosquitoes: 64, 96, 100, 102, 109, 111, 114, 136
Mount Sinai: Kellogg's writings on, 36 n., 45, 52
Mount Vernon, Indian Territory: 74
Mullins, John: 150

National Academy of Design: shows Kellogg paintings, 40, 45, 46
Nessler, Frederic: 49
New Boggy, Indian Territory: 159
New Harmony, Indiana: Robert Owen project, 24; Kellogg's memories of, 24–25; as seen by Sheldon Kellogg, 26–27
New Jersey: Kellogg's experiences in, 30
New Jerusalem Society: Kellogg as member of, 32, 49
Newman, ———: of Expedition, 112, 114, 142
New York Ethnological Society: 44
Nichols' Hotel: 149
Niles, Juliet: letter to, cited, 9
Nineveh: Layard report on, 39

Obeonesser, Balthazar: 25
Oswego, New York: 22
Overland Transportation Company: 66
Owen, Robert: plans of, for New Harmony, 24, 25; and loan to Kelloggs, 27
Owen, Robert Dale: portrait of, by Kellogg, 26 n.

Parsons, Judge: 76 and n.
Patten, D. W.: guide, 88 n., 103, 152, 153, 163
Peale, Rembrandt: 29
Pease, Mrs. E. M.: letters of, cited, 9
Pendleton, E.: 10

INDEX 181

Pennsylvania Academy of Fine Arts: 34, 46
percussion-cap factory: 10
Perponcher, Count: 38, 39
Perryville, Indian Territory: 66, 67
Peters, Richard (?): assistant manager of Expedition, 61; Kellogg's opinion of, 98, 100, 107; mentioned, 65–151 *passim*
Peters' Colony: 18
Peveler, David: 149 n.
Peveler (Peverel) Ranch: 149
Pilot Point, Texas: 155, 156
Plummer, Satterlee Clark: surveyor, 17, 18, mentioned, 6, 64 and n., 95, 113, 128, 142, 144, 148
Poinsett, Joel R.: Secretary of War, 30; commissions portrait, 33; letter of, to Kellogg, 35; mentioned, 31, 32, 52
Polk, James Knox: Kellogg portrait of, 33, 45
Polk, Mrs. James Knox: poses for Kellogg, 45
Pope, John: engineer, 120 n.
Pope's Wells: 115
Porter, Admiral: 14
Potato Hills: 151
Powers, Hiram: bust by, of Kellogg, 28; youth and training of, 34; advice of, to Layard, 39; and dispute with Kellogg, 42–43, 46; on the Kellogg pamphlet, 43; as seen by Hawthorne, 43–44; mentioned, 35, 40
prairie dogs: 131, 132, 133, 134, 140
prairie fire: 122–123, 158, 160
Preble (sloop): 34
Pruet, ———: 132

Quinby, Ira: quartermaster, 128 and n.; mentioned, 129, 130, 147

railroad construction: interest in, 13
rangers: 76, 90
Rapp, (Johann) George: 26
Rappites: 24
Ream, Anna Guy (Mrs. Robert): 61 and n., 62, 63
Ream, Lavinia McDonald (Mrs. Robert Lee): 61
Ream, Robert: 61 and n., 65
Ream, Vinnie. SEE Hoxie, Vinnie Ream

Red River: copper reported on, 8; reached by Expedition, 74, 156
Reschid Pasha (Mustafá Mehemed): grand vizier of Turkey, 37–38
Richard, E. P.: article by, on Kellogg, 21, 22
Riggs, George W.: 46
rival surveyors and expeditions: 18, 64–65, 82, 83, 90, 96, 102
Riza Pasha (Riza Hasan Baja): portrait of, by Kellogg, 37, 40
Robb, James A.: 41, 42, 46
Robbins, Samuel Marshall: engineer, 6, 93 and n., 95, 104, 113, 114, 144
Rock Bluff Ferry: 158
Rockyford: 159
Roessler, Anton R.: birth and education of, 9; marriage of, 9; report of, on Texas ordnance, 9–10; on Texas minerals, 12–13, 139; quarrels with Buckley, 12; recommended for state geologist, 17; invites Gant to join Expedition, 61 n.; as participant of Expedition, 75–84 *passim*, 107, 109, 119, 141, 142, 148, 149; injured and ill on Expedition, 100, 104, 111, 112, 114, 118, 129; Kellogg's opinion of, 129, 131; mentioned, 6, 7, 8, 11, 18
Roessler, Mrs. Octavia (Baker): marriage of, 9
Royal Academy of Arts: 46
Russell, Samuel H.: 54

Salt Creek: scene of Indian massacre, 150
Saranac (ship): 39
Satanta (Indian chief): 150 and n.
Say, Thomas: zoologist, 25 and n.
Schell City, Missouri: 59
Scott, Tom: 13, 14
Scott, Winfield: 45
Secor, ———: 118, 121
Sedalia, Missouri: 59
Shannon, William R.: 10
Sherman, Texas: 63, 75
Shields, Captain: 141, 142, 143, 146, 147
Shoemaker, A. H.: 154 and n.
Shumard, Benjamin Franklin: 9
Shumard, George Getz: 9
Simonds, Frederic W.: 4
Smith (Indian guide): 143
snakes: 103, 114, 115, 119, 128, 146

Snyder, Walter H.: 56 n.
soil: 103, 130, 151
Somers, Lady Virginia Pattle: 48, 49
Somers, Charles (Viscount Eastnor): 48
Song, N. S.: 150
Southard, Samuel Lewis: U.S. senator, 30
Southern Hotel, St. Louis: 59
Spence, Carrol: 46
stampede: 62, 67
Staughton, Dr. James M.: 29
Sternau, Count Bentzel: 49
Steubenville, Ohio: 162
St. Louis, Missouri: 14, 59, 159, 161
storms: experienced during expedition, 60–64 *passim*, 79, 89–100 *passim*, 104, 105, 128, 129, 131, 149, 151
Stringtown, Indian Territory: 68, 69
Succhi Mountain: 62
Sugarloaf Hill: 114
Surratt, John: 52
surveyors: appointed and resident, 94
Suydam, Henry: 52
Suydam, James Augustus: 46
Suydam, Peter M.: 35, 52, 53, 124 and n., 125, 126, 162
Swartwout, Robert: 30
Swenson, S. M.: 11
Swing family: 27
Swisher, James Monroe: 18 n., 79 and n., 94, 95
Switcher. SEE Swisher, James Monroe

Taney, Roger B.: 45
Tasso, Joseph: 28
Taylor, ———: Kellogg letter to, 49
Taylor, Bayard: on Kellogg, 40; mentioned, 44
Taylor, David Brown: 125 and n.
Taylor, M. D. K.: legislator, 10
10th Cavalry: 60 and n., 61 n.
Texans: regret annexation, 122
Texas: conditions of, in 1871, 15–16
Texas and Pacific Railway: 13, 156
Texas and Southwestern Land and Immigration Company: 16
Texas Bureau of Immigration: 3, 4
Texas Central Railroad: 13
Texas Copper Mining and Manufacturing Company: 10, 11, 130 n.
Texas Emigration and Land Company: 18
Texas Emigration Company: 102 n.

Texas Geological Survey: 9, 10, 11, 16; maps of, missing, 12
Texas Immigration Company: 16
Texas Land and Copper Association: described by McConnell, 5–7; objectives of Expedition of, 14; area traversed by Expedition of, 17; Kellogg's opinion of, 138, 139; mentioned, 13, 18, 53. SEE ALSO Expedition of Texas Land and Copper Association
Texas Land and Immigration Company: 16
Texas Road: 69 and n.
Texas State Troops: 10
Thompson, Henry: 97 n.
Thompson, "Mammy": 31
Thompson Hotel: 97, 153
Throckmorton, James Webb: 10, 11
Throop, Enos Thompson: 34
Tonkawa Indians: guides, 6, 10, 128; mentioned, 123, 127, 130
Tonkawa war dance: 136
Trollope, Frances Milton: 28, 29
Troutman, A. C.: photographer, 6, 8; on Expedition, 89–146 *passim*
Troy, New York: 22
Tuckerman, Henry T.: evaluation of, of Kellogg, 51, 52; mentioned, 45
tumblebugs: 101
Tuthill, Abraham G. D.: 29

United States General Land Office: 11, 12
United States Military Academy. SEE West Point

Van Buren, Martin: befriends Kellogg, 30; orders portrait, 33
Vandalia, Illinois: 161
Vanderlyn, John: 29
Veal Station: 154 n.
Vernet, Horace: 47
Vevay, Ohio: 27, 28
Vevay, Switzerland: 50
Victoria Peak: 83 and n., 84
Vorhees, Captain: of U.S. Navy, 34

Waldo, Samuel L.: 30
Wall, Garret Dorset: U.S. senator, 30
Walters, ———: of Expedition, 93, 100, 111, 131
Ward, Lord: 41

INDEX

Ward, Charles Richard: 62 and n.
Washington, George: 30
Washington, D. C.: Kellogg residence in, 51, 52; mentioned, 14, 30, 33, 162
Washington and Texas Land and Copper Company. SEE Texas Land and Copper Association
Waugh, Samuel B.: 34
Weatherford, Texas: 113
Webb, William W.: of U.S. Army, 93, 98 and n., 109
Webster, Mason: expedition of, 18, 114, 117, 122, 123, 132, 152; land agent, 102 and n.
Wegefarth, Major C.: 13
Wegefarth County: 14 n.
Wegefarth Expedition: 18
Weir, Robert Walter: 31, 32
Wenckebach, Enno F.: on Expedition, 6, 68 and n., 69, 95, 96, 114, 137
West Point: Kellogg's life at, 31–32; mentioned, 52, 53, 148
White, C. K.: wagon master, 65, 95, 97, 112, 132, 143, 147
White, George: driver, 95
White Ridge: 156
Whitesboro, Texas: 79
Wichita area: copper in, 5, 13; sketched by Kellogg, 117; not visited, 151 n.; mentioned, 4
Wichita Colonization, Agricultural, Mining, and Manufacturing Company: 13 and n.
Wilke, Sir David: 37
Williams, James: 150
Williams, L. W.: mayor of Sherman, 76
Williams, Milo G.: 24
Williams, Mrs.: landlady, 162
Willis, Nat P.: 45
Wilson, Joseph S.: commissioner of U.S. Land Office, 11, 12
Winchebach, Winchebaugh, Winklepaugh. SEE Wenckebach, Enno F.
Windus, ———: scout, 140
Wisewell, Dr.: 163
Wolf, Dr.: at Fort Richardson, 89
Wolff, Joseph: 37
Wood, James Frederick: 28
Wood, William H.: commander at Fort Griffin, 124 and n., 126
Woodburn, William: 36
Worth, William Jenkins: 45
Wright, Frances: 25 and n.

Young County: 17
Young Territory: 18

www.ingramcontent.com/pod-product-compliance
Lightning Source LLC
Chambersburg PA
CBHW022059160426
43198CB00008B/288